The Philosophy
of Positive Law

The Philosophy of Positive Law

Foundations of Jurisprudence

James Bernard Murphy

Yale University Press

New Haven and London

Set in Adobe Garamond and Stone Sans types by The Composing Room of Michigan, Inc.

Printed in the United States of America.

Library of Congress Cataloging-in-Publication Data

Murphy, James Bernard, 1958–
    The philosophy of positive law : foundations of jurisprudenrce / James Bernard Murphy.
        p.   cm.
    Includes bibliographical references and index.
    ISBN 0-300-10788-9 (hardcover : alk. paper)
    1. Legal positivism.   I. Title.
    K331.M87 2005
    340′.112—dc22

                                                    2004031032

A catalogue record for this book is available from the British Library.

The paper in this book meets the guidelines for permanence and durability of the Committee on Production Guidelines for Book Longevity of the Council on Library Resources.

10 9 8 7 6 5 4 3 2 1

Matri Patrique

Contents

Preface

At the foundation of philosophical jurisprudence, from Plato to Hans Kelsen, are three sets of concepts: natural law, customary law, and positive law. Each of these sets of concepts can be understood only in relation to the other two. They are united by a set of analogies and contrasts within a circle of interdefinability. Positive law is contrasted with both natural law and customary law; customary law is sometimes "second nature" and sometimes "unwritten law"; natural law (*ius naturale*) is sometimes described as inherent, like custom, and sometimes as externally stipulated (*lex naturalis*), like positive law. In other contexts, these three sets of concepts form a progressive hierarchy such that customary law presupposes natural law just as positive law presupposes customary law. All of these interrelations reflect the attempt to work out the relation of what is natural to what is conventional in law, of what has intrinsic moral force to what does not.

In this book I explore the set of concepts known as positive law from Plato to John Austin; I show that there is a striking continuity in the discourse about positive law across the whole tradition of philosophical jurisprudence. In the future, I plan to write companion volumes about natural law and about customary law, thus completing the foundations of philosophical jurisprudence.

Unless otherwise explicitly noted, all translations and all paraphrases from the Greek, Latin, German, and French are mine. All the Greek is transliterated according to the standard conventions: long vowels have a macron, and iota subscripts are indicated by an *i* immediately following the long vowel. In all quotations, the emphasis is that of the original author.

Acknowledgments

I have had the privilege of presenting the various chapters of this book in faculty seminars at Dartmouth College, Yale University, the University of Chicago, Newnham College, University of Cambridge, and the School of the Ius Commune, Erice, Sicily. I have learned a great deal from these discussions. I have benefited even more from an extensive correspondence with many scholars; I shall list only those who provided substantial comments on one or more chapters. Naturally, I absolve them from all responsibility for the mistakes herein.

Introduction: Douglas Edlin, Mark Stein, Kent Greenawalt, Ned Lebow. *Plato:* Christie Thomas, Michael Pakaluk. *Aquinas:* Roger Masters, Walter Sinnott-Armstrong, Fred Schauer, Brian Tierney, James Gordley, Gerald Postema, Annabel Brett, Amanda Perreau-Saussine, Martin Golding, Rogers Smith, Bruce Ackerman, Louis Dupré, Joseph Cropsey, Nathan Tarcov, Russell Hittinger, Denis Sullivan, Charles Stinson, Mark Murphy, John Witte, Joan O'Donovan, Kenneth Pennington, Emmanuele Conte, John Finnis. *Hobbes:* Arlene Saxonhouse, Al Martinich, Gerald Postema, Deborah Soles, Lucas

Swaine, Matthew Kramer, Ted Miller. *Austin:* Wilfrid E. Rumble, Matthew Kramer.

I must also acknowledge the inestimable help I received from my research assistants, including Kevin Walsh, Conor Dugan, Karen Liot, Emily Mintz, Anna Jenkins, and Magdalena Panz.

I am deeply indebted to the Pew Charitable Trusts, the Earhart Foundation, and Dartmouth College for Fellowships that supported this book project.

Abbreviations

CS—*Commentum in Libros Sententiarum,* Thomas Aquinas

D—*A Dialogue Between a Philosopher and a Student of the Common Laws of England,* Thomas Hobbes

DC—*De Cive,* Thomas Hobbes

DH—*De Homine,* Thomas Hobbes

DK—*Die Fragmente der Vorsokratiker,* Diels and Kranz

DL—*A Discourse of Laws,* Thomas Hobbes

Dt.—*Deuteronomy*

Ex.—*Exodus*

L—*Leviathan,* Thomas Hobbes

LJ—*Lectures on Jurisprudence: Or the Philosophy of Positive Law,* John Austin

PJD—*The Province of Jurisprudence Determined,* John Austin

ST—*Summa Theologica,* Thomas Aquinas

Introduction: Natural,
Customary, and Positive Law

WHAT IS POSITIVE LAW?

Legalism pervades Western culture. Whenever we wish to honor some pattern or regularity that we discover in nature, or any rule or norm we discern or devise in society, we call it a law. We call causal relations in the natural world physical, chemical, or biological laws, just as we call precepts we frame for human conduct moral or civil laws. We even call the rules governing the technical arts the laws of logic, or of grammar, or of engineering. Given the prestige of law in both the Hebraic and the Hellenistic sources of our culture, we should perhaps not be surprised by the bewildering profusion of very different kinds of law: divine law, moral law, customary law, natural law, laws of physics, mathematical laws, canon law, international law, municipal law, by-laws, and the laws of etiquette, just to name a few. And yet, despite this profusion, we also speak simply of the law, usually meaning the law enforced by courts. Of the immense diversity of kinds of law, few have been or ever will be enforced by courts. What distinguishes law enforced by courts from all the other kinds of law, which are not so enforced?

Many lawyers and jurists delimit their object of inquiry by speaking of "law enforced by courts," but that does not help us understand why courts enforce this law and not all the other potentially enforceable kinds of law. How do courts know what kind of law should be enforced by courts? These questions are even more perplexing when we consider that the norms enforced by courts, though less diverse than the entire universe of what is called law, nonetheless come in a remarkable variety of kinds. Courts enforce statutory law, administrative law, constitutional law, international law, foreign law, customary law, common law, admiralty law, and the law of equity, to name just a few. Moreover, these very different bodies of law include very different kinds of norms: some are basic moral principles, some quite technical rules; some are ancient, while others change daily; some arise from spontaneous commercial practices, and others are deliberately imposed by legislators; some stem from lay customs, while others stem from the customs of the courts themselves; some arise from actual court decisions, while others arise from learned commentary. What could these diverse laws and legal norms possibly have in common, other than simply being enforced by courts?

Many important legal philosophers, from Thomas Aquinas in the thirteenth century to Hans Kelsen in the twentieth, have attempted to answer these questions by saying that the law that human courts enforce is positive law. By identifying the law enforced by courts as positive law, legal philosophers claim that such law has a certain kind of source and a certain kind of content. Let us begin by looking at the sources of law, for our legal philosophers have a more demanding understanding of source than do practical jurists. The jurists of the ancient Roman law, for example, describe law (*ius*) as a reservoir fed by many different springs or sources of law (*fontes iuris*). The task of the courts was to harmonize these heterogeneous sources into a coherent body of law for the administration of justice. The exact of list of these sources varies over time and place: in the classical Roman law they included statutes (*leges*), enactments of the plebeians, senate resolutions, enactments of the emperors, edicts of the magistrates, and learned commentary (*responsa prudentium*). A modern jurist lists the sources of English law as legislation, custom, precedents, and equity.[1] John Chipman Gray describes the sources of law as the raw material processed by courts into genuine law; he lists the sources of American law as statutes, precedents, opinions of experts, custom, and equity.[2]

1. C. K. Allen, *Law in the Making* (Oxford: Clarendon Press, 1927).
2. J. C. Gray, *The Nature and Sources of Law,* 2nd edition (Gloucester, MA: Peter Smith, 1972).

The exact list of sources varies, but the heterogeneity remains. Lawyers learn how to find, interpret, harmonize, and apply these different kinds of norms. Principles play a role different from rules in legal reasoning, statutes are interpreted differently from precedents, customs are proven differently from statutes, constitutional provisions might control the effect of statutes, and so on. For practical legal purposes, the analysis of law into its constitutive sources is generally adequate. But the philosophy of positive law has aspired to a deeper, simpler, and more unified account of the law enforced by courts. How do courts know where to look for valid sources of law? Are the conventional sources of law irreducibly heterogeneous, or do all recognized sources of law have something essential in common? Is there a single source to which all the various sources of law might be traced and from which they all derive their authority?

According to the leading philosophers of positive law, courts enforce not just any rules but only those rules "laid down" or imposed by the supreme authority within a political community. Behind or above the conventional list of diverse sources of law is a single unifying source that tells us which sources and which particular rules ought to be enforced by courts. The simplicity and parsimony of this theory of law is very appealing, and it only seems right that the law enforced by courts somehow stem from the supreme authority within a political community. Moreover, rational coherence and consistency in law would seem to demand a single, unified chain of command from the highest authority down to every subordinate legislator, judge, mayor, sheriff, and police officer. As we shall see, however, this notion of positive law as law "laid down" by the supreme authority in a community applies more naturally to some sources of law than to others. Statutes clearly get their authority by being "laid down," but custom, equity, and precedents seem to get their authority, not so much by being laid down as by being repeatedly "taken up" by successive judges in the course of administering justice. Nonetheless, the philosophy of positive law will develop a host of strategies for showing how all valid sources of law are in fact "laid down" by the supreme authority within a political community.

In addition to a claim about the source of all law, the philosophy of positive law also makes claims about the content of law. Courts of law are also called courts of justice, suggesting that law ought in some way to serve justice. Indeed, the ancient Roman jurists, and many of their successors, have closely identified law with justice and the art of applying law to disputes with the art of bringing about justice. The main Roman word for law (*ius*) is the etymological basis for the Roman word for justice (*iustitia*). Lawyers in every age are professionally in-

clined to assume, we might venture to say, that the enforcement of the law just
is the administration of justice. In the opening of Justinian's *Digest,* we find the
great jurist Ulpian saying that "jurisprudence comprehends affairs both divine
and human and is the science of what is just and unjust."[3] William Blackstone
is no less confident of the justice of human law when he defines law as a "rule of
civil conduct prescribed by the supreme power in a state commanding what is
right and prohibiting what is wrong."[4]

The philosophers of positive law differ among themselves about the exact relation of law to justice and to morality more broadly, but all of them want
clearly to distinguish the law enforced by courts from the demands of justice
and morality. To call the law enforced by courts positive law is to claim that it
differs in content from the principles of justice and morality. Why should we
distinguish positive law from the pure requirements of moral law? First of all,
the philosophers of positive law all insist that just because a law is enforced by a
court does not conclusively prove that it is consistent with the demands of justice. It is essential to the whole project of criticism and reform of law that we
not confuse the existence of a law with its justice. Second, even when consistent
with the demands of justice, law plays a role in regulating human conduct
different from that played by rules of morality. Legal precepts must provide
much more specific guidance to human conduct than do moral precepts because law must provide clear and determinate guidelines if it is to coordinate
myriad human endeavors. Moral law tells us not to steal, but positive law must
define what counts as property, what counts as stealing, and what legal consequences flow from stealing. Third, in any system of social interdependence, we
cannot achieve our goals without relying on our expectations of the conduct of
others. Within broad moral boundaries, we value, above all, that others' conduct is stable and predictable. In law, as Justice Brandeis famously observed, it
is often more important that a rule be settled than that it be settled right.
Fourth, moral law has a much wider and deeper jurisdiction than positive law
has. Moral law governs all thoughts, words, and deeds, while positive law governs only that which is publicly manifest; courts can take no notice of thoughts,
words, or deeds that are purely private. Moral law forbids coveting your neighbor's property; positive law forbids only stealing it.

Positive law is law whose content is clear, specific, and determinate enough

3. *The Digest of Justinian,* Latin text edited by Theodor Mommsen and Paul Krueger, vol. 1
   (Philadelphia: University of Pennsylvania Press, 1985), 1.1.10.
4. *Blackstone's Commentaries,* vol. 1, intro., sec. 2. Dublin: John Exshaw et al., 1773.

to guide and coordinate human conduct, to create stable expectations, and to be enforceable in court. The principles of natural or moral law are too general, too open ended, take in too much private conduct, and admit of too many conflicting interpretations to function as positive law. Natural law has intrinsic moral force quite apart from whether or not it is enforced or obeyed by anyone, but positive law gets its moral force from contingent facts about its use or adoption within a particular society. Since there are innumerable ways to specify the general norms of the natural law, positive law will vary widely over time and place. The content of positive law, especially procedural requirements and other formalities, is often disparagingly called "arbitrary," as if what is not intrinsically moral must therefore be wholly groundless or adventitious. The content of positive law can and does vary widely, but it usually bears a relation to the moral (or immoral) purpose of that branch of law, even if that relation is sometimes difficult for a layman to discern. Still, as we shall see, to describe the content of law as positive makes more sense for some kinds of law than for others.

What is most deeply puzzling about the philosophy of positive law is that to define human law as positive can mean at least two different things. In one sense, something is positive because it has been deliberately laid down, imposed, or enacted—as opposed to what arises spontaneously by custom or nature; but in another sense, something is positive because it lacks intrinsic rational or moral force, its content is "arbitrary," in the sense that it could be different—as opposed to what has intrinsic rational or moral force by its essence or nature. The first sense of positive is a descriptive or empirical claim about the origins of a law, namely, that it stems from deliberate imposition; positive law is here posited or enacted law. The second sense of positive is a normative claim about the content of a legal norm, namely, that it lacks, on various accounts, intrinsic moral necessity, moral universality, or moral force; positive law here seems arbitrary, such as the English rule of driving on the left side of the road. As we shall see, many writers use positive law in these two senses, but almost none explicitly distinguishes between them. For one of myriad possible examples, William Blackstone in one place contrasts "positive" to "common" law, in the sense that positive law is imposed by statute, while common law is unwritten custom. But in another place, without warning, Blackstone also contrasts "positive" to "natural" legal duties, in the sense that positive duties, he says, forbid what is evil because prohibited, while natural duties forbid what is intrinsically evil.[5] Are we to assume from these two different uses that only pos-

---

5. *Blackstone* [5th edition, 1773], intro., vol. 1, sec. 3.10 and sec. 2.

itive (enacted) law imposes duties whose content is positive in the sense of lacking intrinsic moral force? Does natural law impose natural duties? Or does positive law impose both natural and positive duties?

The discourse of positive law involves an array of fundamental descriptive and normative concepts and a set of contrasts that go to the heart of philosophical jurisprudence. Is law rooted in human nature or is it merely conventional? Is law always deliberately imposed or does it also arise from custom? Does all law have some kind of moral force or do many legal norms lack moral force? What relation is there, if any, between being deliberately imposed and lacking intrinsic moral force? In other words, from descriptive claims about the origin of law, can we infer any normative claims about its moral force? Is all law artificial in the sense of the product of deliberate design? If a law is artificial, does that mean that its content is arbitrary, in the sense of willful or adventitious? Or might a law be artificial without being arbitrary? In this book, we shall explore how this complex and deeply puzzling set of concepts known as positive law both illuminates and obscures the attempt of legal philosophers to answer these questions. In the end, I believe, we shall all be much less positive about the meaning of positive law.

NATURE OR CONVENTION?

The philosophy of law in general, and the discourse of positive law in particular, emerged as part of a larger discourse about social institutions. Just as the discourse of positive law combines descriptive claims about the origin of law with normative claims about its content, so the larger discourse about what is natural and what is conventional includes both descriptive and normative claims. What is most characteristic of this theoretical and critical enterprise in the West has been our inexorable tendency to question whether our manners, morals, and institutions are natural or conventional. Indeed, nothing is more controversial today than the questions of whether our gender relations and our sexual norms stem from nature or from nurture. Is male aggressiveness by nature or by social convention and education? Is homosexuality rooted in biology or in rearing? Is marriage rooted in human biology or in social practices? We even continue to argue about which parts of language are innate and which are merely socially learned. And legal practices and institutions are sometimes ascribed to natural necessity and sometimes to arbitrary conventions.

In one sense, these debates are purely theoretical matters to be decided by philosophers and scientists. Biologists, anthropologists, historians, linguists, and psychologists, among others, have long framed their investigations to shed light upon the relative importance of nature and convention in explaining many kinds of human conduct. But the intensity and partisanship characteristic of debates between champions of nature and champions of nurture strongly suggests that these are more than purely theoretical questions. The recent arguments between sociobiologists who champion nature and their critics who champion culture reach an astonishing level of rhetorical and sometimes even actual violence. These debates embody much more than a clash of alternative theoretical perspectives; they embody a fundamental clash of moral and political commitments. Ever since the time of the ancient Greek Sophists, those who favor a certain practice, such as slavery, have often argued that it is natural, hence associating their preferred agenda with all the prestige commonly associated with what is natural—namely, that it is inherent, permanent, fixed, real, and, perhaps, optimal. Similarly, those who attack slavery will typically argue that it is merely conventional, hence associating the object of their scorn with the lack of prestige commonly associated with mere conventions—that they rest on mere force or interest and are transient, insubstantial, and, often, out of date.

Even today, champions of women's equality almost always insist that gender relations are conventional, while defenders of patriarchy argue from nature; similarly, champions of gay rights tend to argue that homosexuality is natural, while their critics usually insist that it is not. Although, in these debates, what is natural is usually taken to provide the norm for what is conventional, this is not always so. Some ancient Greek Sophists argue, as does Thomas Hobbes, that what is natural is brutish, primitive, and dangerous, and that social order depends upon salutary artifice and convention. Thus, both champions of nature and champions of convention (culture and nurture) draw normative implications from factual claims about the sources of social order; all sides see practical implications to these theoretical claims about the origins of various practices and institutions.

Many philosophers have argued that these kinds of arguments simply rest on a mistake; they insist that from factual and theoretical claims about what is natural, we cannot infer anything directly about what is morally desirable. We cannot assume that what is natural is moral any more than we can assume that what is conventional is not. No doubt many kinds of inferences from what is natural or conventional to what is normatively justified or not are fallacious. But it is still the case that the debate over nature and convention has been, and always will be, both factual and normative, both theoretical and practical. Why?

To begin with, simply to raise the question of whether a custom, practice, or institution is natural or conventional already has profound normative and practical implications. Every human custom, practice, or institution either needs no explicit justification (having never been challenged) or, more typically, includes its own kind of justification (often by reference to divinity or tradition). Even if we defend an existing practice as natural, we have inalterably changed the basis on which it was previously justified. Just to debate whether a practice is natural or conventional is to subject it to reflective rationality and to standards of rational argument. Even if a putative practice or institution survives such critical scrutiny, it will be a changed practice or institution because it now rests on (or rather includes) a new and theoretical justification. In short, debating whether a practice is natural or conventional, even when aimed at shoring up or defending the status quo, is always a subversive activity. Social and political theory is never simply theoretical; it always has normative and practical implications and effects. As the philosopher G. A. Cohen says: "The Sophists' distinction between nature and convention is the foundation of all social criticism."[6] To the extent that they alter our understandings and justifications of our practices, debates about nature and convention are subversive even when the arguments are wielded by conservatives.

Second, even if the empirical study of human nature and human conventions cannot conclusively decide normative or practical questions about how we ought to live, such empirical study is still deeply relevant and often crucial in making good normative judgments. Some practices and some institutions are more compatible with what we know about human nature than are other practices and institutions; such compatibility is not decisive, but surely quite significant and often burden shifting in debates about what is normatively desirable. What we know or could learn about the biology of sexual desire does not conclusively rule out the social practice of encouraging homosexuals into heterosexual marriage; that practice might still be justified, but current understanding of human sexual orientation does shift the burden of proof to those who favor it. Similarly, we have learned from bitter experience that our normative judgments about what kinds of laws we ought to support should be keenly sensitive to the question of how compatible those laws are with existing social customs. No doubt, some customs ought to be abolished, but whether it is wise to attempt to do so by means of law is largely, though not wholly, an empirical

6. G. A. Cohen, *Karl Marx's Theory of History* (Princeton: Princeton University Press, 1978), p. 107.

question. In short, the debates about nature and convention are simultaneously empirical and normative, theoretical and practical because our deliberation about social practices and institutions rightly includes both kinds of premises.

TRANSCENDING THE NATURE-CONVENTION DICHOTOMY[7]

Positive law is contrasted not only with natural law but also with customary law. What this means is that the discourse of positive law already presupposes the significance of the contrast between what is deliberately stipulated and what is tacitly practiced, a contrast that is obscured by the simple dichotomy between nature and convention. So the discourse of positive law takes its starting point from theories that have already transcended the nature-convention dichotomy. The ancient Greek Sophists are famous for framing our analysis of human social institutions in terms of a stark choice between what is natural and what is conventional. Yet the greatest of the Sophists had already begun to transcend this stark dichotomy. Protagoras said: "Learning from teaching [*didaskalia*] requires both nature [*phusis*] and practice [*askēsis*]."[8] Plato also developed a version of this triad when he observed that "if one has the natural capacity [*phusei*] for rhetoric, one can become a famous rhetorician, provided that one also acquires knowledge [*epistēmē*] and practice [*meletē*]."[9] And Aristotle agrees on the need for all three qualities: "Now some think that we become good by nature [*phusei*], others by habit [*ethei*], still others by teaching [*didakē*]."[10]

---

7. My discussion here and in the next section of the kinds of social order and the logic of social order draws freely from my own work. See *The Moral Economy of Labor: Aristotelian Themes in Economic Theory* (New Haven: Yale University Press, 1993) and "Nature, Custom, and Reason in Aristotelian Political Science," *Review of Politics* 64 (summer 2002): 469–95.

8. Protagoras in *Die Fragmente der Vorsokratiker*, ed. Hermann Diels and Walter Kranz (Berlin: Weidmannsche Verlagsbuchhandlung, 1954), frag. 3. Usually *didaskalia* is rendered as "teaching," but Paul Shorey is right to argue that "learning" fits the context better, since the focus is on the conditions that promote successful learning in the student, of which teaching is only one. Shorey traces the history of Protagoras's triadic conception of education through Plato and all the way to Cicero's *ingenii, exercitatio dicendi, ratio aliqua* (*Pro Archias*). See his "*Physis, Meletē, Epistēmē*," *Transactions and Proceedings of the American Philological Association* 40 (1909): 185–201.

9. Plato, *Phaedrus*, 269D.

10. Aristotle, *Nicomachean Ethics*, 1179b 20.

All of these writers are rejecting the simple dichotomy between what is natural and what is artificial or conventional. Some Sophists argued that intellectual and moral excellences come from natural genius; others argued that these virtues come from deliberate teaching. But Protagoras, Plato, and Aristotle reframe the analysis. Rather than accept the choice of nature or convention, they insist on both. In this view, man is by nature a conventional animal: social conventions are how we actualize our natural potential. A recent book attempting to transcend the contemporary debate over nature and nurture adopts the same strategy: it is entitled *Nature Via Nurture.*[11]

Why attempt to transcend the Sophistic dichotomy? First, as we have seen, many thinkers, ancient and modern, see human language, law, and culture as involving both natural capacities and artificial conventions. A human being apart from all cultural artifice would lack his or her very nature. So the challenge is to understand how nature and culture interact both in the development of each individual person and in the development of human social and political life. Second, the Sophistic dichotomy of nature and convention fails to distinguish the tacit and implicit practices of individual habit and social custom from the deliberate practices of teaching and law making. The Greek word *nomos,* like our "convention," is ambiguous as to what is deliberately and explicitly instituted, such as statutes, and what is only implicitly or tacitly practiced, such as customs. Individuals acquire their intellectual and moral excellence both by tacit emulation and by explicit instruction; societies acquire their conventions both by tacit practices of social custom and by the deliberate institution of legislation. So this triadic conception of human life sees our complex individual and social achievements as the products of natural potential, tacit practices, and deliberate stipulation and institution. That this fundamental insight into the complex sources of individual and social human life should arise from a reflection upon education is characteristic of the Greek mind. For, as John Dewey was fond of saying, there is an important sense in which all of Greek philosophy is the philosophy of education.

Aristotle made more use of this tradic logic of explanation than any other ancient thinker. He says, for example, "In order to become good and wise requires three things; these are nature, habit, and reason [*phusis, ethos, logos*]."[12] Here Aristotle is speaking of the components of moral and intellectual self-realization: we must begin with the right natural capacities, we cultivate these capaci-

---

11. Matt Ridley, *Nature Via Nurture* (New York: HarperCollins, 2003).
12. Aristotle, *Politics,* 1332a 38.

ties into the right dispositions and habits of character, and we use reason reflectively to adjust our habits in light of our ideals. In this model of self-realization, our habits presuppose our nature but cannot be reduced to it, just as our rational ideals presuppose our habits but cannot be reduced to them. Aristotle extended his triad beyond individual self-realization to the actualization of the political community. Thus, he says in many places (e.g., *Politics* 1332b 8–11), the legislator, in the deliberate stipulation of law, must take into account the natural capacities of his citizens as well as their social customs.

Although this triadic model of social explanation never achieved the ubiquity and familiarity of the Sophistic dichotomy, it appears frequently throughout the history of Western theories of language and of law. In the theory of language, we find John Poinsot (John of St. Thomas) asking "whether the division of signs into natural [*naturale*], stipulated [*ad placitum*], and customary [*ex consuetudine*] is a sound division."[13] By natural signs he means those signs that relate to their objects independent of human activity: smoke is a sign of fire. By customary signs he means those signs that arise from the tacit social practices of human communities: napkins on a table are a sign that dinner is imminent. By stipulated signs he means those signs whose meaning is deliberately appointed by an individual, as when a new word is introduced.[14] In the history of jurisprudence, our triad appears in a variety of guises. The author of the *Rhetorica ad Herennium* (II, 19) says that law (*ius*) can arise by nature (*natura*), by statute (*lege*), and by custom (*consuetudine*) as well as in other ways. The jurist Ulpian famously distinguishes natural law, the customary law of nations, and civil law (*Digest* 1.1.1). And Cicero deploys this triadic scheme in his famous description of the evolution of law from the principles of nature, through custom, to the deliberate stipulation of statutes: "Law [*ius*] initially proceeds from nature, then certain rules of conduct become customary by reason of their advantage; later still both the principles that proceeded from nature and those that had been approved by custom received the support of religion and the fear of legislation [*lex*]."[15] Here Cicero sees that the deliberate imposition of law does not create social or legal order but reinforces, revises, or supplements the exist-

---

13. John Poinsot, *Tractatus de Signis* [1632], ed. and trans. John Deely (Berkeley: University of California Press, 1985), p. 269.

14. For a critique and reconstruction of Poinsot's doctrine of signs, see James Bernard Murphy, "Nature, Custom, and Stipulation in the Semiotic of John Poinsot," *Semiotica* 83, nos. 1/2 (1991): 33–68.

15. Cicero, *De inventione*, 2.53.160.

ing natural and customary order. Both Thomas Aquinas and John Austin cite this passage from Cicero with approval.[16]

Recently, Friedrich Hayek has argued that the nature-convention dichotomy embodies the assumption that all social order is either natural or deliberately instituted, thereby ignoring the crucial role of spontaneous order, such as we find in language, law, and the market. "Yet much of what we call culture is just such a spontaneously grown order [e.g., custom], which arose neither altogether independently of human action [nature] nor by design [stipulation], but by a process that stands between these two possibilities, which were long considered as exclusive alternatives."[17] Hayek traces his notion of spontaneous order to Adam Ferguson: "Nations stumble upon establishments, which are indeed the result of human action, but not the execution of any human design."[18] Hayek argues that the totalitarian disasters of the twentieth century all shared the hubris of attempting to impose a deliberately stipulated order on society without regard for the existing natural and customary social orders in place. In his view, these totalitarian projects were not just crimes, they were also mistakes—the mistake of thinking that natural and customary social order could be replaced by deliberately designed order. In other words, for Hayek the theoretical question of how to account for the kinds of order we find in society has direct normative implications: if we fail to acknowledge the fact of diverse kinds of social order, our moral and legal projects will come to naught, or worse.

THE LOGIC OF NATURE, CUSTOM, AND ENACTMENT

We can see Aristotle's view of the different kinds of social order in his terms for describing "good social order": *eukosmia, eunomia,* and *eutaxia;* here *kosmos* connotes natural social order, *nomos* connotes customary or legal order, and *taxis* connotes deliberately stipulated order, as in the order of battle.[19] Knowing the kinds of order in society gives us the basis for forming reliable expectations

16. Aquinas, *Summa Theologica* (ST), I-II, 95.2c, and Austin, *Lectures on Jurisprudence,* lec. 30.

17. F. A. Hayek, "Kinds of Order in Society" [1964], in *The Politicization of Society,* ed. Kenneth Templeton Jr. (Indianapolis: Liberty Press, 1979), p. 509.

18. Adam Ferguson, *An Essay on the History of Civil Society* (Edinburgh: A. Millar and T. Caddel, 1767), p. 187.

19. See *Politics,* 1299b 16, *Nicomachean Ethics,* 1112b 14, and *Politics,* 1326a 30.

about human conduct: order is the basis for inference.[20] The development of our understanding of natural, customary, and legal order, however, often proceeded through a series of analogies. The order of nature is understood by analogy to legal order, as when we speak of the "laws of physics"; or the legal order is understood by analogy to the order of nature, as when we speak of "natural law." Scholars are not sure whether the Greek word *kosmos* was first used about social order and then applied to nature or was first used about natural order and then applied to society.[21] In the first document in the history of Western philosophy, Anaximander develops an elaborate analogy between the natural cycle of the seasons and the legal cycles of transgression and retribution. This fragment (DK 12 A9) is the first expression of natural law because Anaximander describes the uniformities of nature as just (*dikē*).[22] Indeed, the Greek word for natural cause (*aitia*) is a legal term for guilt—the cause is guilty of the effect.[23] So law is natural, and nature is lawful. What about custom? Here we move within the same circle of analogies, since custom is both "second nature" and

20. Order, says Hayek, is "a state of affairs in which a multiplicity of elements of various kinds are so related to each other that we may learn from our acquaintance with some spatial or temporal part of the whole to form correct expectations concerning the rest, or at least expectations which have a good chance of proving correct." Hayek, *Law, Legislation, and Liberty,* vol. 1 (Chicago: University of Chicago Press, 1973), p. 36. Hayek here draws on Stebbing: "When we know how a set of elements is ordered we have a basis for inference." L. S. Stebbing, *A Modern Introduction to Logic* (London: Methuen, 1950), p. 228.

21. "It may be that, from the beginning, *kosmos* was applied to the world of nature by conscious analogy with the good order of society." Charles Kahn, *Anaximander and the Origins of Greek Cosmology* (New York: Columbia University Press, 1960), p. 223.

22. In Kahn's translation: "And the source of coming-to-be for existing things is that into which destruction, too, happens, according to necessity; for they pay penalty and retribution to each other for their injustice according to the ordinance of time." According to Kahn's interpretation of this fragment, "the elements feed one another by their own destruction, since what is life to one is death for its reciprocal. The first law of nature is a *lex talionis:* life for life." *Anaximander and the Origins of Greek Cosmology,* p. 183.

23. Hans Kelsen sees the word *aitia* as central to early Greek conceptions of natural law: "It is significant that the Greek word for cause, *aitia,* originally meant guilt: the cause is guilty of the effect, is responsible for the effect. . . . One of the earliest formulations of the law of causality is the famous fragment of Heraclitus: 'If the Sun will overstep his prescribed path, then the Erinyes, the handmaids of justice, will find him out.' Here the law of nature still appears as a rule of law: if the Sun does not follow his prescribed path he will be punished." Kelsen, *Pure Theory of Law,* ed. Max Knight (Berkeley: University of California Press, 1970), p. 84.

"unwritten law." In one passage, Aristotle compares habit or custom both to nature and to law: "We should consider the organization of an animal to resemble that of a city well-governed by laws [*eunomia*]. For, once order [*taxis*] is established in a city, there is no more need of a separate monarch to preside over every activity; each man does his own work as assigned, and one thing follows another because of habit [*ethos*]. In animals, this same thing happens because of nature: specifically because each part of them, since they are so ordered, is naturally disposed to do its own task."[24] In other words, habit or custom is like nature, in that it operates as an internal constraint on human conduct; but habit or custom is also like law, in that it might have its origin in deliberate stipulation. Even today, a social theorist, Pierre Bordieu, descibes custom (*habitus*) both as "immanent law" and as "history turned into nature."[25] We cannot seem to escape this circle of analogies among nature, custom, and law.

But Aristotle also offers us another way to understand the relations among nature, custom, and enactment. In his classification of the kinds of souls, Aristotle does not define a genus of soul and the species of plant, animal, and human souls. Instead, Aristotle says that the plant soul is living (that is, nutritive and reproductive), the animal soul is living plus sensitive, and the human soul is living and sensitive plus rational.[26] I think Aristotle thought that nature, custom, and enactment also formed such a nested hierarchy: "In every case the lower faculty can exist apart from the higher, but the higher presupposes those below it."[27] Nature represents the physical, chemical, and biological processes of the cosmos; nature can and did exist apart from human custom and enactment. Human custom is rooted in the physiology of habit but transcends habit by becoming a social system of norms. Custom presupposes nature but can exist without being the object of rational reflection and stipulation: language existed before grammarians, just as custom existed before legislators.

This nested hierarchy of nature, custom, and rational stipulation is pervasive in Aristotle's thought. First, for Aristotle, nature, custom, and rational stipulation articulate the hierarchy of the *scala naturae:* "The other animals for the most part live by nature, though in some respects by habit as well, while man

24. Aristotle's "On the Motion of Animals," 703a 29. Translation from Martha Nussbaum, *Aristotle's De motu animalium* (Princeton: Princeton University Press, 1978), p. 52.
25. For Bordieu's theory of *habitus,* see his *Outlines of a Theory of Practice,* trans. Richard Nice (Cambridge: Cambridge University Press, 1977), pp. 78–81.
26. *De Anima,* 414a 29 to 415a 13.
27. R. D. Hicks, *Aristotle: De anima* (Cambridge: Cambridge University Press, 1907), 335.

lives also by reason, for he alone has reason."[28] Second, nature, custom, and rational stipulation form the same nested hierarchy in individual development as they do in the ladder of nature. Aristotle says that there are three kinds of human faculties (*dynameis*): those that are innate (*suggenēs*), those that come by practice (*ethos*), and those that come from teaching (*mathēsis*). These three faculties form a hierarchy: "The contribution of nature clearly does not depend on us . . . while argument [*logos*] and teaching [*didakē*] surely do not influence everyone, but the soul of the student must have been prepared by habit [*ethos*]."[29] So habit presupposes nature while rational argument presupposes habits. Third, this hierarchy is found in Aristotle's discussions of legal order: "We have already determined what natures are likely to be most easily moulded by the hands of the legislator. All else is the work of education; we learn some things by habit and some by instruction."[30] Just as the legislator is responsible for attempting to shape the natural potential and the tacit customs of his city, so all people are responsible for making the best they can of their natural potential and their habits of character.

In the Aristotelian logic of explanation, we must distinguish the levels of analysis from units of analysis. Natural order studied by natural sciences, customary order studied by social sciences, and rationally stipulated order studied by the social and the normative sciences are levels of analysis; human practices and institutions are units of analysis. What this means is that a given human practice or institution usually must be understood as embodying all three levels of analysis. Human language is natural, customary, and stipulated, so the science of language involves the physiology of speech, the science of tacit language habits, and the normative science of grammar. Similarly, human law is natural, customary, and deliberately enacted, so that the science of law must involve the ethology of animal and human norms of justice, the science of tacit legal growth through the evolution of popular and judicial customs, and the descriptive and normative sciences of deliberate enactment. We do not want to confuse a unit of analysis, such as language or law, with a level of analysis by saying, for example, that all law is customary or that all law is enacted. Law, like all complex human enterprises, has a natural, customary, and stipulated dimension.

28. *Politics,* 1332b 2.
29. Aristotle, *Metaphysics,* 1047b 31, and *Nicomachean Ethics,* 1179b 21.
30. *Politics,* 1332b 8. "Now, in men reason and mind are the goal of nature, so that the birth and training in custom of the citizens ought to be ordered with a view to them." *Politics,* 1334b 15. I have here adopted Jowett's translation.

Yet, as we shall see, legal philosophers will talk about natural law, customary law, and positive law instead of talking about the natural, customary, and positive dimensions of law. Is all human law positive? Can human law be divided into natural, customary, and positive norms? Or, given the organic unity of the rule of law, in which every legal norm gets its meaning, force, interpretation, and application in relation to many other norms, does virtually every law and legal institution have a natural, customary, and stipulated dimension?

POSITIVE LANGUAGE AND POSITIVE LAW

Historians have shown that the discourse of positive law emerged from ancient Greek debates about language. This should not be surprising, since explicit analogies between law and language pervade the history of Western thought. Socrates says that the original maker of names was a linguistic legislator, and Hobbes frequently compares legislative authority to linguistic authority. Later, Savigny famously compares the tacit evolution of national languages to the tacit evolution of national law, and Lon Fuller says that law, like language, does not have its own purpose but is the medium for the realization of myriad individual purposes.

But what, precisely, was it about certain ancient Greek debates about language that should inspire the discourse of positive law? In what sense, or senses, is language positive? As we shall see, the whole larger discourse about what is natural (*phusei*) and what is conventional (*nomōi*) stemmed from certain Greek views about language. The pre-Socratic philosophers frequently contrasted "what is said" (by convention) about the world with "what is true" (by nature) of it. In this way, what is natural often became associated with what is real, objective, and true, while what is conventional often became associated with what is illusory, subjective, and false. I shall argue that Plato's dialogue about language, the *Cratylus,* deeply illuminates the whole conceptual logic and puzzles of the discourse of positive law. In this dialogue, we see the transition from general debates about what is natural and what is conventional to specific debates about what is natural and what is positive. Moreover, Plato here explores both sets of contrasts that will define the later discourse of positive law: he contrasts what is positive with what is natural and with what is customary. Finally, the *Cratylus* even combines descriptive claims about the origin of language with normative claims about the intrinsic force of language in ways that anticipate the combination of empirical and normative claims in the discourse of positive law.

Let me say something more about why a book about positive law begins with a chapter on Plato's *Cratylus*. In the dialogue, Cratylus argues that names (meaning both proper names and words) are correct by nature; but he asserts two quite distinct theses. First, he says that the content of each name is intrinsically related to what it names as an image; second, he argues that this image arose by spontaneous, natural growth. Conversely, Hermogenes argues that the correctness of names is by convention; and he also asserts two distinct theses. First, he says that the content of a name has no intrinsic relation to what it names; second, he asserts that names do not grow up naturally but emerge by agreement or imposition. Neither Cratylus nor Hermogenes seems to be aware that each of their theses is logically independent of the other. But Socrates dialectically transcends this debate and illuminates its ambiguities by proposing that names acquire their correctness from the deliberate enactment of a name giver who designs names that are natural images of what they name. To Cratylus he says: you are right that names are natural images but wrong to suppose they they emerge by nature; to Hermogenes he says: you are right that names emerge from artificial convention but wrong to suppose they they are not natural images of what they name.

Socrates has transcended the standard debate about what is natural and what is conventional by offering an account of names that is both naturalist and conventionalist: he says that names (ideally) are natural in content but conventional in origin. Indeed, Socrates's account of names marks the transition to the new discourse of positivity because he claims not just that names are conventional (*nomōi*, that is, either statutory or customary) but also that names are deliberately imposed (*thesei*)—the term that will become translated into Latin as *positiva*. What is especially important and illuminating about this dialogue is how Socrates carefully and explicitly distinguishes his normative account of the correctness of names from his descriptive account of the origin of names: he says that names ideally are natural in content but positive in origin. By contrast, our theorists of positive law rarely distinguish in any explicit way between law positive by origin and law positive by content. In the legal context, the Socratic strategy for making this distinction explicit would be to observe that natural law might be posited or that law that is positive in content might well be customary. In short, Socrates argues that names are artificial without being arbitrary, just as many legal philosophers argue that law is artificial without being arbitrary.[31] But his insight is difficult to convey in the language of positive law, un-

---

31. David Hume famously observed: "Tho' the rules of justice be *artificial,* they are not *arbitrary.*" See *A Treatise of Human Nature* (Oxford: Clarendon Press, 1978), III, 2.2, p. 484.

less one explicitly distinguishes what is positive in source from what is positive in content, and that distinction will turn out to be astonishingly rare.

QUANDARIES OF POSITIVE LAW

When philosophers and jurists speak of positive law, they can be understood to make at least two quite different claims: either that law finds its source in some authoritative enactment (in contrast to custom) or that law lacks intrinsic moral force (in contrast to natural law). But these philosophers and jurists rarely, if ever, explicitly distinguish these two very different senses of positive law. As a result, the meaning of positive law oscillates unstably between them, and even in the context in which it is deployed, the reader is often not sure whether the focus of law's positivity is on the source of a law in deliberate enactment or on the morally contingent content of a law. As we shall see, a deep conflation of meanings is intrinsic to the concept of what is "positive," from its origins in Greek debates about language, through the discourse of positive law, up to the present. Thomas Gilby, when explaining what Thomas Aquinas means by positive law, offers this definition: "The low Latin term '*positivus*' signified what was accidental and imposed, not essential and inherent."[32] Notice that this definition actually compounds two distinct meanings: that positive law is law imposed and that law has an adventitious content. We find the same compound of meanings in the first definition of "positive" in the *Oxford English Dictionary*: "Formally laid down or imposed; arbitrarily or artificially instituted; proceeding from enactment or custom; conventional; opp. to *natural*." Here again positive means both "laid down" and "arbitrary." In one sense positive refers to a descriptive claim about the source of law, while in the other sense it refers to a normative claim about the content of law.

This conflation of meanings makes sense on the implied assumption that what possesses intrinsic moral force needs no enactment, while what lacks such moral force requires enactment. Such a basic moral principle as "you shall not kill" (properly restricted) possesses whatever force it has quite apart from whether or not it is or ever was enacted, while "drive on the left" would seem to have no moral force unless it were enacted. So it seems to make sense to conflate what is deliberately imposed with what lacks intrinsic moral force.

The conflation of these two meanings would not create quandaries for legal theory if they were coextensive: if every law laid down were arbitrary in content

32. Gilby in the Blackfriars edition of the *Summa Theologiae,* at I-II, 95.2c.

and if every legal norm arbitrary in content were laid down. But these two meanings are far from coextensive: sometimes basic moral principles are formally enacted (as in the Decalogue and the Constitution of the Federal Republic of Germany), while at other times legal rules that arise from custom are arbitrary or adventitious in content. We want to distinguish factual and empirical questions about law from normative and moral questions about law, even though, ultimately, we also want to understand the subtle interrelations of the empirical and the normative dimensions of law. Unfortunately, because the term *positive* is used to mean both "enacted" and "lacking in intrinsic moral force," the discourse of positive law often creates the impression that there is some necessary connection between what it enacted and what lacks intrinsic moral force. What is positive in source need not be positive in content; what is positive in content need not be positive in source.

At a deeper level, the discourse of positive law raises profound questions about the nature of a legal system and the individuation of laws. In this discourse, as we shall see, we find everywhere not only such expressions as natural, customary, and positive "law" but also natural, customary, and positive "laws." How are we to understand these distinctions? Is the law an aggregate of laws in the sense of discrete precepts to be sorted into mutually exclusive classes of natural, customary, or positive precepts? Or do we want to say that every legal norm, practice, and institution has natural, customary, and positive dimensions? Some writers strongly distinguish positive laws from customary laws on the basis of their different and often mutually exclusive sources. Positive international law, for example, is thought to come from, chiefly, treaties, conventions, and U.N. resolutions, while customary international law is thought to come from the actual practices of states. Positive municipal law, similarly, is thought to come from, chiefly, written constitutions, statutes, administrative regulations, and local ordinances, while customary municipal law is variously said to come from commercial usage, private ordering, and the usages of courts. Can we classify the various precepts of law into mutually exclusive categories on the basis of their source? Does customary law cease to be customary if adopted by a court or legislature and hence transmuted into positive law?

A very different way of understanding the relation of positive to customary law is developed by Lon Fuller, when he discusses the "implicit elements in made law" and the "made elements in implicit law."[33] Here, instead of sorting positive and customary laws into mutually exclusive classes based on their

33. Fuller, *Anatomy of the Law* (New York: Mentor, 1968), pp. 91–132.

sources, Fuller shows how a statute cannot be drafted, interpreted, or applied apart from a complex set of customs determining the promulagation, interpretation, and application of that law. New statutes, for example, are implicitly understood to revoke earlier statutes regulating the same matters; statutes are implicitly understood to remedy, not just declare, common law; the canons of interpreting statutes and applying them to specific cases are largely customary. Similarly, Fuller shows how customary practices of commercial bargaining are subtly shaped by the formalities of contract law and processes of arbitration. So all positive law has a customary dimension, just as all customary law has a positive dimension. The best example of the interpenetration of positive and customary law is common law. Although Hobbes claims that common law is positive law, because the judge's opinion is "the king's law, whosoever pens it," and although Blackstone and others claim that common law is customary law, the best accounts of common law acknowledge the important role of statutes in the formation and control of common law as well as of judicial customs, such as reasoning from precedents.

Our legal philosophers will also contrast natural law to positive law by focusing on the content of legal norms. This distinction was developed by medieval theologians in the context of deciding which parts of Mosaic law were natural (and, hence, binding also on Christians) and which parts were merely positive (and, hence, binding only on Jews). Thomas Aquinas sorts the 613 precepts of the Mosaic law into three mutually exclusive classes according to their normative content. The Mosaic precepts with intrinsic moral force he calls "natural" or "moral" laws, such as "you shall not kill" (Ex. 20:13); Mosaic precepts lacking intrinsic moral force, such as the precept "you must not wear clothing of wool and linen woven together" (Dt. 22:11), he calls the "positive" or "ceremonial" laws. Still other laws that regulate political and judicial institutions in ancient Israel he describes as a mixture of natural and positive. Since Mosaic law includes precepts of startlingly different normative content, it is tempting to think that laws can be sorted into mutually exclusive classes of natural and positive precepts. John Austin will also distinguish, within human positive law, natural law precepts from positive law precepts on the grounds that the natural law precepts of human law are universal whereas the positive law precepts are unique to each legal system.

At the same time, however, Thomas Aquinas insists that in every valid positive law we can discern the law of nature, showing that he does not always attempt to sort laws into mutually exclusive categories but insists upon the interlocking quality of moral and legal obligations. And Thomas Hobbes famously asserts that the natural law and the civil law contain each other. So the distinction between natural law and positive law can be meant to sort laws into very different classes of precepts, or it can be meant to draw our attention to the interpenetration of moral principle and legal convention in every law. Theorists of positive law disagree about whether every valid positive law must be consistent with objective morality.

The discourse of positive law, with its contrasts to customary law and to natural law, thus raises fundamental questions about how we understand a legal system. What is a law? Is it a discrete statute, judicial holding, administrative rule, or constitutional provision? Or are these items merely the focal point of a complex cluster of rules, principles, canons of interpretation, and judicial customs that define the scope, force, meaning, and application of the discrete precept? Is law an aggregate of rules, or is each law a web of rules, principles, standards, canons, and practices? When legal philosophers contrast positive law to natural law or to customary law, it is not usually clear whether they believe that a legal system can be sorted into natural, customary, and positive laws, or whether they believe that every legal rule, practice, and institution has a natural, customary, and positive dimension.

LEGAL POSITIVISM AND THE END
OF POSITIVE LAW

This is a book about positive law, emphatically not about legal positivism. I studiously avoid the whole complex and contentious question of legal positivism so that I might bring into focus the theory of positive law. Indeed, legal positivism turns out to have only a contingent relation to the discourse of positive law. Some of the major theorists of positive law, such as Thomas Aquinas, have never been described as legal positivists, while some major legal positivists, such as Jeremy Bentham, almost never refer to positive law. The discourse of positive law emerged among the theological humanists of the cathedral school of Chartres in the early twelfth century. Thomas Aquinas made extensive use of various expressions for "positive law" in his accounts of both divine and human law; to a lesser extent, so did Thomas Hobbes in both his Latin and his English works. The discourse of positive law reached its apotheosis in the work of John Austin, who subtitled his *Lectures on Jurisprudence,* "The Philosophy of Positive Law." Hans Kelsen was the last major legal theorist to make extensive use of the discourse of positive law. Ironically, legal positivism today has achieved its greatest sophistication and success after shedding the discourse of positive law.

And although the meaning of legal positivism has been subjected to a searching critical analysis by several contemporary theorists, the meaning of positive law has almost entirely escaped critical attention.[34] The leading contemporary legal positivists almost never refer to positive law—to find a contemporary analysis of law's positivity we must turn to the natural law theorist John Finnis.[35]

That a study of positive law is quite distinct from a study of legal positivism does not, of course, mean that the one will not illuminate the other. For example, the fact that law can be positive both in source and in content helps us to understand the twofold nature of the critique of legal positivism. Champions of customary and common law, from Henry Sumner Maine and James Bryce to James C. Carter and C. K. Allen, have focused their critique of Austinian positivism on the claim that all law is imposed by the sovereign. What they chiefly reject is the claim that all law can be traced to a single source in sovereign command. At the same time, champions of the moral claims of law, who insist that legal obligations are at least presumptively moral obligations and that the law that is cannot be understood apart from the law that ought to be, such as Jacques Maritain, Lon Fuller, Ronald Dworkin, and John Finnis, focus their critiques of legal positivism on the claim that the content of positive law has no necessary relation to objective morality. Indeed, so much of the recent debate about legal positivism has focused on issues about the relation of law to morality that it is easy to forget that Fuller and Dworkin, for example, also attacked the claim that all law finds its source in a single master norm or rule of recognition. Legal positivists today, having jettisoned the discourse of positive law, explicitly distance themselves from Austinian positivism. Still, most variants of legal positivism retain a twofold set of claims about the source of law and about its content: namely, that law can be identified and distinguished from other norms by a set of empirical criteria and that the content of law has no necessary connection to moral truth.

Throughout this book I tend to speak of the "discourse" of positive law

34. See H. L. A. Hart's analysis in *The Concept of Law*, 2nd edition (Oxford: Clarendon Press, 1994), p. 302; Joseph Raz, "The Purity of the Pure Theory," in *Essays on Kelsen*, ed. Richard Tur and William Twining (Oxford: Clarendon Press, 1986), pp. 79–97, at 81–82; and Matthew Kramer, *In Defense of Legal Positivism* (Oxford: Oxford University Press, 1999).

35. See Finnis's analysis of law's "positivity" in "The Truth in Legal Positivism," in *The Autonomy of Law: Essays on Legal Positivism*, ed. Robert P. George (Oxford: Clarendon Press, 1996), pp. 195–214.

rather than the "theory" of positive law precisely because the whole problematic of positive law has so rarely been subjected to explicit theoretical analysis. The discourse of positive law is ubiquitous in scholastic Latin and modern European jurisprudence, but this discourse is used more as a tool of legal analysis rather than as an object of legal analysis. Positive law is wrapped in the mystery of its own familiarity.

In the aftermath of Kelsen's jurisprudence, the discourse of positive law has fallen into desuetude; "positive law" never attained the level of theoretical reflection necessary to be deliberately revoked. In the Conclusion, I shall assess the rise and fall of the discourse of positive law. After showing some of the ways in which the discourse of positive law evolved from Aquinas to Kelsen, I shall consider some reasons why positive law remained at the center of legal philosophy for so long and why contemporary legal theorists have generally ceased to make use of it. I shall briefly argue that underlying both the rise and the fall of positive law is a deeper transformation of legal philosophy from a focus on legislatures to a focus on courts as the center of a legal system.

Chapter 1 Positive Language
and Positive Law in Plato's
Cratylus

The English expression *positive law* is by origin a direct translation of a variety of Latin expressions, such as *ius positivum* and *lex positiva;*[1] these Latin expressions, however, do not have their origin as translations or even paraphrases of any Greek expressions.[2] Instead, as Kuttner and others have shown, these Latin expressions for "positive" law find their origin in Greek debates about whether language is natural (*phusei*) or positive (*thesei*). The source of the new discourse of "positive" law and justice among the theologians and canonists of the twelfth-century cathedral school of Chartres seems to have been the rediscovery of Chalcidius's ancient commentary on Plato's *Timaeus,* in which Chalcidius speaks of "positive justice." Chalcidius himself in

1. The French *droit positif* and *loi positive* and the German *positives Recht* and *positiv Gesetz* are much better translations of the original Latin expressions.
2. As we shall see, some other related Latin expression for "positive law"—expressions central to the legal theory of Thomas Aquinas, such as *lex posita, ius positum,* and *legem ponere*—are direct translations of Greek expressions.

the fourth century likely drew the term *positiva* from Aulus Gellius, who used it in the second century to render Greek debates about language.[3] Gellius tells us that the Roman Pythagorean philosopher and friend of Cicero, P. Nigidius Figulus, "taught most shrewdly that names are not positive, but natural."[4]

My concern, however, is not lexical but philosophical. I am interested not in the origin and history of the Greek, Latin, and modern terms for positive law but rather in the concepts expressed by those terms. As we have observed, the first sense of "positive" is a descriptive thesis about the origins or source of a word or of a law: a positive word or law is one whose meaning or content was deliberately imposed. The second sense of "positive" is a normative thesis about the meaning of a word or the content of a law: a positive word lacks an intrinsic connection to its meaning just as a positive law lacks an intrinsic connection to morality. One cannot "see" the meaning of the word *green* in the word itself, nor does "green" sound green; its relation to the concept of green is purely contingent. Similarly, one cannot "see" the justice of paying a tax at 33.65 percent; that requirement has only a contingent relation to justice. By contrast, ono-

3. On the rediscovery of Chalcidius's commentary in the twelfth century in Latin (probably a translation of a Greek original) and on his reliance on Gellius, see Stephen Kuttner, *Repertorium der Kanonistik (1140–1234)*, vol. 1 (Vatican City: Biblioteca Apostolica, 1937), p. 176: "Aus welchen Quellen die französische Scholastik und Dekretistik den Ausdruck 'positives Recht' bildete—es wäre z. B. an des Chalcidius Kommentar au Platons Timäus zu denken—bedarf noch philosophiegeschichter Erforschung"; and p. 176 n. 2: "Da der Kommentar selber wohl nur eine Uebersetzung einer griechischen Kommentarkompilation ist, lässt sich vermuten, dass das Begriffspaar 'naturalis–positiva' eine Latinisierung von *physei–thesei* ist, wie sie auf grammatisch-sprachlogischem Gebiet schon bei Gellius . . . begegnet." Cf. Kuttner, "*Sur les origines du terme 'droit positif,'*" *Revue historique du droit français et étranger* 15 (1936): 728–40 at 739. Raymond Klibansky also claims that Chalcidius (circa A.D. 350) "reproduces in a Latin form the substance of a Greek exegesis," in *The Continuity of the Platonic Tradition During the Middle Ages* (London: Warburg Institute, 1939), pp. 22 and 27.

4. "Quod P. Nigidius argutissime docuit nomina non positiva esse, sed naturalia." Gellius then points to the Greek origin of this debate: "Quaeri enim solitum aput philosophos, *physei ta onomata* sint *ē thesei*." Aulus Gellius, *Noctes Atticae,* ed. P. K. Marshall, vol. 1 (Oxford: Clarendon Press, 1990), X, 4, p. 307. Other variants of *pono,* later used to describe positive law, were also derived from Greek debates about language: "Illi qui primi nomine imposuerunt rebus fortasse an in quibusdam sint lapsi." Varro, *De lingua Latina,* L, 8, 7. "Qui primus, quod summae sapientiae Pythagorae visum est, omnibus rebus imposuit nomina." Cicero, *Tusculan Disputations,* I, 25, 62. In my translations, I have benefited from Méridier's (Paris: Belles Lettres, 1931) and Reeve's (Indianapolis: Hackett, 1998) translations of Plato's *Cratylus* and from Arens's translation of Ammonius in *Aristotle's Theory of Language and Its Tradition* (Amsterdam: John Benjamins, 1984).

matopoetic words are said to have a natural relation to what they mean, while "you shall not kill" is said to have a natural relation to justice.

The first sense of "positive" is a descriptive thesis about the origin of a word or of a law: here the implicit contrast is usually with what is customary. The second sense of "positive" is a normative thesis about the content of a word or of a law: there the implicit contrast is with what is natural. Why is the word *positive* used to pick out both of these quite different conceptual contrasts? Perhaps because of the assumption that a sound can have a merely contingent or arbitrary relation to what it signifies or a law can have a merely contingent relation to morality only by deliberate imposition. Since the word does not have intrinsic meaning and the law has no intrinsic moral force, each must acquire that meaning or force by deliberate decision. Conversely, a word with an intrinsic relation to its meaning, such as "bang!", or a law with an intrinsic relation to morality, is often supposed to have no need of deliberate imposition. However, these inferences would be false: natural words and laws can (also) be deliberately imposed, just as contingent words and laws can arise from custom without deliberate imposition. So the two senses of positive law, while undeniably related, are far from coextensive. From the normative thesis about the content of a word or of a law we cannot infer a particular descriptive thesis about its origin, nor from a descriptive thesis about origins can we infer a particular normative thesis.

This conceptual conflation is not peculiar to English. A semantic analysis of the Latin terms for "positive" law (based on variants of *pono: legem ponere, lex posita, lex positiva, ius positivum*) as well as its Greek prototypes (variants of *tithēmi: thesis, keitai, thetikos, thesmos*) and modern European progeny (positive, *positif, positiv*) reveals a striking continuity from Greek antiquity to contemporary usage: in each language one word yokes together two quite different concepts.[5]

---

5. In the *Liddell-Scott-Jones Greek-English Lexicon* (Oxford: Oxford University Press, 1996) we see under "thesis": definition 2 a laying down, e.g., of arms and 5 (3) arbitrary determination; under *thetikos*: definition 1 imposition of names and 5 arbitrary usage. In the *Thesaurus Linguae Latinae* (Leipzig: B. G. Teubner, 1980) we read under *positio: actus vel effectus ponendi* (83.42) and *in quaestionibus philosophicis significatur modus, quo constituta sunt ea, quae putantur non naturaliter facta esse* (87.30); under *positivus* we read: *positione existens* and *quod non natura, sed positione, arte constitutum est* (90.21); under *positus* we read: *imponendo vel efficiendo* (92.61). That the Latin authors rendered the Greek *tithēmi* and variants with *pono* and variants is demonstrated in the *Corpus Glossariorum Latinorum*, ed. Georgius Goetz (Lipsiae: G. B. Tuebner, 1923); in vol. 2 (*Glossae Latinograecae et Graecolatinae*, 1888) we find these equivalences attested: *thesis = hicsituspositio,*

NATURE AND CONVENTION IN GREEK DEBATES
ABOUT LANGUAGE

The historians of "positive law" merely point to the ancient Greek debates about language as the lexical source of the discourse of positive law. Because they have not unpacked the conceptual complexity of "positive" law, they do not see how the Greek debates about language give rise not just to the terms but also, and more important, to the concepts and confusions of the whole discourse of law's positivity. Indeed, when we widen our horizons from the lexical to the conceptual, we shall discover that we cannot understand this newer discourse about what is natural (*phusei*) and what is positive (*thesei*) until we grasp how and why it grew out of the older discourse about what is by nature (*phusei*) and what is by convention (*nomōi*). The transformation of what is "conventional" into what is "positive" has profound significance for debates about language and about law across many thinkers and over many centuries; here we must restrict ourselves to a few pertinent observations.

The discovery of the contingent and the accidental is one of the latest and least welcome of human insights. We much prefer to think of our words and of our rules as grounded in nature or at least in tradition: thus, in coining new words we rarely invent new sounds, and our purely conventional measures, such as a meter or a yard, pretend to be based on natural dimensions.[6] The claim that many of our beliefs, practices, customs, and laws are not natural but conventional emerged originally from ancient Greek reflection upon language. As Felix Heinimann shows in detail in his classic study *Nomos und Physis,* the contrast of what is merely conventional to what is natural grew out of earlier contrasts in Greek thought between what is merely verbal and what is actually real. In every archaic society, language is thought to have, under certain circumstances, an intrinsic and even a causal relation to reality; this is the basis of

---

thetikos = positivus, positum = keimenon, positio = thesis; in vol. 7 (*Thesaurus Glossarum Emendatarum,* 1901) we find this: *pono = tithēmi.*

6. As Richard Robinson says: "We should probably acknowledge the arbitrary element in language more than we do; for that would encourage us to invent new sounds for our new names, instead of taking an old sound and thus creating a new ambiguity." From "A Criticism of Plato's *Cratylus*," in *Essays in Greek Philosophy* (Oxford: Clarendon Press, 1969), pp. 118–38, at 138. Guthrie says that an English act of 1824 provided that a "standard yard" should be "in terms of the length of a pendulum which, swinging in a vacuum in the latitude of London, should have a periodic time of two solar seconds exactly." See W. K. C. Guthrie, *A History of Greek Philosophy,* vol. 5 (Cambridge: Cambridge University Press, 1978), p. 21.

magical incantations, in which speech and reality, word and deed are inseparable. The philosophy of language begins with a reflection upon the contrast of word and deed. Homer emphasizes the heroic ideal of the unity of word and deed in the *Iliad* against the backdrop of awareness that they often diverge; and Odysseus became the compelling exemplar precisely of the possible contradiction between word and deed. Gradually, "mere" words or, as we still say, "mere" rhetoric" became devalued in favor of "real" deeds.[7] Over time these literary contrasts of word to deed (*epos, glotta, logos* to *ergon, pragma*) developed into philosophical contrasts of word to reality (*onoma* to *pragma, ergon, ontos*), of mere opinion to truth (*doxa* to *alētheia*).[8] Even in the heyday of the Sophistic contrast of what is by nature (*phusei*) and what is by convention (*nomōi*), Euripides would still invoke the older contrast: "They were friends in speech, but not in deeds."[9]

Several early Greek philosophers of nature reflected upon the chasm between what is said about the world and what is really true of it. Parmenides strongly contrasts the language of change with the reality of changelessness; our language of "coming into" and "passing out of" being and generally of change reflects only our beliefs, not reality.[10] Similarly, Empedocles says that the mingling and exchange of elements involves no birth or death; but he admits that

7. "Sondern hier erwächst aus der Erfahrung des Widerspruchs zwischen Worten und Taten die Höherbewertung der *erga* als des eigentlich 'Wirklichen' und entsprechend die Geringschätzung der *logoi*." Felix Heinimann, *Nomos und Physis* (Basel: Friedrich Reinhardt, 1945), p. 44.

8. See Heinimann, *Nomos und Physis*, pp. 42–58. For a critique of aspects of Heinimann, see Max Pohlenz's "Nomos und Physis," in *Kleine Schriften,* vol. 2, ed. Heinrich Dörrie (Hildesheim: Georg Olms, 1965), pp. 341–60.

9. Euripides, *Alcestis,* 339: "Logōi gar ēsan, ouk ergōi philoi." Cited in Heinimann, *Nomos und Physis,* p. 45. Note the instrumental dative construction across these various contrasts.

10. There are scholarly disputes about the exact text and translation of this passage in Parmenides. In Hermann Diels and Walter Kranz, *Die Fragmente der Vorsokratiker* (Berlin: Weidmannsche Verlagsbuchhandlung, 1954), hereafter DK, 28 frag. B 8, vss. 38ff.: "Tō panta'onom(a) estai, hossa brotoi katethento pepoithotes einai alēthē." They translate: "Darum wird alles *blosser* Name sein, was die Sterblichen *in ihrer Sprache* festgesetzt haben, überzeugt, es sei wahr." Kirk and Raven: "Tō pant'onomastai, hossa brotoi katethento pepoithotes einai alēthē." They translate: "Therefore it has been named all the names which mortals have laid down believing them to be true." See G. S. Kirk, J. E. Raven, and M. Schofield, *The Presocratic Philosophers,* 2nd edition (Cambridge: Cambridge University Press, 1983), p. 252. Parmenides's term for "positive" words (*kata tithēmi*) will also be used for "positive" law.

even he cannot avoid speaking of the combination and dissolution of these elements as a coming-into-being and a passing-out-of-being. By speaking of birth and death "they do not call them [the elements] what is just [to call them]; even I must say them with custom [*nomōi*]."[11] Here language is identified with mere opinion in contrast to the essential nature of reality. Democritus was famous for contrasting our merely subjective common speech to what is objectively real: by convention (*nomōi*), he says, there is sweet, bitter, hot, cold, and color; but in reality (*eteēi*), only atoms and the void.[12]

Recall that in one sense "positive" means contingent or accidental, as opposed to what is required by reason or nature. In the above passages, words are described as "positive" or conventional (*nomōi*) in this sense, as opposed to the reality of nature. However, "positive" can also mean what is deliberately "imposed or posited," in contrast to what spontaneously grows up by nature or custom. Because the Greek word for convention (*nomos*) could refer to either custom or statute, when Greek writers wished to emphasize the imposition of positive law, they would usually modify *nomos* with some variant of the verb *to impose* or *to set down* (*tithēmi*). If "positive" language and law is what is deliberately imposed, then we see the emergence of the discourse of "positive" language and of "positive" law in the same passage. The standard term employed by Plato, Aristotle, and others for a legislative enactment (*nomothetēma*) has its first attested use in describing words as "posited." Here (*De arte* 2), the Hippocratic writer says that names follow from the forms of things, "for it would be illogical and impossible for the forms [*eidea*] to have grown from the names, for names are legislative impositions on nature [*nomothetēmata* (*phuseōs*)], whereas forms are not legislative impositions, but natural growths."[13] In this passage, names are said to be positive not because they are adventitious but because they

---

11. See Empedocles in DK, 31 B, frags. 9 and 10. "Hē themis [ou] kaleousi, nomōi d' epiphēmi kai autos" (frag. 10).

12. Democritus in DK 68 B frag. 9. As Steinthal sums up: "Wir haben wohl bemerkt, wie Parmenides, Empedokles, Anaxagoras, Demokrit, auch Protagoras gewisse Wörter, weil sie *nomōi* seien, verwarfen; das heisst aber nur, dass die gewisse Vorstellungen, welche das Volk hatte, für falsch erklärten." H. Steinthal, *Geschichte der Sprachwissenschaft bei den Griechen und Römern,* vol. 1 (Hildesheim: Georg Olms, 1961), p. 75.

13. "Alogon gar apo tōn onomatōn hēgeisthai ta eidea blastanein kai adunaton. ta men gar onomata [phuseōs] nomothetēmata estin, ta de eidea ou nomothetēmata, alla blastēmata." DK, 87 B frag. 1. Of course, as Martin Ostwald suggests, this employment of *nomothetēma* in a linguistic context might well have been a deliberate borrowing from legal terminology. See Ostwald, *From Popular Sovereignty to the Sovereignty of Law* (Berkeley: University of California Press, 1986), p. 93.

are impositions on nature, rather than growths from nature. This is a descriptive thesis about the origin of names and the origin of natural forms: names are deliberate impositions, while natural forms are spontaneous growths.

Even the terms *natural* and *conventional,* then and now, mix normative and descriptive meanings. We often use "natural" to refer both to the spontaneous origin of something and to its essence. Similarly, Greek philosophers frequently used the term *nature* (*phusis*) to mean both the origin of a substance and its essence. In the passages cited above, Empedocles uses *phusis* to mean "birth," while the Hippocratic writer says that the forms are natural growths. In perhaps the first use of the nature/convention contrast in an ethical context, Archelaus, the teacher of Socrates, said that "living things first emerged from slime and that what is just and what is shameful are not by nature but by convention."[14] Here the claim seems to be a descriptive one: what is just did not emerge spontaneously in human evolution (as living things emerged from slime) but was deliberately invented. At the same time, of course, "nature" also means, especially when contrasted with "convention," what is permanent, real, and essential. Scholars have long debated whether *phusis* primarily refers to the origin (*genesis*) of things or to their essence (*ousia*).[15] But Aristotle tells us that nature means both, and that the two meanings are related, because "nature in the sense of origin is [oriented] toward nature [in the sense of essence]."[16] Greek philosophical thought about nature did not sharply distinguish empirical questions about the origins of things from normative and metaphysical questions about their essences.

In the case of what is "conventional" we find a similar set of contrasting meanings: to describe something as "conventional" can mean that it arose not spontaneously but by human artifice, either tacitly, through custom, or deliberately, through enactment; at the same time, one can use "conventional" as a term of normative appraisal, as when it means "merely believed, adventitious, or illusory"—what John Kenneth Galbraith calls "the conventional wisdom."

14. "Ta zōia apo tēs iluos gennēthēnai kai to dikaion einai kai to aischron ou phuei, alla nomōi." Archelaus in DK, 60 A 1; cf. A 2.
15. On *phusis* as *genesis,* see William Arthur Heidel: "*Peri Physeōs,*" *Proceedings of the American Academy of Arts and Sciences* 45 (1910): 79–133; on *phusis* as *ousia,* see Arthur Lovejoy, "The Meaning of *Physis* in the Greek Physiologers," *Philosophical Review* 18, no. 4 (July 1909): 369–83, and John Burnet, *Early Greek Philosophy* (London: A. & C. Black, 1920), appendix.
16. "Eti d' hē phusis hē legomenē hōs genesis hodos estin eis phusin." Aristotle, *Physica,* 193b 12, ed. W. D. Ross, Oxford Classical Texts (Oxford: Claredon Press, 1950).

For example, Socrates's disciple, Antisthenes, famously said that "according to convention there are many gods but according to nature only one."[17] What is merely said or believed (*nomizetai*) is contrasted with what is actually real and true (*phusei kai eteēi*). We have already seen how Parmenides, Empedocles, and Democritus denigrate what is merely conventional as illusory, subjective, and false; but the normative appraisal of convention need not be negative: Protagoras, among others, champions convention as our artful escape from the misery of the state of nature. Where nature is described as primitive and "red in tooth and claw," convention becomes valued as the basis of security, peace, the arts, and sciences.[18] Yet so great was the normative prestige of nature that even champions of convention resorted to appeals to it. One writer observes that, by nature, human beings are individually vulnerable and insecure in a state of nature, so that "by reason of these necessities law and the just were enthroned among men—and by no means to be overthrown, for by nature these things are strongly embedded."[19] Here the argument is that although conventions are artificial, they are not arbitrary, reflecting instead the necessities of natural survival. The author clearly wants to associate human conventions with the necessity, objectivity, and reality usually associated with nature.

Finally, the whole messy mixture of normative and descriptive theses at stake in the discourse of nature and convention is best revealed in the fragment of Antiphon, who notoriously counsels us to obey conventional laws only when we fear getting caught; otherwise, he says, we should follow the precepts of nature: "For the affairs of law are arbitrarily imposed [*epitithēmi*], while the affairs of nature are necessary; and the affairs of law are agreements, not natural growths, while the affairs of nature are natural growths, not agreements."[20] Antiphon not only describes how natural growths differ from artificial impositions; he also prescribes following nature, not convention, because nature is

---

17. "Kata nomon einai pollous theous, kata de phusin hena." Antisthenes, cited in Heinimann, *Nomos und Physis*, p. 42. Aristotle says: "For convention [*nomos*] is the opinion of the many, while the wise speak according to nature [*kata phusin*] and truth." *Sophistici elenchi*, ed. W. D. Ross, Oxford Classical Texts (Oxford: Clarendon Press, 1958), 173a 29.

18. The "Great Myth of Protagoras" is his story of how moral conventions rescue mankind from a bestial state of nature (see DK, 80 C1).

19. "Dia tautas toinun tas anagkas ton te nomon dai to dikaion embasileuein tois anthrōpois kai oudamēi metastēnai an auta. phusei gar ischura endedesthai tauta." Anonymous Iamblichi in DK, 89 6(1).

20. "Ta men gar tōn nomōn epitheta, ta de tēs phuseōs anagkaia. kai ta men tōn nomōn homologētheta ou phunt' estin, ta de tēs phuseōs phunta ouk homologēthenta." Antiphon in DK, 87 B 44 A 1.

necessary, true, and real. Moreover, Antiphon's conception of convention is "positivistic" in the sense that he sees conventions as deliberately "imposed" (*thesei*) rather than the tacit growth of custom.

PLATO'S *CRATYLUS* AND THE DISCOURSE OF POSITIVITY

The full significance of the transformation of the older discourse about what is natural or conventional into the new discourse of positivity is evident only when we turn to Plato. Plato's dialogue *Cratylus* has a uniquely pivotal role in the history of philosophical reflection upon language. No doubt Proclus, in his fifth-century commentary, oversimplifies when he says that "Pythagoras and Epicurus take the view of Cratylus while Democritus and Aristotle take the view of Hermogenes";[21] nonetheless, he is right that the dialogue canvasses virtually all the prior philosophical views on language, dialectically transforms the existing terms of the debates, and inspires the whole new discourse about what is natural and what is positive in the Stoic, Epicurean, Pythagorean, and Aristotelian traditions. Of special interest to us is the way in which this dialogue both exemplifies and playfully illuminates the ambiguities of the whole discourse of positivity both before and after Plato.[22] As we have seen, the pre-Socratic debates about whether language or other institutions were by nature or by convention oscillated between two sets of concerns: first, whether the content of names or other practices reflected reality and truth or merely illusion and opinion; second, whether the origin of names and other practices is to be found in spontaneous growth (of nature or of custom) or in deliberate imposition. In the context of such a two-front war it is often difficult to know whether a defender of nature or a defender of convention is making a claim about the origin or about the content of language. Moreover, this double contrast opens the possibilities for many mixed positions, such as that language is natural in content but conventional in origin or natural in origin but conventional in content. Socrates playfully exploits this mixed position in the dialogue.

Hermogenes opens the dialogue by framing the debate about words within the framework of the common Sophistic contrast of what is natural and what is

---

21. *Procli diadochi in Platonis Cratylum commentaria,* ed. Georgius Pasquali (Lipsiae: B. G. Teubner, 1908), p. 5.25.

22. Thus, a recent commentator on this dialogue describes Hermogenes as a defender of the correctness of "positive" names. See Rachel Barney, "Plato on Conventionalism," *Phronesis* 42, no. 2 (1997): 143–62, at 146.

conventional.[23] Hermogenes tells Socrates that Cratylus argues that "in the name for each being there is a correctness that grows up by nature, and names are not simply what people agree to call things."[24] Here, even before the use of the term *convention* (*nomos*), we find the familiar opposition, in all its ambiguities, between what is natural and what is conventional, for what "people agree" (*sunthemenoi*) to call things implies "what people ordinarily believe" (*nomizetai*).[25] Hermogenes has perhaps unwittingly ascribed to Cratylus two quite separate theses: first, that the content of each name is by its nature (*phusei*), meaning by its essence, intrinsically related to a being; and, second, that this correct relation between words and beings arose by natural growth (*pephukuian*). Socrates will later show us that the first thesis in no way depends upon the second.

If Cratylus's naturalism is ambiguous, so is Hermogenes's conventionalism. Hermogenes seems to deny both kinds of naturalism: he rejects the view that there is an intrinsic relation between each name and each being by asserting that names for the same slave can vary over time (384 D) and that names for the same things vary over space (385 E). He also denies that names grow up naturally by saying that they arise from agreement (*sunthēma,* 383 A, *sunthēkē, homologia,* 384 D) or from individual stipulation (*thētai,* 384 D, *ethemēn,* 385 D) or from custom and habit (*nomōi kai ethei,* 384 D). Hermogenes thus offers several mutually inconsistent views about the origins of names, and he has often been taken to task by commentators for effacing the distinction between stipulative and lexical (or customary) definitions. An individual act of stipulation does not an agreement or a custom make. The two prongs of his attack on Cratylus's naturalism are perhaps related by the ordinary assumption that if names lack an intrinsic relation to their objects, then they must find their ori-

23. Robinson appears to deny this when he says: "Many interpreters, however, have falsely said or implied that the *Cratylus* does oppose nature to law." It is not clear, however, how a dialogue, especially a Platonic dialogue, could speak so univocally; does Robinson mean that Plato (or Socrates) does not oppose nature to law? Whatever might be said about "the *Cratylus,*" Robinson concedes that Hermogenes initially opposes *phusis* to *nomos.* See Richard Robinson, "The Theory of Names in Plato's *Cratylus,*" in *Essays in Greek Philosophy* (Oxford: Clarendon Press, 1969), pp. 112–13.

24. Plato, *Cratylus,* 383 A, in Louis Méridier's edition of the Greek text: *Platon: Oeuvres Complètes,* vol. 5, part 2 (Paris: Belles Lettres, 1931).

25. Of this contrast of *phusei* to *sunthemenoi* in 383 A, Goldschmidt says: "Qui recouvre sans doute l'antithèse *nomōi–physei.*" Victor Goldschmidt, *Essai sur le "Cratyle"* (Paris: H. Champion, 1940), p. 40.

gin and their correctness in the agreements, choices, and decisions of men and of communities.

Hermogenes concludes his framing of the debate by deploying the classic terms in all their ambiguity: "For a name does not naturally grow [*pephukenai*] for each being by nature [*phusei*] but by the custom [*nomōi*] and habit [*ethei*] of those habituated" (384 D). Is the dispute here about the intrinsic content of names or about the origin of names? Whether names have an intrinsic relation to their objects or not directly raises the normative question of the "correctness" of names, that is, whether names are revelatory of real beings. This fundamental ambiguity in how the debate is framed helps to explain why scholars have never been able to agree on the theme of the dialogue.

Despite the ancient title of the dialogue—"Concerning the Correctness of Names"[26]—many commentators have argued that the object of inquiry is actually the origin of language.[27] Other scholars insist that the primary issue is not the origin of names but their content and the relation of that content to reality, that is, their correctness.[28] Those who summarily reject the salience of the

26. "Peri onomatōn orthotētos."

27. Max Leky cites Sütterlius with approval: "Plato . . . untersucht in seinem *Kratylus* schon die Frage, ob die Wörter das Ergebnis natürlicher Entwicklung oder des Menschen willkürliche Erfindung, ob sie *physei* entstanden seien oder *synthēkē*." Leky announces: "Die Frage nach dem Sprachursprung bildet ja den Kerninhalt dieses Dialoges." Max Leky, "*Plato als Sprachphilosophe*," in *Studien zur Geschichte und Kultur des Altertums,* vol. 10, no. 3 (Paderborn: Ferdinand Schöningh, 1919), p. 2 n. 1 and *Vorwort.* A. E. Taylor says that "the ostensible subject of discussion is the origin of language" in *Plato* (London: Methuen, 1929), p. 77. H. N. Fowler, in his introduction to his translation of the *Cratylus,* sees no distinction between the two possible themes: "Socrates is further requested to set forth his own opinion concerning the correctness of names or, in other words, the origin of language." *Plato,* vol. 6, Loeb Classical Library (London: Heinemann, 1926), p. 3.

28. Steinthal cites Julius Deuschle with approval: "Plato unternahm es nicht, die Natur der Sprache um ihrer selbst zu entwickeln, sondern um ihren gewähnten Wert für de Erkenntnis der Wahrheit und des Wesenhaften in seiner Unbegründung aufzuzeigen." Deuschle says of Plato: "Dass seine Methode nicht genetisch, sondern ontisch war." See Steinthal, *Geschichte der Sprachwissenschaft,* vol. 1, p. 92. Robinson: "Since the *Cratylus* is solely about the correctness of names, it is not about the origin of names, either wholly or in part." See "The Theory of Names in Plato's *Cratylus,*" p. 103. "Plato's *Cratylus* repeatedly declares itself to be an investigation of 'correctness of names,' and that is what it is. But generations of commentators have described it as something else—usually as a fantasy on the origin of language." Norman Kretzmann, "Plato on the Correctness of Names," *American Philosophical Quarterly* 8, no. 2 (April 1971): 126–38, at 126. Friedländer begins dogmatically: "The debate, to begin with, has nothing to do with the problem of the origin of language . . . ," but later he says of Robinson's view, quoted above, that it

issue of the origin of names too often assume that an exploration of origins must mean a historical investigation. Plato, however, seems quite interested in other kinds of origins, such as hypothetical origins in the act of a name giver or logical derivation from elements. Still, even conceding that the primary focus of the dialogue is the correctness of names, a number of views of the origin of names (not necessarily just historical origins but also hypothetical and logical origins) are discussed, if only to shed light on the source of the correctness of names.[29] Some commentators implicitly reveal the focus of their inquiry by their descriptions of the role of nature and convention in the dialogue. To ask whether *names* are natural or conventional focuses attention on the descriptive question of the origins of language; by contrast, to ask whether the *correctness* of names is natural or conventional focuses attention on the normative question of the truthfulness of language.[30]

Because they do not distinguish their claims about the origins of names from their claims about the content of names, Cratylus and Hermogenes do not articulate what kind of relation they see between them. Does Cratylus think that names arise spontaneously because of their intrinsic connection to their objects, or do names have that intrinsic relation because they arise spontaneously? Does Hermogenes think that names lack an intrinsic relation to their objects because they are deliberately imposed, or the converse? Does Cratylus think that a name with a natural content simply cannot have its origin in deliberate stipulation?[31] Does Hermogenes think that names lacking a natural content

---

"is much too narrow." Paul Friedländer, *Plato,* vol. 2 (New York: Bollingen, 1964), pp. 196 and 340 n. 2.

29. "Plato wants to prove the correctness of the *physei*-principle by explaining it as one of the ways in which words fulfill their basic aim as means of communication. This could not be proved in a better way than by looking at the very moment when words are being created for this purpose." Alfons Nehring, "Plato and the Theory of Language," *Traditio* 3 (1945): 13–48, at 21. W. K. C. Guthrie observes that we find rival views of the origin of language in Plato's *Cratylus* in his *History of Greek Philosophy,* vol. 2 (Cambridge: Cambridge University Press, 1965), p. 474.

30. Thus Steinthal contrasts the questions "ob die *onomata physei* oder *nomōi* seien" and "bei der Frage von *nomōi* oder *physei* oder *orthotēs* gar nicht der Ursprung der Sprache in Betracht, sondern nur ihr Verhältnis zur Erkenntnis, zum Wissen." Steinthal, *Geschichte der Sprachwissenschaft,* vol. 1, pp. 75 and 78. Friedländer chides a commentator: "Is not the antithesis *nomōi-physei* incorrectly transferred to language instead of the *orthotēs*?" in *Plato,* vol. 2, p. 342 n. 11.

31. Bernard Williams ascribes this view to Cratylus: "There is no act which a *nomothetēs* or anyone else can perform to *make* 'N' the name of Y—'N' either bears the required φ-relation to Y or it does not." Williams, "Cratylus' Theory of Names and Its Refutation,"

might have a natural origin, as the *m* sound in mother seems to arise naturally in many languages? Neither the participants in the dialogue nor generally their commentators ask or attempt to answer these questions, because of the lack of a clear acknowledgment of the two dimensions of these arguments.

Plato invites us to explore these questions by having Socrates develop one of his familiar arguments from the arts. If a name is a kind of tool (388 A)—a tool for dividing things by their natures (388 B)—and if a tool is to be effective it must designed according to the nature of the material in which it is to work.[32] The craftsman must make his tools not arbitrarily (*boulēthēi*) but naturally (*pephuke*).[33] Recall the view in the Hippocratic *De arte* that the arts take their terms from natural kinds. For Plato, the arts are paradigms and proofs that what is artificial need not be arbitrary. Indeed, the very power of true artifice depends upon a disciplined naturalism: one cannot deliberately impose a form upon matter without genuine knowledge of what forms are by nature suited to what kinds of matter. In Plato's view, the arts represent convention working in cooperation with nature: by origin, the arts are conventional, stemming, as they do, from particular human purposes and decisions; but in content, the arts are natural, because they rest on the knowledge of natural kinds, on the essential properties of things.[34]

For these reasons, Plato's appeal to the arts—to names as tools and to name givers as craftsmen—is generally regarded as his strategy for transcending the Sophistic antithesis of convention and nature.[35] Socrates proceeds to develop a political and legislative model for the ideal origin and correctness of names.

---

in *Language and Logos,* ed. Malcolm Schofield and Martha C. Nussbaum (Cambridge: Cambridge University Press, 1982), pp. 83–93, at 89–90.

32. Socrates says that the craftsman must put into each tool the form or nature (*phusin*) that is naturally (*pephuke*) most appropriate for a particular task (389 B–C).

33. 389 C.

34. As evidence that the content of the arts is natural, Socrates says that blacksmiths make the same tool for the same task both in Greece and among the barbarians (389 E to 390 A).

35. Steinthal observes: "So wäre denn, wenn die Untersuchung rücksichtlich der *onomata* glückte, im allgemeinen wenigstens und an einem besondren Fall der Gegensatz von *nomōi* und *physei* aufgelöst." See *Geschichte der Sprachwissenschaft,* vol. 1, p. 94. Goldschmidt also says: "Ainsi l'antagonisme de ces deux concepts sophistiques s'evanouit devant la dialectique platonicienne." In *Essai sur le "Cratyle,"* p. 64. Friedländer also says: "*Nomos* here appears also in a peculiar conjunction with *physis,* and we begin to realize that the customary contrast between *nomos* and *physis* does not penetrate to the depth of the real problem." See *Plato,* vol. 2, p. 201.

The highest, or royal, art is political (*Statesman,* 289 D), and the craftsman of names is a legislator or lawgiver (*nomothetēs,* 388 E, 428 E, 429 A, 431 E). Socrates repeatedly refers to the maker of names (*onomatourgos*) as a legislator (*nomothetēs*), who is, he says, the craftsman most rarely met among humans (389 A). In his ideal account, Socrates consistently uses the Greek verb *to set down* or *to impose* (*tithēmi*) when describing the origin of names: the law imposer (*nomothetēs*) is responsible for imposing names (*onomata thēsesthai,* 390 D). Just as few have a craftsman's knowledge of the natural kinds with which he works, so few are qualified to be a legislator of names—only he who knows the name by nature (*phusei*) suited to each thing (389 D and 390 E).

Socrates's dialectical transformation of the dispute between Hermogenes and Cratylus sheds a great deal of light on the deep ambiguities of the whole discourse about what is conventional and what is natural. To Cratylus he says: you are right that (at least ideally) names ought to reflect the nature or essence of what they name; but you are wrong to suppose that names must grow up naturally or spontaneously. To Hermogenes he says: you are right that names do not grow up naturally but are the product of human conventions; but you are wrong to think that names ought not reflect the nature of what they name. In other words, Socrates reveals the conceptual conflation of the standard discourse about what is natural and what is conventional by offering an account that is both naturalist and conventionalist: he says that names are (or ought to be) natural in content but are conventional in origin, challenging the assumption that what is natural in content must be natural in origin or that what is conventional in origin must be conventional in content. Names are artificial but not arbitrary. It is not quite accurate to say that Socrates has transcended the antithesis of nature and convention; rather, he has distinguished two kinds of antitheses and offered a mixed account. He continues to contrast what is natural in content with what is merely adventitious and he continues to contrast what grows up naturally with what is deliberately imposed. Socrates has greatly clarified and deepened the traditional antithesis rather than transcended it.

Ammonius (c. 445–526) is the only commentator on Plato's *Cratylus,* to my knowledge, who argues that Socrates draws his mixed solution from two sets of antitheses. He says of the characters in the dialogue that those who claim that names are by nature (*phusei*) use that expression in a twofold way, just as those who claim that names are by convention (*thesei*) use that expression in a twofold way.[36] According to Ammonius, Cratylus believes that names are by

---

36. Ammonius's commentary on the *Cratylus* appears in his commentary on Aristotle's *On*

nature in the sense of being "the works of nature" (*dēmiourgēmata phuseōs*) while others believe that names are by nature in the sense that names are artificial pictures (*homoiōmata*) of real things.[37] In other words, "by nature" can refer to the origin of a name or to its content. Similarly, says Ammonius, when Hermogenes says that names are "by convention" he means that anyone can name anything as he pleases (*ethelēi onomati*); but others mean "by convention" (*thesei*) that a name is imposed or laid down (*tithesthai*) by a single name giver (*hypo monou tou onomatothetou*).[38] Here the first sense of "by convention" refers to the adventitious content of names, while the second refers to the origin of names in deliberate imposition. Ammonius rightly observes that Socrates shows the compatibility of the second sense of "by nature" with the second sense of "by convention": a wise lawgiver of names can deliberately impose names whose content is natural.[39]

Socrates has also subtly transformed the traditional antithesis by revealing the ambiguity of the concept of convention (*nomos*). The Greek and the English terms are ambiguous as to those institutions that grow and evolve from custom and those that are deliberately imposed by stipulation or law. All conventions are the product of human action but not necessarily of any human design. In many contexts, the ambiguity does not matter: all conventions are in certain respects unnatural. When Greek philosophers wish to emphasize customary conventions, they speak of custom or habit (*ethos*), of unwritten law (*agraphos nomos*), or of cooperative agreement (*sunthēkē* or *homologia*); when they wish to emphasize deliberate stipulation and imposition by a superior to an inferior, they modify the words for name (*onoma*) or for law (*nomos*) with a variant of the verb *to impose* (*tithēmi*).

As we saw above, Hermogenes has no consistent vocabulary for describing the conventions by which, in his view, names come about: often he uses terms suggesting that they emerge from custom by spontaneous agreement (*sunthēma* or *homologia*) or from custom and habit (*nomōi kai ethei*); but he also uses terms suggesting deliberate stipulation or imposition (*thētai* or *ethemēn*). Socrates, by contrast, in his ideal account, consistently deploys the vocabulary of deliberate stipulation or indeed of legislative enactment when he discusses

---

Interpretation, see text in *Ammonius in Aristotelis De interpretatione commentarius,* ed. Adolfus Busse, in *Commentaria in Aristotelem Graeca,* vol. 4, part 5, p. 34.20.

37. *Ammonius in Aristotelis De interpretatione commentarius,* pp. 34.23 and 35.8.
38. *Ammonius in Aristotelis De interpretatione commentarius,* p. 35.15–16.
39. *Ammonius in Aristotelis De interpretatione commentarius,* p. 36.22ff.

the origin of names; he repeatedly says that names are laid down just as laws are "laid down" (*keisthai* or *keitai,* 429 A to C) by a lawgiver (*nomothetēs*).

Socrates's appeal to the lawgiver as the source of names transforms the whole discourse about what is natural and what is conventional. Socrates has radically sharpened and simplified the vague notion of convention (custom and/or law) into the clear notion of deliberate stipulation. In other words, the traditional discourse about what is natural and what is conventional now becomes a discourse about what is natural (*phusei*) and what is positive (*thesei*)—a discourse that, beginning in the twelfth century, will come to dominate philosophical jurisprudence.

The question, then, is not whether the lawgiver is meant to be a historical figure or a mere personification; the question is what idea of order is represented by the lawgiver.[40] Some scholars argue that Socrates's appeal to the stipulation of an expert craftsman is deeply rooted in Plato's own view that all true order, whether natural or conventional, must be understood as if it were the product of deliberate design.[41] The demotion of custom as a source of linguistic or legal order is the most significant aspect of this new discourse of positivity. When convention was contrasted with nature, convention included custom; but when stipulation is contrasted with nature, custom is assimilated to nature as a "second nature." If names are posited by a lawgiver, then they do not

40. Some scholars interpret the lawgiver as the personification of deliberate stipulation and enactment. Guthrie describes the contrast of Socrates and Hermogenes as: "The opposition is between *thesis* (*kata physin*) by a single, mythical divine or heroic *heuretēs* and the collective action (*homologia* or *synthēkē*) of an evolving society." See *History of Greek Philosophy,* vol. 3 (Cambridge: Cambridge University Press, 1969), p. 206n. Goldschmidt agrees: "Hermogène entend par *nomos* l'usage, tandis que Socrate, en postulant le nomothète le prend au sens de loi." *Essai sur le "Cratyle,"* p. 63. But other scholars reject this contrast by interpreting the lawgiver as merely a personification of custom: "And if we demythologize the theory we find behind the device nothing so simple as Solon or Peisistratus, but something like the interacting combination of good English usage and the Oxford English Dictionary." Kretzmann, "Plato on the Correctness of Names," p. 129.

41. "Right and legitimate name-giving is declared to be an affair of science or art, like right and legitimate polity: it can be performed by the competent scientific or artistic namegiver, or by the lawgiver considered in that special capacity . . . the Platonic point of view comes out—deliberate authorship from the scientific or artistic individual mind, as the only source of rectitude or perfection." George Grote, *Plato, and the Other Companions of Sokrates,* vol. 3 (London: John Murray, 1888), pp. 281 and 329–30. "Everything starts by voluntary imposition, according to Plato's usual assumption." Robinson, "Theory of Names in Plato's *Cratylus,*" p. 111.

grow up either by nature or by custom. The new contrast is between what is imposed from the top (*thesei*) and what grows up from below (*phusei* or *ethei*), between what is made and what has grown.[42] As we shall see, the view that names and laws are posited will have a profound effect on the capacity of philosophical reflection on language and law to grasp the role of custom as an independent source of social order.

We have seen that the Socratic ideal for the correctness of names is for them to be posited, according to nature, by a lawgiver supervised by a dialectician (390 D), just as Plato's ideal republic is governed by guardian dialecticians (*Republic* 532 A). But Plato is concerned to understand not just the best possible regime but also the second-best or practically best regime. Near the end of the *Cratylus*, Socrates comes to accept custom and agreement as a second-best basis for the correctness of names. Socrates observes that the name "hardness" (*sklērotēs*), with its liquid *l* does not sound like what it names (435 A), yet we can use this name correctly because of habit (*ethos*), custom, or covenant (*suntheto, sunthesis*). Indeed, Socrates says that habit (*ethos*) can ground signification by names both like and unlike what they name (435 B). Here Socrates is again distinguishing between the origin of a word and its content: words having their origin in habit, he says, can be in content natural or not. Similarly, when it comes to the names of the numerals, says Socrates, surely we must rely on agreement and covenant (*homologia kai sunthēkē*, 435 B). Yet Socrates emphasizes that such reliance on custom is unfortunate and purely *faute de mieux:* "We'll have to resort to that burdensome thing, covenant" (435 C).[43] Most commentators see this passage (435 A to D) as reflecting Socrates's concessions,

---

42. Grote cites Mill that "languages are not made, but grow"; Grote says that Plato rejects this emphasis on nature or custom as a source of order: "A Kosmos which grows by itself and keeps up its own agencies, without any extra-kosmic constructor or superintendent: in like manner, an aggregate of social customs, and an aggregate of names, which have grown up no one knows how." *Plato, and the Other Companions of Sokrates,* vol. 3, pp. 328. Robinson says of Plato: "His conservatism is not the English idea that the constitution has grown by itself and what has grown naturally is best. It is the Greek conservatism that some great legislator or god has made the natural constitution and we must see that his work is not defaced." In "Theory of Names in Plato's *Cratylus*," p. 111.

43. "In the absence of such a best standard, we are driven to eke out language by appealing to a *second-best*, an inferior and vulgar principle approximating more or less to rectitude—that is, custom and convention." Grote, *Plato, and the Other Companions of Sokrates,* vol. 3, p. 282.

if grudging, to Hermogenes's opening arguments, but this is not accurate. Recall that Hermogenes lumped everything into his notion of convention (*nomos*)—habit and custom as well as stipulation and imposition (*thesis*). Socrates, by contrast, through his language, has carefully distinguished the deliberate imposition of the lawgiver from the organic habits and customs of language users.[44]

We observed above that the whole discourse about what is natural and what is conventional seems to have emerged from archaic Greek reflections upon the gap between words and deeds—which in turn inspired early Greek philosophical reflections upon the gap between conventional language and natural reality. Many of the original Greek philosophers commented upon the chasm between what is or even can be said about nature and what is actually true of nature. In the *Cratylus,* Greek thought about convention and nature comes full circle when, at the end of the dialogue, Socrates frames the whole debate about whether names derive their correctness from nature or from convention within the larger and older debate about the relation of language itself to reality. Even assuming an original or ideal name giver, who deliberately creates and imposes names correctly according to natural kinds, there will still be a chasm between the name and the object of which it is an image. Reverting to the ancient contrast, Socrates says that names (*onomata*) are not deeds or affairs (*pragmata*) but merely images (*eikonas*) of them (439 A). And, says Socrates, it is better to learn from the truth (*alētheia*) than from a mere image (439 A to B), just as it is better to learn from real beings (*ta onta*) than from mere names (*onomata,* 439 B). Deeper than the contrast of names correct by convention or by nature is the contrast between everything artificial (including all names) and what is truly by nature real. We find a similar point made about law in the Platonic *Minos:* we don't find the truth in names or in laws but only in what is real, though names and laws might be useful heuristics in discovering what is truly real. Thus, a name that fails to name anything real is no name, just as a law that violates moral reality is no law.[45]

---

44. Compare Socrates's use of variants of *tithēmi* in connection with the lawgiver of names (389 to 391) and the absence of those variants in 435 A to D.

45. "Thus law is a judgment discovering what is real" (*ho nomos ara bouletai tou ontos einai exeuresis*), *Minos,* 315 A. "It would not be fitting to take an evil resolution to be a law" (*ouk ara harmottoi an to ponēron dogma nomos einai*), *Minos,* 314 E. Rachel Barney points to these parallels in the *Minos* in her "Plato on Conventionalism," p. 160 n. 24.

THE RISE OF THE ANTITHESIS OF WHAT
IS NATURAL AND WHAT IS POSITIVE

If the *Cratylus* pivots back into the origins of Greek philosophy, it also pivots forward into the future discourse of positivity. When Socrates describes a lawgiver who imposes names according to nature, he thereby distinguishes what is positive in origin from what is positive in content. As we shall see, Plato is more explicit about the two senses of positivity than are the legal philosophers from Thomas Aquinas to John Austin and beyond. Moreover, by contrasting what is deliberately imposed (*thesei*) with what grows up, either by nature or by custom, Socrates has launched a transformation of the whole discourse of what is natural and what is conventional into the discourse of what is natural and what is positive.

It is curious that the debate between Hermogenes and Cratylus should become the exemplar among ancient commentators for the contrast between what is posited (*thesei*) and what is natural (*phusei*), since the Platonic characters frame their debate in terms of what is conventional and natural; and with respect to Socrates, far from sharply contrasting what is posited with what is natural, he tries to join them.[46] Nonetheless, in the subsequent Hellenistic and Roman discussions of language and law, the debates both before and after Plato are now discussed in terms of what is natural and what is positive.[47] Most scholars see the natural/positive contrasts as Hellenistic in origin, but our concern is not with the origin but with the significance of this new discourse.[48] As

46. Robinson says of the speakers of the *Cratylus:* "They never oppose nature to *positing, physis* to *thesis.*" Robinson, "Theory of Names in Plato's *Cratylus,*" p. 110. True, Socrates does expressly unite what is positive in origin with what is natural in content; but Socrates also implicitly contrasts what is imposed with what grows up by nature or by custom.

47. Proclus not only says that the debate between Hermogenes and Cratylus is about what is respectively positive (*thesei*) or natural (*phusei*) but also says that Democritus and Aristotle side with Hermogenes, while Pythagoras and Epicurus side with Cratylus. See *Procli diacochi in Platonis Cratylum commentaria,* pp. 4, X, and 5, XVI.

48. Steinthal is typical: "*Thesei* . . . aus der späteren alexandrinischen Zeit stammt." See his *Geschichte der Sprachwissenschaft,* vol. 1, p. 76. Nehring refers to "the replacement of the term *nomōi* by *thesei* that took place at some time during the Hellenistic period." See Alfons Nehring, "Plato and the Theory of Language," p. 34. Cf. Detlev Fehling, "Zwei Untersuchungen zur Griechischen Sprachphilosophe," *Rheinisches Museum für Philologie* 108, no. 3 (1965): 212–29, at 218ff. Gregory Vlastos, however, defends *thesei ta onomata* as authentically Democritean in *Studies in Greek Philosophy,* vol. 1 (Princeton: Princeton University Press, 1995), p. 353n.

we have seen in the *Cratylus,* Socrates describes a name giver who posits names according to nature; this positing (*thesei*) sharply contrasts with what grows up by nature or by custom. However, in the context of the Hellenistic discourse about what is natural and what is positive, *thesei,* like *nomōi,* became ambiguous and could refer either to the origin of words or of laws in deliberate imposition or to the adventitious content of words or of laws. What was "positive" was assumed to be both deliberately imposed and adventitious, yet Socrates' ideal lawgiver gave names that were artificial but not at all arbitrary.[49]

Aristotle's treatise *On Interpretation* (*Peri hermēneias*) is the first major interpretation and critique of Plato's *Cratylus.*[50] As we shall see, Aristotle's views about the origin of language are transformed beyond recognition by Hellenistic Greek and later Latin commentary; this transformation will contribute a great deal to the new discourse of positive law from Aquinas to Hobbes. In the second chapter of this treatise, Aristotle says about names: "A name is a spoken sound meaningful according to covenant or agreement (*kata sunthēkēn,* 16a 19) . . . of names, there is none by nature (*phusei*) but only when it has become a symbol" (16a 27).[51] It is understandable, although misleading, to say with Proclus that Aristotle takes the side of Hermogenes,[52] since the latter does say, among other things, that names arise from covenant or agreement (*sunthēkē*). Aristotle's account of language is embedded in an account of cognition in which spoken names are conventional symbols of the affects of the soul, but these affects of the soul are said to be natural likenesses of the things themselves; in short, Aristotle's full account weaves natural likeness and conventional symbol together in a way that transcends the debate between Hermogenes and Cratylus.[53]

49. "The new term [*thesei*] was meant to indicate the way in which the conventional connection between word and thing . . . arose, namely, by an absolutely arbitrary act of the word-creator." Nehring, "Plato and the Theory of Language," p. 34.

50. "Aristotle in the first chapters of *De interpretatione* obviously has his eye on the *Cratylus.*" Guthrie, *History of Greek Philosophy,* vol. 3, p. 208n (Cambridge: Cambridge University Press, 1969).

51. Greek text from Oxford Classical Texts, ed. L. Minio-Paluello.

52. Unfortunately, even Guthrie says this in his *History of Greek Philosophy,* vol. 3, p. 208n.

53. Ammonius rightly observes that in Aristotle's overall account of language and cognition (16a, 3–8), there are both natural and conventional elements, though Ammonius turns Aristotle's "by convention" into a deliberate "by imposition": "According to Aristotle, there are four elements, two by nature and two by imposition; the things themselves and the concepts are by nature while the spoken words and the written marks are by imposition": "Toutōn de tōn tettarōn ta men duo phusei einai phēsin ho Aristotelēs, ta de duo

What is difficult to understand is how commentators could equate Aristotle's view that names have significance according to covenant (*kata sunthēkēn*) with the view that names are significant by deliberate imposition (*thesei*). Still, the ancient Greek commentators began to equate these expressions, despite the great differences between them.[54] These Greek expressions convey very different understandings of language, differences that will prove decisive for the new theory of positive law. First, covenants and agreements are not imposed from above but grow up gradually and tacitly from below; second, impositions can be unilateral, while covenants must be multilateral. To say that language is based on covenants is to say that language presupposes a community of speakers and listeners who share a set of common expectations about the meanings of words.[55] By contrast, to say that language is based on imposition is to imagine that language is based on the individual, authoritative act of giving names to things—not unlike Adam naming the beasts.[56] Hermogenes himself, when il-

---

thesei. phusei men ta te pragmata kai ta noēmata, thesei de tas te phōnas kai ta grammata." Text in *Ammonius in Aristotelis De interpretatione commentarius,* pp. 30.31, 19.1

54. Origen says in *Contra Celsum:* "Poteron, hōs oietai Aristotelēs, thesei esti ta onomata, ē hōs nomizousin hoi apo tēs Stoas, phusei." Cited in J. Engels, "Origine, sens et survie du terme boècien *secundum placitum,*" *Vivarium* 1, no. 2 (1963): 87–114, at 100. Ammonius directly equates them: "To kata sunthēkēn, tauton sēmainon tōi thesei." Text in *Ammonius in Aristotelis De interpretatione commentarius,* p. 30.31; cf. pp. 35–37 passim.

55. What Engels says of Plato also applies to Aristotle: "Même chez Platon, *synthēkē* est 'concurrence' par des termes tels que *homologia,* 'accord (tacite),' *nomos,* 'loi, usage,' *ethos,* 'coutume.'" Engels, "Origine," p. 99. Arens says of *kata sunthēkēn:* "It presupposes a language community; we may even say that such a community consists of nothing but such conventions, it is the embodiment of the speaker-hearer relation, the precondition of communication and understanding, of the social product language." Given this solid understanding of linguistic covenant, it is astonishing that Arens should go on to say: "*Kata synthēkēn* seems to become the equivalent of *thesei* (*positione*): by position or arbitrary determination or by institution." He even cites Socrates's *thesis onomatos* (*Cratylus,* 390 D) as an explication of Aristotle's doctrine! See Arens, *Aristotle's Theory of Language and Its Tradition,* p. 38.

56. "Le sens propre et littéral de *thesei,* que les Grecs ne paraissent jamais avoir cessé d'analyser ainsi, est 'par position' . . . *thesei* énonce expressément cette seule idée que les noms ont été poses par l'homme, contrairement aux sons vocaux naturels." Engels also cites W. S. Allen: "The English translation of *thesis* by 'convention' is not entirely accurate: it represents only one aspect of *thesis,* that which Aristotle calls *synthēkē,* a joint agreement made by a number of people, whereas *thesis* admits the possibility of a system arbitrarily made by one man and subsequently imposed upon his fellows." Engels, "Origine," pp. 101 and 101n.

lustrating the origin of language by means of giving names (*thētai*), cites the example of naming slaves (384 D)—hardly based on a covenant.

The usage of the Greek commentators on Plato was not of decisive importance for the rise of the discourse of positive law in the Latin West—except insofar as they influenced key Latin writers like Gellius, Chalcidius, and Boethius. In particular, Boethius's rendering of Aristotle's *kata sunthēkēn* by the Latin *secundum placitum* (according to the pleasure [of the name giver]) was crucially significant for the discourse of positive language and law from Aquinas to Hobbes. Let us look at Boethius's translation of the two sentences from Aristotle cited above explaining how words are significant "according to covenant (*kata sunthēkēn*): "A name therefore is significant according to the pleasure [of the name giver] . . . certainly according to pleasure, because nothing is by nature a name, except when it becomes a token."[57] Whereas Aristotle's focus is on the agreement between speaker and listener, Boethius's focus is on the willful decision of the name giver.

Boethius's two commentaries on this passage will shed important light on this profoundly influential translation of Aristotle. In the first, Boethius says that, according to Aristotle, a name is a vocal sound (*vox*) having significance not by nature but "according to the positing (*secundum positionem*) of men and therefore according to the positing of men in such a way as is pleasing to them, by whom names were formed . . . in this way, therefore, words, which are according to positing, are according to the pleasure of those positing."[58] He goes on to explain that names have significance "according to the pleasure of the imposers and authors and those by whom names themselves are impressed on the things."[59] Boethius's reference to plural name givers hints at a social context, but it seems to be a community of independent name givers rather than a com-

---

57. "Nomen ergo est vox significativa secundum placitum . . . secundum placitum vero, quoniam naturaliter nominum nihil est, sed quando fit nota." Text in *Anicii Manlii Severini Boetii Commentarii in librum Aristotelis* Peri hermēneias, 2 vols., ed. Carolus Meiser (Lipsiae: Teubner, 1880), vol. 1, p. 4.2.

58. "Tales igitur voces quae secundum positionem sunt hominum, et ita secundum positionem, quaemadmodum ipsis hominibus placuit, a quibus nomina illa formata sunt. Huiusmodi ergo voces, quae secundum positionem sunt, secundum ponentium placitum sunt." Text in *Anicii Manlii Severini Boetii Commentarii in librum Aristotelis* Peri hermēneias, vol. 1, p. 46.17.

59. "Secundum placitum sunt scilicet ponentium atque auctorum et a quibus nomina ipsarebus impressa sunt." Text in *Anicii Manlii Severini Boetii Commentarii in librum Aristotelis* Peri hermēneias, vol. 1, p. 47.4.

munity of speakers and hearers. If there is not one authoritative name giver, then how do these plural name givers coordinate their denominations?[60]

In the second commentary, these references to plural name givers now curiously become references to a singular name giver. Here Boethius explains "according to pleasure" as "according to a certain positing and pleasure of one imposing" and "according to the pleasure and the will of one imposing" and "pleasing to him who first gave names to things."[61] The many references to the singular name giver in this commentary, says Engels, suggest a belief that names are significant because of the arbitrary pleasure of the original or authoritative name giver.[62] Whereas Aristotle's "according to covenant" drew attention to the agreement of the community of speakers and listeners, Boethius's language draws attention to the willful and arbitrary power of the authoritative name giver.[63] Hans Arens points out that an obscure Latin commentary rendered Aristotle's "according to covenant" as "*secundum consensum*," but this felicitous version would play no role in medieval or early modern thought about language.[64]

In the context of late imperial Rome, especially in the culture of the early sixth-century Romano-Byzantine court, it is not surprising that Boethius would see language as whatever is pleasing to the namegiver—after all, Justinian at that time was just codifying the maxim that "whatever pleases the prince has the force of law."[65] In the case of both language and law, the deliberate impositions of authorities do play an important role; but the tacit consensus of the community plays an equally important role, though not a salient one in the discourse of positive law. When we examine Aquinas's commentary on Aristotle's

60. Arens asks of this account: "Did they act independently of each other? Were they a group representing the community and the *synthēkē*?" See "*Aristotle's Theory of Language and Its Tradition*," p. 220.

61. "Secundum quandam positionem placitumque ponentis" (vol. 2, pp. 54–55); "secundum placitum voluntatemque ponentis" (vol. 2, p. 56.17); "placuit ei qui primus nomina indidit rebus" (vol. 2, p. 59.7). Engels calls attention to the transition from *potentium* in the first commentary to *potentis* in the second in his "Origine," pp. 108–09.

62. "La conclusion s'impose: Boèce prend *placitum* dans le sens de 'bon plaisir individuel.'" Engels, "Origine," p. 109.

63. Arens says of Boethius's translation, "The background of the language community that agrees in a certain appellation is lost, '*placitum*' does not remind of it, and so 'conventionally' became 'arbitrarily.'" See *Aristotle's Theory of Language and Its Tradition*, p. 219.

64. Arens, *Aristotle's Theory of Language and Its Tradition*, 219.

65. "Quod placuit principi, legis habet vigorem." This is cited by Aquinas, who says that it must be qualified by the proviso that the will of the prince be ruled by reason (ST, I-II, 90.1 ad 3).

On Interpretation, we find ourselves not in the world of covenant and agreement but in the Boethean world of authoritative stipulation and imposition. According to Aquinas, Aristotle asks whether vocal sounds get their signification by nature or by imposition—thus omitting the possibilities of habit, custom, and consensus central to Aristotle's actual account.[66] Aquinas says that while the voice is natural, the noun and verb are by human institution.[67] When he discusses Aristotle's view (via Boethius) that a name is a vocal sound significant according to pleasure (*secundum placitum*), Aquinas explains this expression as meaning that "a name does not signify by nature but from institution [*ex institutione*]."[68] According to Aquinas, Aristotle says that speech signifies *secundum placitum,* "that is, according to the institution of human reason and will."[69] Because the concept of "according to pleasure" so strongly suggests arbitrary willfulness, Aquinas usually qualifies it, whether he is speaking of the imposition of laws or of names, by adding the proviso "according to reason." Whether the emphasis is on the will or the reason of the name giver, Aquinas's focus remains on language as a deliberate artifact, rather than as a customary agreement between speaker and listener.[70]

Aquinas's doctrines of language and of law come together in his discussion of the sacraments, which are both signs of divine grace and commands of divine law. Speaking of sacrifices, he says that, generically, they belong to natural law, but that the particular ways in which sacrifices are offered belong to positive law, whether divine or human. As signs, he adds, sacraments are also both natural and positive: "It is natural for man to signify his concepts, but the particular signs he uses are according to human pleasure" (*secundum humanum placitum,* ST, II-II, 85.1 ad 1 and 3). We shall now see how law can be both natural and positive on Aquinas's account and what this dichotomy means for his understanding of customary law.

66. *In Libros Perihermeneias,* in *S. Thomae Aquinatis Opera Omnia,* vol. 4, ed. Roberto Busa (Stuttgart: Friedrich Frommann, 1980), I, 2.1: "Utrum sit ex natura vel ex impositione."
67. *In Libros Perihermeneias,* I, 2.4: "Ex institutione humana."
68. *In Libros Perihermeneias,* I, 4.11.
69. *In Libros Perihermeneias,* I, 6.8: "Ad placitum, idest secundum institutionem humanae rationis et voluntatis."
70. Where custom appears in his account of language, it serves mainly to distort the meanings originally imposed on words: "Quod consuetum est quod nomina a sui prima impositione detorqueantur ad alia significanda." ST II-II, 57.1 ad 1. He speaks of the "original imposition" (*secundum primam impositionem*) of the name *judgment* in ST, II-II, 60.1 ad 1, and "according to the original imposition of the name" (*secundum primam impositionem nominis*) in ST, II-II, 62.1 ad 2.

Chapter 2 Law's Positivity in the Natural Law Jurisprudence of Thomas Aquinas

THE SCIENTIFIC DIMENSION OF POSITIVE LAW: THE KINDS OF ORDER IN SOCIETY

According to Thomas Aquinas, the methods and logic of every science must conform to the inherent order found in its specific object of inquiry. Indeed, Aquinas even defines rationality as the capacity both to establish and to discern order. As he says in the prologue to his commentary on the *Nicomachean Ethics* of Aristotle: "To be wise is to establish order. The reason for this is that wisdom is the most powerful perfection of reason, whose characteristic is to know order."[1] The student of Aquinas who completed his commentary on the *Politics* of Aristotle certainly understood the hierarchical structure of Aristotle's three concepts of order: "There ought to be harmony among them, namely, nature, custom, and reason: for always the latter presupposes

---

1. *S. Thomae Aquinatis Opera Omnia,* vol. 4, *Sententia Libri Ethicorum,* ed. Roberto Busa (Stuttgart: Friedrich Frommann Verlag, 1980), Prologue, n. 1. Unless otherwise explicitly noted, all Latin texts of Aquinas are from this edition.

the former."² And in his commentary on Aristotle's *Nicomachean Ethics,* Aquinas analyzes the mutually complementary roles of nature, habit, and doctrine in the moral development of an individual.³ Yet in his formal account of the kinds of order, in the prologue of his commentary on the *Ethics,* Aquinas does not refer to the Aristotelian hierarchy. He says that there are four kinds of order: the first is the order that reason does not make but only beholds, the order of nature; the second is the order that reason makes in its own acts, as when it arranges concepts and signs of concepts; the third is the order that reason makes in the operations of the will; and the fourth is the order that reason makes in the external things it produces.⁴

In terms of our Aristotelian triad, Aquinas's four orders actually reduce to two: order independent of human action (namely, the order of nature) and the order made by deliberate human action (namely, the order stipulated by reason in thought, deeds, and artifacts). There seems to be nothing corresponding to the order of custom, an order that is the product of human action but not the execution of any design. Yet this kind of order is precisely the kind of order powerfully illustrated in language and in law. When one considers that every utterance made by a speaker in English shapes the language, and that every judicial decision, indeed, every decision to obey or enforce the law or not, shapes the law, we begin to appreciate the complexity of this kind of order. By contrast, in this prologue Aquinas focuses on the order found in an army, as does John Finnis in his exposition of Aquinas.⁵ But the deliberately stipulated order of battle is a very misleading exemplar of the complex and evolutionary order found in social life. Indeed, the attempt by several modern societies to reorder language and law on the model of the order of battle shows how dangerous it is to reduce the spontaneous order of custom to the order of deliberate stipulation. Of course, Aquinas is aware of this danger when he warns against attempting to use legislation to repress all customary vices (ST, I-II, 96.2), but he tells us very little about what is distinctive of customary social order.

---

2. The commentary on *Politics* 1332a 38 reads: "Quare hoc oportet consonare inter se, scilicet naturam, consuetudinem, et rationem: semper enim posterius praesupponit prius." In *In Libros Politicorum Aristotelis Expositio,* ed. Raymundi Spiazzi (Turin: Marietti, 1951), 386.

3. See Aquinas, *In Decem Libros Ethicorum Aristotelis Ad Nicomachum Expositio,* ed. Raymundi Spiazzi (Turin: Marietti, 1949), bk. VII, lec. 10.1.14, pp. 2143ff.

4. *Sententia Libri Ethicorum,* Prologue, n. 1.

5. Aquinas, *Sententia Libri Ethicorum,* Prologue, n. 5; John Finnis, *Aquinas: Moral, Political, and Legal Theory* (Oxford: Oxford University Press, 1998), pp. 32–35.

THE THEOLOGICAL DIMENSION
OF POSITIVE LAW

Aquinas's consistent focus on the order of deliberate stipulation and, in law, his consistent focus on law deliberately imposed, stem from the fundamental theological orientation of his thought. For Aquinas, God is the source of all order, and the order of nature embodies the deliberate order of God's providential design. Human beings are made in God's image, in the sense that just as God orders all things through his rational will, so we order all of our deeds and affairs by our own rational wills.[6] If God is the supreme legislator of natural order, then, as social and political animals, we participate in his divine providential government through deliberate moral choice and through deliberate legislation. As we shall see, Aquinas does admit that custom can obtain the force of human law, but his account of customary law is deeply legislative, as when he says that custom stems from the reason and will of man (ST, I-II, 97.3c).

The theological dimension of Aquinas's legal thought is almost always obscured by modern editions of his "Treatise on Law" (ST, I-II) and by modern commentary on it. To begin with, by ripping the "Treatise on Law" out of its context in the overall design of the *Summa Theologiae,* we are likely to misunderstand Aquinas's view of the role of law in the larger drama of salvation. The *Prima Secundae,* of which the "Treatise on Law" is a part, begins with the intrinsic principles by which human beings are led toward the good and to God, namely, the basic natural desires and their modifications through acquired virtues. But, says Aquinas, in addition to being led toward good (or evil) by the intrinsic principles of the virtues and vices, we are also led toward good (or evil) by extrinsic principles, namely, God and the devil. Now God has two main instruments for leading men to their natural good and supernatural salvation: "He instructs us through law and helps us through grace."[7] In short, when we put both the intrinsic and extrinsic principles of human salvation together, we get a theological version of Aristotle's triadic model of human self-realization: men become good and holy, says Aquinas, by the right natural desires, modi-

---

6. "Man is said to be made in the image of God, according to which is signified that he is intelligent, master of himself, and with free judgment; now since we have agreed that God is the exemplar cause of things and that they issue from his power through his will, it remains to consider his image, that is to say, man as the source of his own deeds, having free judgment and power over his deeds." Aquinas, ST, prologue to IaIIae.

7. Aquinas, prologue to ST I-II, QQ. 90–108.

fied by virtuous habits, which are acquired by practice and through the instruction of law and the gifts of grace. So, by comparison with natural desires and acquired habits, all kinds of law are extrinsic principles of human good; laws are means by which we are instructed by our divine and human teachers. Although we might well learn how to be good by means of customary law, we are not deliberately taught or instructed by that kind of law. When Aquinas describes law as an extrinsic source of instruction, he is thinking of law deliberately enacted, from the Decalogue to every subsequent enactment. What about natural law? By comparison with both human and divine law, natural law is an intrinsic principle of human good. But even natural law belongs to the extrinsic principles of human good, when compared to natural desires and acquired habits, for natural law is a standard by which natural desires and acquired habits are to be evaluated.

Although Aquinas tells us in the prologue to the "Treatise on Law" that it will include Questions 90 to 108, I know of no modern edition of this treatise that extends beyond Question 97. In other words, for modern students of legal theory, Aquinas's treatise on law does not include his analysis of the Mosaic law (QQ. 98–105) or his analysis of the law of the Gospel (QQ. 106–108), despite the fact that Aquinas devotes many more pages to divine law than to human law. Moreover, the discourse of positive law, both in history and in Aquinas's own work, arose mainly in the context of the analysis of divine law and of church law by theologians. We shall see that Aquinas's understanding of both senses of the positivity of human law stems from his analysis of divine and church law. First, just as God laid down divine law through Moses, so the human legislator lays down the law (*lex posita*) on human communities. Second, all of Mosaic law is positive in the sense of law laid down or enacted, but within Mosaic law, Aquinas will distinguish natural law precepts (*ius naturale*) from positive law precepts (*ius positivum*) on the basis of their content. Similarly, within human law, which Aquinas takes to be positive in the sense of laid down (*lex posita* or *lex positiva*), Aquinas will also distinguish natural law from positive law on the basis of its content. Most important, just as Aquinas sorts the precepts of divine law into mutually exclusive classes of natural and positive precepts, so he also sometimes sharply divides natural from positive precepts within human law.

The failure to understand Aquinas's theory of positive human law, in the context of his analysis of positive divine and church law, has led commentators to misunderstand the meaning of positive law in Aquinas's thought. Thus even eminent contemporary authorities will say of Aquinas's doctrine: "Positive law . . . is the law produced by human legal institutions"[8] or speak of "positive law's variability and relativity to time, place, and polity, its admixture of human error and immorality, its radical dependence on human creativity"[9]—as if there were for Aquinas no positive divine law. Although Aquinas in his *Summa Theologiae* uses various expressions for "positive law" mainly in connection to human law, he also uses them in reference to divine law. Moreover, Aquinas explicitly compares the relation of the moral to the ceremonial Mosaic law in the *Summa* to the relation of the natural to the positive law in human law. So, despite Aquinas's verbal tendency to limit "positive" law to human law in the *Summa,* he deploys the full conceptual apparatus of law's positivity to his analysis of divine law. Despite, then, his modern commentators, Aquinas sees nothing essentially "human" about positive law.[10] All of divine law, on Aquinas's account, is authoritatively laid down or posited by God, and some of divine law is positive in the sense of being the product of God's particular determinations of natural law. So, for Aquinas, there is a strict analogy between divine law and human law: both kinds of law are deliberately imposed by a legislator and both kinds of law include precepts whose content is natural and positive. God, on Aquinas's account, both lays down law and lays down particular determinations of natural law. To attempt to understand his account of law's positivity apart from his account of divine law is just as anachronistic and misleading as to attempt to understand his philosophical analysis of law apart from its theological context.

Throughout this chapter I shall be drawing upon Aquinas's analysis of divine law in order to illuminate his understanding of law's positivity, but here it is worth briefly reviewing the theological dimension of Aquinas's analysis of positive law, since it is so often denied by his modern commentators. In Aquinas's first major work, *The Commentary on the Propositions of Peter Lombard* (c. 1255), he discusses the authority of precepts of divine law and of church law that lack intrinsic moral force. In discussing whether all of divine law might be led back to the natural law precepts of the Decalogue, he says that "the ceremonial precepts or the precepts of positive law cannot be led back to the natural precepts

---

8. R. J. Henle, S.J., ed., *Saint Thomas Aquinas: The Treatise on Law* (Notre Dame: University of Notre Dame Press, 1993), p. 38.

9. John Finnis, "The Truth in Legal Positivism," in *The Autonomy of Law: Essays on Legal Positivism,* ed. Robert P. George (Oxford: Clarendon Press, 1996), pp. 195–214, at 195.

10. Finnis, for example, says of Aquinas's view: "*Positive law* . . . can be studied as the product of human deliberation and choice." In "The Truth in Legal Positivism," 195.

as if they had the force of obligation from nature itself."[11] Similarly, in discussing whether a person might be dispensed from confessing his sins to another person, Aquinas considers the argument that a person might be dispensed by a church official, since the law of confession is a positive law (*de iure positivo*); but Aquinas replies that "the precepts of the divine law are not less obligatory than the precepts of natural law, and just as dispensation is not possible from natural law neither is it from positive divine law [*in iure positivo divino*]."[12] Later in the same discussion, he refers to the precepts of the church as precepts of positive law.[13] In short, in this first major work, Aquinas refers to positive Mosaic law, positive church law, and positive civil law. Later, in his *Summa contra Gentiles* (c. 1259–1266), he says: "If, however, the law is divinely posited [*divinitus posita*], it can be dispensed by divine authority."[14]

In the *Summa Theologiae* (c. 1270), Aquinas tends to use the expression *positive law* in reference mainly to civil law, but he applies the full conceptual apparatus of law's positivity to the Mosaic law as well. For example, when he considers what is just or lawful (*ius*), he asks whether it is aptly divided into natural law and positive law. He considers the objection that divine law is neither natural, since it transcends human nature, nor positive, since it does not rest upon human authority. So the objector assumes that positive law must essentially refer to human law. But Aquinas replies: "Divine law is that which is promulgated by God and partly these things are naturally just, though a justice hidden to men, and partly they become just by divine institution. Hence just as divine law is divided into these two [parts] so is human law. For the divine law enjoins certain things because they are good and prohibits others because they are evil, while still other things are good because enjoined and evil because prohibited."[15] Even though Aquinas does not here explicitly label part of divine law as "positive," he does explicitly defend the application of the distinction between natural law and positive law to both divine law and human law. Moreover, as

---

11. "Praecepta caeremonialia vel juris positivi." The use of *vel* shows the equivalence of these terms. *Commentum in Libros Sententiarum*, vol. 3, d. 37, q. 1, a. 3, ad 2. [Hereafter CS.]

12. CS, vol. 4, d. 17, q. 3., a. 1e, ob. 1 and ad 1.

13. CS, vol. 4, d. 17, q. 3, a. 3d ad 5. "Nec in hoc transgreditur aliquis praeceptum ecclesiae; quia praecepta juris positivi non se extendunt ultra intentionem praecipientis."

14. "Si autem lex sit divinitus posita, auctoritate divina dispensatio fieri potest." *Summa contra Gentiles*, lib. 3, cap. 125. Kevin Flannery cites this passage to show "that in Aquinas there is also such a thing as divine posited (i.e., positive) law." See his *Acts amid Precepts: The Aristotelian Logical Structure of Thomas Aquinas's Moral Theory* (Washington, D.C.: Catholic University of America Press, 2001), p. 73 n. 54.

15. ST, II-II, 57.2 ob. 3 and ad 3.

we shall see, one of the conceptual bases of the distinction between natural law and positive law is the distinction between what is evil (or good) in itself and what is evil (or good) because prohibited (or enjoined). And here Aquinas applies this conceptual distinction to both divine law and human law.

In many other places, Aquinas will draw explicit analogies between natural and positive divine law and natural and positive human law. Aquinas's technical term for how law that is positive in content is created is *determinatio:* this is the process whereby the generalities of natural law are concretized and particularized into specific norms of conduct. Throughout the *Summa,* Aquinas compares the determinations of human positive law to the determinations of divine law. In considering, for example, whether religious sacrifice is by natural or positive law, Aquinas says: "Some things are generically from natural law of which their particular determination is by positive law. . . . Similarly, to offer a sacrifice is generically from natural law, but the particular manner in which a sacrifice is made is from divine or human institution."[16] Thus, in the "Treatise on Law," he frequently says: "The precepts of natural law are general in character and require particular determination; such determination is by human and by divine law."[17] He argues that the judicial and the ceremonial precepts of divine law are determinations of the natural moral precepts, just as human positive law is a determination of the natural moral law.[18] In these and many other ways, as we shall see, Aquinas's analysis of the positivity of divine law both mirrors and illuminates his analysis of human law.

THE NORMATIVE DIMENSION OF POSITIVE LAW
IN RELATION TO NATURAL LAW

The centerpiece of Thomas Aquinas's account of human law is his understanding of the relation of natural law to positive law—or, as we might say, of morality to law. Aquinas aims to show that law and morality are two distinct, though overlapping, modes of practical reason, and that legal obligation is a species of moral obligation. Still, law is not simply the pursuit of moral ends by coercive means. True, according to Aquinas, both law and morality aim to make men good, but each ought to do this in a distinct, and mutually supportive, manner. Morality has a more comprehensive role in cultivating the full range of moral virtues and in directing the full range of human acts, reaching even to the har-

16. ST, II-II, 85.2 ad 1.
17. ST, I-II, 99.3 ad 2. Cf. I-II, 99.4c.
18. ST, I-II, 100.11 ad 2 and 101.1c. ST, II-II, 122.2 ad 2.

mony of our thoughts, words, and deeds; law, by contrast, has a much more limited role in cultivating mainly the virtue of justice (and, only secondarily, the other virtues supportive of the disposition to justice) and in regulating only deeds, not mere intentions and dispositions.[19]

Law, in short, can play its necessary role in protecting and promoting the common good only by substantially distinguishing itself from morality. A merger of law and morality would be deeply immoral for Aquinas because law cannot by its nature reach into the deeper springs of human morality; moreover, the attempt to reach the full range of moral motives and deeds would undermine the capacity of law to fulfill its distinctive office of regulating the justice of the (mainly) external dealings of human beings. To be just, law must be compatible with the permanent requirements of practical reason—and one of those requirements is precisely that law not usurp the distinctive office of morality.

Before we can understand Aquinas's account of the relation of positive law to the moral requirements of the natural law, we must first determine why Aquinas so frequently calls human law "positive." What does it mean for law to be "positive"? We have seen that the Greek discourse for what is positive (*tithēmi* and its variants) included two quite distinct concepts: what is deliberately imposed and what is in content contingent, indifferent, or adventitious. When the Greek discourse was rendered in Latin (*pono* and its variants), the same conceptual ambiguity followed. Aquinas became the first major theorist of positive law because he inherited two major, though quite distinct, traditions of legal discourse. The first is the discourse about statutory law found in Roman law, the Vulgate Bible, and contemporary translations of Aristotle's *Politics*; here statutory law is contrasted to customary law and described as "imposed" or "posited" (*legem ponere* or *lex posita*). The second is the discourse about whether names are natural or positive—a discourse that in the twelfth century was increasingly extended to the question of whether justice and law were natural or positive; here positive law is often contrasted with natural law and described as morally contingent, indifferent, or adventitious in content (*ius positivum*). Unfortunately, as we shall see, Aquinas's use of the term *positive law* often oscillates ambiguously between these two very different concepts. Only by disambiguating the discourse of positive law can we develop and clarify

---

19. For an argument that Aquinas understood law to have a limited role in promoting virtue and repressing vice, see John Finnis, *Aquinas: Moral, Political, and Legal Theory* (Oxford: Oxford University Press, 1998), pp. 222–28.

Aquinas's very subtle and underdeveloped account of the twofold relation of positive law to the natural law requirements of the common good.

What are the requirements of the common good? And what is the twofold relation of positive law to those requirements? First, in many contexts, the common good requires a single determinate and a precisely calibrated rule to coordinate a particular activity—for example, that a tax be payable at a rate of 33.65 percent and postmarked by 5 P.M. on April 15. Positive law, as publicly promulgated and authoritatively imposed, answers that requirement by (ideally) a uniquely valid rule. Second, the common good requires that, in the framing of laws, legislators have wide scope for creative adaptation to local circumstances and yet avoid violating the fundamental principles of morality—for a law that attacks basic aspects of human good undermines the essential rationale of the legal system; positive law answers this requirement with a content that, though in many details is morally neutral, is at least compatible with the fundamental requirements of morality. In short, positive law must be authoritatively imposed if the good of a political community is to be genuinely common, and the detailed specifications of positive law must not violate morality if what is common to a community is to be good. Thus the natural law requirements of the common good justify a prima facie moral duty to obey positive law merely as imposed—even apart from the issues presented by the content of a law. That same natural law justifies the right (and sometimes the duty) to disobey positive law by establishing limits to what is permissible in its content. In this way, from each distinct sense of "positive" there arises a distinct relation of positive law to the moral requirements of the common good.

Let us, then, explore the curious ambiguity of positive law and see how that ambiguity can be made to illuminate the complex relation of positive law to natural law in the thought of Thomas Aquinas. Does the common good require that social coordination arise from rules deliberately imposed or might those rules arise from custom? We shall see that Aquinas's understanding of law is thoroughly legislative—as is his understanding of custom. And even though the central claim of his jurisprudence is that positive law is essentially law to the extent that it has the force of natural law, he sometimes says that positive law lacks the force of natural law. Just as he divides the Mosaic law, so he sometimes divides human law, into mutually exclusive classes of natural and positive precepts. So in his account of human law, sometimes natural and positive precepts form an interlocking whole and sometimes not.

WHAT MAKES LAW POSITIVE?

Although Thomas Aquinas is best known in jurisprudential circles as a classic expositor of natural law theory, there is a growing recognition of his strikingly original contributions to the theory of law's positivity. For example, the historian of legal theory Sten Gagnér makes the astonishing claim that "in the *Prima Secundae* of the *Summa Theologiae*" is found "for the first time in Western Latinity, a full-blown ideology of legal positivism."[20] Similarly, the philosopher John Finnis, though without any reference to Gagnér, underscores the decisive originality of Aquinas's mature theory of positive law: "It is in the *Summa Theologiae* that Aquinas most decisively affirms law's positivity," which involves a "break with all previous philosophical and juristic analyses" and leads to "a systematic position quite fresh and new. *Positive law* is put forward as a properly distinct category and subject of study in its own right."[21] Both Gagnér and Finnis seek to show that in the "Treatise on Law" (ST, I-II, 90–108, especially 90–97) Aquinas develops the first systematic philosophical account of the positivity of law.[22]

That two eminent authorities should independently make such dramatic claims for the originality and power of Aquinas's account of positive law is remarkable. Given the inherent ambiguity in the discourse of positive law, we should expect different interpretations of what Aquinas means by "positive law." Jacques Maritain sees positive law as being morally contingent in content, as opposed to the morally necessary content of natural law: "*Positive Law,* or the body of laws (either customary law or statute law) in force in a given social group, deals with the rights and the duties which are connected with the first principle [of natural law], but in a *contingent* manner, by virtue of the determinate ways of conduct set down by the reason and the will of man."[23] Here Maritain understands positive law in Aquinas to refer to the morally contingent content of a legal norm, whether it arises by custom or by deliberate imposition. Other distinguished students of Aquinas interpret positive law quite

20. "In der Ia IIae der Summa Theologiae des heiligen Thomas de Aquino ist, zum ersten Mal in der abendländischen Latinität, eine vollständige Ideologie des Gesetzespositivismus zu finden." Sten Gagnér, *Studien zur Ideengeschichte der Gesetzgebung* (Stockholm: Almqvist and Wiksell, 1960), p. 279.
21. Finnis, "The Truth in Legal Positivism," pp. 201 and 195 (emphasis his).
22. Finnis properly avoids Gagnér's highly tendentious description of Aquinas's "legal positivism" in favor of the more precise, if more awkward, "positivity" of law in Aquinas.
23. Maritain, *Man and the State* (Chicago: University of Chicago Press, 1951), p. 99 (emphases his).

differently. For Gagnér, the positivity of law in Aquinas stems from its statutory character: law is positive in the sense of being imposed by a lawgiver, in contrast to the tacit agreements of custom.[24] Similarly, says Finnis, "[w]hat makes law positive is that it is laid down. Period."[25] Curiously, both Gagnér and Finnis also define positive law in terms of its contingent content, as if being deliberately imposed were coextensive with having a contingent content. Finnis, as we have seen, speaks of positive law's "variability and relativity to time, place, and polity, its admixture of human error and immorality, its radical dependence on human creativity."[26] These qualities, of course, refer not to the source of law but to its content. Even customary law has the same contingent content that Finnis ascribes to law that is laid down. Despite these varying criteria for what constitutes positive law, Gagnér and Finnis ultimately define positive law as what is authoritatively laid down.[27] These mutually inconsistent definitions of law's positivity require us to be somewhat less positive about the meaning of positive law. Indeed, what makes Aquinas such a seminal figure in the history of philosophical reflection on human law is precisely his role in bringing together these two very different senses of law's positivity—making his account of human law an ideal context for thinking through the perplexing quandary of law's positivity.

The conflation of these two senses of "positive" makes sense on the (usually unexamined) premise that what is formally imposed must have, at best, only contingent moral force—after all, the necessary requirements of morality (that is, the natural law) need no formal enactment. It is easy to suppose, then, that formal enactment somehow presupposes a lack of intrinsic moral necessity. Indeed, we often associate what is deliberately imposed with what is morally adventitious or dubious. Because of the tremendous power of statutes to revoke long-standing custom and law, statutes have long been regarded with suspicion

24. Gagnér cites Conor Martin: "The idea that law was something consciously created by a legislator, and not merely the legacy of custom, was brought to the fore by the *Politics* [of Aristotle] and its commentators." *Studien,* p. 199n.

25. Finnis, correspondence to author of 22 September 1997.

26. Finnis, "The Truth in Legal Positivism," p. 195. Gagnér similarly connects *iustitia positiva* with what is *ab hominibus inventa,* with *lex temporalis* and *lex mutabilis, Studien,* pp. 231, 261, 275–76.

27. "I don't think there are two concepts of positivity. There's just one—being laid down." Finnis, correspondence to author of 22 September 1997. Gagnér similarly emphasizes "being laid down" by rendering *positiva iustitia* as "*gesetztes Recht*" and *lex posita* as law "*Stellen, setzen, bestimmen, einrichten.*" *Studien,* pp. 243 and 207.

by many jurists in our tradition, both Roman and English.[28] Statutes are the most lethal weapons in the legal arsenal, with the power to effect great good or evil. As F. A. Hayek says, "Legislation, the deliberate making of law, has justly been described as among all inventions of man the one fraught with the gravest consequences, more far-reaching in its effects even than fire and gun-pow-der."[29] As a favorite instrument of autocratic rulers, statutes suffer from guilt by association with the exercise of morally dubious power; the body of law built up by jurists over time, by contrast, seems more rational if only because it is re-sistant to radical change.[30] Nonetheless, the association of what is imposed with what is morally contingent, though understandable, is not defensible. The content of statutes need not be less intrinsically moral than the content of com-mon law rules, and customs can be as immoral as deliberate enactments. Clear thinking about law requires us carefully to distinguish the empirical source of a law from its normative justification, even if, at a deeper level, the source of law has important implications for its justification.

Positive Law as Statutory Law

Thomas Aquinas had available to him two words for "law": *ius* and *lex*. Far from being two different words for the same concept, each of these words had a very distinctive semantic field. By the time Aquinas deploys them, the two words already have at least eighteen hundred years of history in legal and philo-sophical discourse. The ancient Roman jurists, who deployed these words as

28. Of the Republican and classical Roman jurists, Schulz says: "We may assume that a Ro-man principle existed which read: Romans are basically opposed to codification and maintain a strict reserve in regard to statutes. The law-inspired nation is not statute-inspired." See Fritz Schulz, *Principles of Roman Law*, trans. Marguerite Wolff (Oxford: Clarendon Press, 1936), p. 7. As for English lawyers and judges, Frederick Pollock says that their attitude toward statutes "cannot well be accounted for except upon the theory that Parliament generally changes the law for the worse, and that the business of the judge is to keep the mischief of its interference within the narrowest possible bounds." Cited in Harold Berman and William Greiner, *The Nature and Functions of Law* (Mine-ola, NY: Foundation Press, 1980), p. 568.

29. Here Hayek is paraphrasing Bernhard Rehfeldt, *Die Wurzeln des Rechts* (Berlin: Duncker und Humblot, 1951). See Hayek, *Law, Legislation, and Liberty*, vol. 1 (Chicago: Univer-sity of Chicago Press, 1973), p. 72.

30. "Laws [i.e., statutes] are easily made instruments of dictators. Law, by which a reasoned technique is applied to laws in order to achieve an ideal relation among men, is the arch enemy of dictators." Roscoe Pound, *Jurisprudence*, vol. 5 (St. Paul: West Publishing, 1959), p. 715.

technical terms, did not subject them to philosophical analysis. Still, systematic study of those deployments by modern scholars of Roman law provides a fairly clear picture of the main meanings of these terms. *Ius* is the main word for law in Republican and classical Roman jurisprudence. The Roman jurists used *ius* to refer to "the law" as an integral whole—as when our lawyers speak of "the law of England" or "the law of contract." *Ius* was almost always used in the singular, such as *ius civile,* and the law (*ius*) was certainly not thought of as an aggregate of laws (*iura*).[31] Rather, *ius* was a body of law built up by juristic interpretation from very heterogeneous sources—ranging from statutes, to resolutions of the Senate, to plebiscites, to edicts, to customs, to juristic commentary, to imperial decrees, and so forth.[32] *Ius,* in short, to use the figure of the jurists, was a reservoir of law fed by a variety of different sources (*fontes iuris*): the task of the jurist is to blend the norms from these disparate sources of law into a systematic and coherent basis for guiding legitimate expectations and for adjudicating disputes.

Lex, by contrast, originally meant a statute. In the Roman Republic, a *lex* was an enactment of the popular assembly (*comitia*), giving its consent to the proposal of the convening magistrate. As Jochen Bleicken says, *lex* and *ius* are related like statute and law (*Satzung und Recht*).[33] Sometimes, *ius civile* was taken to include *leges,*[34] and sometimes the lawyers' law (*ius civile*) was contrasted with statutory law (*ius legitimum*).[35] In the Republican and classical epochs of Roman law, legislation played a very minor role in the formation of

---

31. By contrast *lex* can often mean an aggregate of *leges,* just as *nomos* can often mean an aggregate of *nomoi.* In other words, legislation is an aggregate of statutes, but the common law is not an aggregate of laws. Finnis observes Aquinas's frequent use of *iura* to refer to an aggregate of laws but fails to remark upon the great gulf this reveals between Aquinas's understanding of law and that of the Roman lawyers. See Finnis, *Aquinas,* p. 134.

32. The lists of the various sources of the *ius civile* vary over time and by jurist.

33. Bleicken, *Lex Publica: Gesetz und Recht in der Romischen Republik* (Berlin: Walter de Gruyter, 1975), p. 56. Bleicken goes on to cite Mommsen's view that *lex* was the *generale iussum populi aut plebis.*

34. As Fritz Schulz insists, "What object could a lawyer have in drawing a line between statutory and non-statutory law, when the two were inseparably interlocked?" See Schulz, *History of Roman Legal Science* (Oxford: Clarendon Press, 1946), p. 74.

35. "In English law we find the distinction between common law and statute law, which exactly corresponds to the distinction between *ius civile* and *ius legitimum.*" Eugen Ehrlich, *Principles of the Sociology of Law,* trans. Walter Moll (Cambridge, MA: Harvard University Press, 1936), p. 439.

the private law;[36] enacted law (*lex*) was used only rarely to supplement the existing body of law (*ius*).[37] The upshot for our purposes is that *lex* is a term that focuses attention on the source of law while *ius* is a term that focuses our attention on the (presumptively just) content of law, whatever its source.

However, with the growth of imperial prerogatives after Diocletian, legislation began to absorb all other sources of law. As legislation eclipsed the lawyers' law (*ius*) in practice during the Dominate, *lex* began to be used interchangeably with *ius* to refer to law as a whole. In the twelfth and thirteenth centuries, *lex* and *ius* were often used interchangeably, though *lex* retained the connotations of legislation and statutory enactment just as *ius* retained the connotations of a body of norms built up by juristic commentary. In his early *Commentary on the Propositions of Peter Lombard* (c. 1255), Aquinas alternates *ius* and *lex* as if there were no distinction between them.[38]

Despite the fact that there is no Greek equivalent for the Latin *ius*,[39] Aquinas, in his commentary on the *Nicomachean Ethics* of Aristotle, equated *ius* with Aristotle's expression for the just thing (*to dikaion*).[40] In his *Summa*

36. On the paucity of statutes in the formation of Roman private law, see W. W. Buckland, *A Text-Book of Roman Law* (Cambridge: Cambridge University Press, 1966), pp. 2–6; Hans Julius Wolff, *Roman Law* (Norman: University of Oklahoma Press, 1951), pp. 66–67; Max Kaser, *Roman Private Law* (Pretoria: University of South Africa Press, 1984), p. 18; Barry Nicolas, *An Introduction to Roman Law* (Oxford: Oxford University Press, 1962), pp. 15–16.

37. Arthur Schiller comments: "Continental scholars as well as those trained in the Anglo-American legal system have recognized that the relation of *lex* to *ius* in Rome was quite similar to that of statute law to common law in an early period of English law." See Schiller, *Roman Law* (The Hague: Mouton, 1978), pp. 226–27.

38. "It seems that all precepts of law [*legis*] cannot be reduced to these ten. For since these precepts contain natural law [*jus naturale*] they cannot be reduced to them unless they proceed from natural law [*jure naturali*]. But certain things are prohibited in law [*lege*] that are not seen to proceed from natural law [*lege naturali*]." CS, vol. 3, d. 37, q. 1, art. 2.

39. *Ius* was rendered in classical Greek alternatively by *dikaion* (the just), *nomos* (law), and *exousia* (authority); see *Thesaurus Linguae Latinae*, s.v. *ius* (679.60). "There is nothing in the Greek language exactly corresponding to the Latin *jus*. The Roman term cannot be translated by *nomos*, which is mainly used for statutory law—*lex*. Nor is *to dikaion* an equivalent, for it signifies 'the just,' and is so employed, for instance, by Cicero, who does not even attempt to translate the term." Paul Vinogradoff, *Outlines of Historical Jurisprudence*, vol. 2 (Oxford: Oxford University Press, 1922), p. 19.

40. Aquinas, *In Decem Libros Ethicorum Aristotelis Ad Nicomachum Expositio,* ed. Raymundi Spiazzi (Turin: Marietti, 1949), lib. V, 12, sec. 1016: "Idem [iuristae] enim nominant ius, quod Aristoteles iustum nominat."

Theologiae (c. 1270), Aquinas attempts systematically to distinguish *ius* as the general pattern of what is ethically just from law (*lex*) as a more particular formulation of that pattern.[41] Where the Roman jurists thought of *lex* as one source or species of law (*ius*), Aquinas defines *lex* as one species of what is ethically just (*ius*). The Roman jurists, not surprisingly, were concerned with the relation of statutory *lex* to other sources of law, while Aquinas is concerned with law in relation to other kinds of moral norms. So whereas the Roman lawyers had a much richer conception of law, of which legislation was only one part, Aquinas has a much richer conception of moral norms (natural, customary, divine), of which law (meaning legislation) was only one part. So *lex* becomes Aquinas's technical term for law in the treatise on law, while *ius* becomes his technical term for what is ethically just in general in his treatise on justice (ST, II-II, 57).[42] Aquinas uses *ius* to refer to the (presumptively) just content of legal norms, whether they have a source in natural, customary, enacted or divine law, while he uses *lex* to refer to the source of a law (statute), divine or human, in authoritative enactment and to the body of such enactments.[43] What this means for the discourse of positive law in Aquinas is that when he focuses on law as positive in the sense of enacted, he usually uses a variant of *lex posita* or *lex positiva* (the statute laid down), as contrasted with custom or law based purely on judicial decisions (ST, I-II, 95.2 ad 2). Here the use of *lex* points us to the source of law in authoritative enactment. But when Aquinas wishes to focus on positive law in the sense of law lacking intrinsic moral force, he usually uses the expression *ius positivum,* as when he distinguishes, within both human law and divine law, natural law (*ius naturale*) from positive law (*ius positivum*). Here *ius positivum* refers not to the source of law but to its content, since Aquinas says that within human statutory law (*leges scriptae,* ST, II-II, 60.5c) we find both *ius positivum* and *ius naturale.*

Given the strongly statutory character of *lex,* it is surprising that Aquinas

41. This is how I read the cryptic: "Lex non est ipsum jus proprie loquendo, sed aliqualis ratio juris. (ST, II-II, 57.1 ad 2). Still, despite this attempt to stipulate an ethical meaning for *ius,* Aquinas continues to deploy both *ius* and *lex* interchangeably to refer to law throughout the *Summa Theologiae.*

42. Aquinas says that *ius* was twisted from its original meaning as "the just thing" to mean "the art by which the just thing is discerned (i.e., law)" (ST, II-II, 57.1 ad 1); but of course it is the reverse that is true.

43. In the *Summa Theologiae,* Aquinas devotes nineteen questions to *lex,* in the treatise on laws (I-II, 90–108), but only one question to *ius,* in the treatise on justice (II-II, 57). In the Treatise on Divine Law in the *Summa contra Gentiles* (III, 2, 114–46), Aquinas virtually never refers to *ius.*

Table 2.1

Latin	ius	lex
French	droit	loi
German	Recht	Gesetz
Italian	diritto	legge
Spanish	derecho	ley
Russian	pravo	zakon
English*	"the law"	"a law" (statute)

*English, like Greek, has no precise counterparts to *ius* and *lex*. We approximate the Latin contrasts of *ius* and *lex* awkwardly through three sets of English contrasts: common law versus legislation, the law versus a law, and equity versus law ("equity," like *ius*, unites the legal and the moral).

should so frequently use the expression *lex naturalis* rather than *ius naturale,* since natural law is thought to have its authority from the intrinsic rational force of its content rather than from its formal enactment. If natural law were simply the rational requirements of morality, then we would expect Aquinas to speak of a moral *ius naturale* rather than of a statutory *lex naturalis.* But we should recall that Aquinas very frequently says that "divine and natural law [*lex divina et naturalis*] proceed from the rational will of God" (e.g., ST, I-II, 97.3c and ad 1). So on the premise that God is a legislator who lays down law for us, both in the human heart and in the Bible, it makes sense to speak of a *lex naturalis.* Still, despite his stipulation of a broadly ethical meaning of *ius,* Aquinas continues to use the expressions *ius naturale* and *ius positivum* to mean natural law and positive law.

The contrast in Roman law between the body of law as a whole (*ius*) and a statute (*lex*) is so fundamental to legal thought that we find it preserved in the vocabulary of European jurisprudence, even apart from the actual Latin terms (see table 2.1).

How can we account for Aquinas's bold innovation of explicitly treating *ius* primarily as an ethical rather than a legal term? To begin with, like its modern counterparts, *ius* meant the unity of what is lawful and what is right: law that is just. Yet, as John Salmond rightly observes, the juridical meaning predominates in the ancient term, while the ethical meaning predominates in the modern terms.[44] To my knowledge, Aquinas is the first legal theorist in the Latin West

44. John Salmond sees a difference between *ius* and its modern counterparts in that *ius* primarily means law, while the modern term primarily means what is right: "The juridical

explicitly to substitute *lex* for *ius* as the primary term for law—an innovation that will be adopted, as we shall see, by Hobbes and Bentham.[45] That Aquinas should favor a statutory conception of law is not surprising: Aristotle's analysis of law focuses mainly on legislation (*nomothesia*); the *Corpus iuris civilis,* even including the Digest of Roman juristic commentary, survived in the form of statutes (*leges*) enacted by Justinian;[46] and, perhaps most important, *lex* is the term used in the Vulgate Bible to capture the statutory character of divine law.

Thus, even a cursory inspection of the contents of Aquinas's treatment of law and justice in the *Summa Theologiae* reveals that what he offers there is a theory essentially of statutory law. Virtually the only source of law he ever mentions is the act of legislation by the supreme legislator, and both his legal concepts and his vocabulary are almost exclusively drawn from the discussions of legislation in Aristotle, the *Corpus iuris civilis,* the emerging *Corpus iuris canonici,* and the Bible.[47] When, for example, Aquinas sets forth his formal definition of law (I-II, 90), he considers whether anyone's reason can make law. He answers (90.3c) that "to make law [*condere legem*] pertains to the whole people or to that public personage who has the care of them." Here he is obviously speaking of legislation, because the power to legislate does belong to the supreme political authority.[48] Similarly, Aquinas's emphasis on promulgation makes sense if we are referring to statutes; he speaks of promulgation in the form of a written code (*lex scripta*).[49] When discussing the interpretation of laws, Aquinas always pro-

---

sense having a much greater predominance over the ethical in the case of *ius,* than in that of its modern representatives *Recht* and *droit.*" Salmond, *Jurisprudence* (London: Stevens and Haynes, 1902), p. 620.

45. Aquinas was obviously not the first writer to use *lex* as his main word for law; rather, he was the first to make an argument that *lex* is the primary legal term, while *ius* is primarily an ethical term.

46. Thus, even the Digest is cited by title and *lex.*

47. The main source, and the glory, of Roman law was juristic commentary (*responsa prudentium*), a source of law all but invisible to Aquinas, who mentions it only in passing as appropriate mainly to aristocratic polities (ST, I-II, 95.4c).

48. True, one could attempt, following Austin, to bring custom and juristic commentary within this conception of legislative supremacy but only by adding several highly controversial premises, such as "judges are agents of the sovereign" and "whatever the sovereign permits, he commands."

49. ST, I-II, 90.4 ad 3: "Present promulgation is extended into the future through the permanence of writing (*per firmitatem scripturae*), which, in a certain manner, promulgates forever." To apply the concept of statutory promulgation to lawyers' law we must narrow the concept to mean "known at least to lawyers"; to apply it to customary law we must widen the concept to mean "promulgated in practice."

ceeds by comparing and contrasting the letter of the law with the intention of the legislator (*verba et voluntas*);[50] such a procedure makes sense if one is interpreting statutes but not if interpreting precedents.[51]

Because he defines law as a deliberate exercise of practical reason,[52] Aquinas is almost inexorably drawn to statutory law: "Every law proceeds from the reason and will of the lawgiver."[53] Whether this understanding of law as deliberate enactment is justified as a general theory of law depends upon how well it can reasonably be made to include other sources of law.[54] Sometimes Aquinas's attempt to extend his account of law to nonstatutory sources of law—such as precedents, juristic commentary, popular custom, or *usus fori*—requires some rather Procrustean methods. For example, when Aquinas discusses how law changes, we see the limits of his account of law as deliberate enactment. Aquinas argues that human law should never be changed unless the future benefits of a new statute significantly outweigh the costs of disrupting existing habits of conduct (ST, I-II, 97.2c.); a legislator must, on this view, make a deliberate judgment as to when, on balance, it is advantageous to change law.[55] Yet common law, because it is based in the evolving factual circumstances of new cases, changes over time despite the often valiant efforts of judges to prevent change.[56]

50. For one of many examples of this contrast, see ST, II-II, 120.1 ad 1.

51. "Where case law is considered, and there is no statute, he [the judge] is not bound by the statement of the rule of law made by the prior judge even in the controlling case. . . . It is not what the prior judge intended that is of any importance; rather it is what the present judge, attempting to see the law as a fairly consistent whole, thinks should be the determining classification." Edward Levi, *An Introduction to Legal Reasoning* (Chicago: University of Chicago Press, 1949), pp. 2–3.

52. "Law is a kind of decree of practical reason" (*lex est quoddam dictamen practicae rationis*), ST, I-II, 91.3c.

53. ST, I-II, 97.3c. On law as an exercise of practical reason, see ST, I-II, 90.1 ad 2 and 90.2c.

54. Aquinas's statutory model of law extends much more easily to other kinds of enactments (referenda, executive orders, administrative regulations, constitutions, decrees) than to common law rules and principles, whose authority rests more upon reception (*imperio rationis*) than upon imposition (*ratione imperii*), to use a later distinction.

55. As when, Aquinas says, a new statute (*novum statutum*) is greatly and obviously superior to the old (ST, I-II, 97.2c).

56. "Even the judicial decision which seems merely to illustrate pre-existing law often adds to it. In purporting to apply a rule, the rule itself is modified. For the rule is held to be found, not in the language of the judges, but in the facts and the decision. Each time a new case is tried these facts are different. Each difference of fact creates new possibilities of interpretation. As a result, the most conservative and timid of judges, however stren-

Although Aquinas does assert that law also emerges from custom, he adopts a civil law understanding of custom that is curiously legislative. He begins his discussion of the legal status of custom by repeating his view that "all law proceeds from the reason and the will of the legislator" (ST, I-II, 97.3c). In the case of a self-governing people, he says, law rests on the consent of the governed—a consent expressed either by an intentional act of assent (for example, voting for a rule) or by external conformity to a rule in our habitual deeds. Aquinas then goes on to make the very striking claim that our internal judgment of reason and will is most effectively declared by our external deeds: "When anything is done repeatedly it seems to proceed from the deliberate judgment of reason."[57] Yet a deliberate judgment of reason is but one of many possible grounds for my conforming to custom: I might act purely from unconscious psychological compulsion or I might fear ostracism. The mere existence of social habits of conduct does not imply the rational consent of individuals to those habits.

It is tempting to interpret Aquinas's view of the normative force of customs in the light of civil law doctrines holding that only those customs accompanied by an intentional attitude of explicit consent to their legal authority (*opinio iuris* or *opinio necessitatis*) were thought to have the force of law. Yet Aquinas seems to reject such appeals to intentional attitudes in his account of what gives custom its force. He says that rational consent "is most effectively [*efficacissime*] conveyed by external acts" (ST, I-II, 97.3c), as opposed, for example, to linguistic reports of internal attitudes.

However, what if we reject Aquinas's claim that rational consent is expressed most effectively through deeds rather than through words? What if we assume that customs have legal force only if accompanied by appropriate internal (and necessarily linguistic) attitudes of explicit approval, demands for conformity, and critical reflection? Such internal attitudes would certainly be stronger evidence of rational consent to custom than are merely external deeds, but even here we must not confuse rational consent to customary morality with consent to legal enforcement of that morality. From my consent to the customary rules of morality forbidding adultery, blasphemy, and casual abortion, with all the appropriate internal attitudes, it would be quite mistaken to infer that I thereby

---

uously seeking to shelter himself behind the authority of earlier decisions, is driven by a power beyond his control to take his place in the ranks of the makers of law!" W. Jethro Brown, *The Austinian Theory of Law* (London: John Murray, 1906), p. 297.

57. "Inquantum scilicet per exteriores actus multiplicatos interior voluntatis motus et rationis conceptus efficacissime declaratur. Cum enim aliquid multoties fit videtur ex deliberato rationis judicio provenire." ST, I-II, 97.3c.

consent to the legal enforcement of these mores. Consent to moral rules does not constitute consent to legal rules. When Aquinas argues that, for a self-governing people whose laws are based on popular consent, custom is the best evidence of that consent, he is clearly echoing the jurist Julian: "What does it matter whether the people declares its will by voting or by the very substance of its actions?"[58] As we have seen, it matters a great deal: avoiding adultery in practice is quite different from voting to legally forbid adultery.

Finally, and most important for Austinian positivism, Aquinas considers a people who are not free to make their own laws. Even here a prevailing custom seems to obtain the force of law according to the maxim "Whatever the sovereign permits, he approves."[59] However, a sovereign may have many other motives for tolerating a custom besides his approval of it—for example, the costs of suppressing the custom may be greater than the benefits. As Aquinas himself noted in the previous question, law may tolerate vices without in any way approving of them (ST, I-II, 96.2c). In short, many difficulties arise out of Aquinas's attempt to treat custom as proceeding, as would a statute, from the will and reason of the legislator.

No one has explored the origins and significance of the vocabulary of positive law in Aquinas more than Sten Gagnér. Although he does not comment on Aquinas's decisive and deliberate substitution of *lex* for *ius* as the primary term for law, Gagnér illuminates Aquinas's language of "positivity" by exploring how Aquinas modifies *lex* and *ius* with the many variants of *pono*. Unlike Stephen Kuttner and others who focus narrowly on variants of the perfect passive participle, such as *lex positiva* and *ius positivum,* Gagnér explores the whole lexical family of *pono,* ranging from the *legem ponere* to *lex positiva.* Gagnér rightly argues that Aquinas's deployments of "positive law" (*lex positiva*) must be understood in relation to his many related deployments of "imposed law" (*legem ponere, lex posita*). Indeed, although Gagnér does not discuss the ambiguity of "positive law," his analysis of the whole lexical family of *pono* reveals the seamless transitions in Aquinas's discourse from the concept of law imposed by statute (*lex posita*) to the concept of law with a morally contingent content (*lex positiva, ius positivum*).

Moreover, Gagnér is also right to emphasize Aquinas's strongly statutory

---

58. Julian, Digest, 1.3.32.
59. Of an unfree people, Aquinas says: "Tamen ipsa consuetudo in tali multitudine praevalens obtinet vim legis, inquantum per eos toleratur ad quos pertinet multitudini legem imponere: ex hoc enim ipso videntur approbare quod consuetudo introduxit." ST, I-II, 97.3 ad 3.

conception of law—one sharply at odds with the emphasis on customary law in other currents of medieval legal thought. Thus Gagnér observes that in the centerpiece of Aquinas's mature theory of human law (I-II, 95.1), Aquinas uses the expression *legem ponere* seven times.[60] Aquinas opens this question by asking "whether it is useful that laws in some way be imposed by men [*leges poni ab hominibus*]." Aquinas, of course, answers in the affirmative several times, deploying the same expressions: "Therefore it is necessary that human laws be imposed [*ponere leges*]." Why? "It is necessary for human virtue and for peace that laws be imposed [*quod leges ponerentur*]." And "it is easier to find a few wise men who suffice to enact rightful laws [*ad rectas leges ponendas*] than the many who would be required to judge rightly about individual cases." Moreover, "those who impose laws [*leges ponunt*] consider with more time what must be framed by law" than do judges who must rule on the cases immediately before them. Earlier in the treatise on law we find Aquinas's most pithy statement of his statutory conception of law when he says that it belongs to the essence of law that "law is imposed on others" (*lex imponitur aliis,* I-II, 90.4c). In addition to illustrating Aquinas's resolutely statutory conception of human law, these deployments of variants of *legem ponere* also show that his understanding of positive law cannot be gleaned from his deployments of *lex positiva* or *ius positivum* alone.

Unfortunately, Gagnér's claim that the primacy of statute in Aquinas's theory of law anticipates and contributes to the primacy of statute in subsequent legal practice cannot be sustained. The best scholarship suggests instead, as one might well expect, that Aquinas's emphasis on statutory law reflects and embodies prior developments toward the supremacy of legislation in medieval legal practice. Gagnér claims that Aquinas is contributing to a new "*Drang zur Kodifikation*" of his day, a quest that would soon issue in the *Sacrosanctae* of Boniface VIII and the *Defensor Pacis* of Marsilius.[61] Michel Villey follows Gag-

60. "Das Wort *ponere* mit Ableitungen ist hier zum Fachwort der Gesetzgebung geworden. Es handelt sich bei Thomas demnach um einem bewussten, etwas programmatischen Sprachgebrauch. Stellen, setzen, bestimmen, einrichten, *ponere*—diese Ausdrucksweise in bezug auf die menschlichen Gesetze lenkt die Aufmerksamkeit auf die gesetzgeberische Tätigkeit, auf den tatsächlichen Ursprung der Gesetz im Menschen der Gemeinwesen dieser Welt." Gagnér, *Studien,* p. 207.

61. "Mit der Gesetzgebungsideologie, die wir aus der IaIIae des Aquinaten kennengelernt haben, besitzen wir offenbar den Schlüssel zum Verstandnis der *Sacrosanctae* Bonifaz VIII. bzw. dem Marsilischen *Defensor pacis,* was die Rechtslehre betrifft." Gagnér, *Studien,* p. 283. Michel Villey agrees with Gagnér about Aquinas's influence on Boniface's plan to codify canon law: "C'est sous l'influence du thomisme que Boniface VIII, à la fin

nér by arguing that Aquinas has restored the legislative office to its ancient, and later modern, supremacy.[62] According to Gagnér, medieval jurisprudence before Aquinas allowed little scope for legislation: Gratian, for example, says that man is ruled by natural law and by custom; he goes on to say that when custom is declared in writing it is called law, otherwise it remains merely usage.[63] Before the thirteenth century, says Gagnér, the king was merely a custodian of the laws; law and statute stood over him, and the new had to find its grounding in the old.[64] With the revival of Aristotle, however, came a revival of the idea that law could be deliberately enacted—that law was not merely ancient custom. In opposition to Gratian's view that law ascends from the customs of the people, Aquinas champions the conception of law as descending from the sovereign power of the lawgiver. In short, says Gagnér, Aquinas contributed greatly to the restoration of the Aristotelian conception of the legislative office with plenary powers for regulating a wide scope of human affairs and for changing laws to meet new circumstances.[65]

Gagnér argues that Aquinas's use of this vocabulary represents a radical innovation in legal discourse in the Latin West. He shows that *legem ponere* and

du XIIIème siècle, propose nouvelle analyse des décrétales pontificales et revendique le pouvoir de 'poser' des lois créatrices d'un droit nouveau." See Villey, *La formation de la pensée juridique moderne* (Paris: Cours d'Histoire de la Philosophie du Droit, 1975), p. 133.

62. "Mais surtout, l'oeuvre de saint Thomas est de rendre aux juristes le sens de la fonction législatrice. . . . Saint Thomas restaure la loi." Villey, *La formation,* p. 133.

63. "Humanum genus duobus regitur, naturali videlicet iure et moribus. . . . Mos est longa consuetudo . . . non differt, utrum consuetudo scriptura, vel ratione consistat, apparet, quod consuetudo est partim redacta in scriptis, partim moribus tantum utentium est reservata. Quae in scriptis redacta est, constitutio sive ius vocatur; quae vero in scriptis redacta non est, generali nomine, consuetudo videlicet, appellatur." Gratian, *Corpus Iuris Canonici,* D 1, cc. 1, 4, 5. Villey agrees that "Gratien ne fait plus aucune place à une fonction créatrice du législateur." Villey, *La formation,* p. 133. But Gagnér and Villey neglect Gratian's repeated insistence that custom yield to truth (D 8, c. 5) and that statutes should remove evil customs (D 11, cc. 1 and 4).

64. Gagnér cites Fichtenau: "Früher war dem Herrscher allein das '*leges custodire*' aufgegeben gewesen, Recht und Gesetz standen ja über ihm und das Neue musste stets im Alten seine Begrundung finden." *Studien,* p. 207n.

65. "Freilich ist er immer durch die *lex aeterna* gebunden . . . aber die Aristelische politisch-soziale Gesetzgebungsauffassung, die Thomas rezipiert hat, gibt dem *legum conditor* eine selbstherrliche Macht. Er ist nicht länger derjenige, der mit einer gewissen Freiheit das Recht im ganzen nur schrifftlich niederlegt, eine *consuetudo in scriptis redacta* herstellt, sondern er entscheidet den Inhalt des Gesetzes, gemäss dessen Zweckmässigkeit im Gemeinwesen. Er ist zum Gestezgeber geworden." Gagnér, *Studien,* p. 274.

its variants are exact renderings of the Greek technical verb for the act of legislation, *nomothetein,* and its variants. Gagnér argues that Aquinas acquired this vocabulary from his careful study of Moerbeke's translation of Aristotle's *Politics,* which occupied Aquinas at the very time he was developing his mature legal philosophy in the *Prima Secundae.*[66] Indeed, Gagnér insists that the expression *legem ponere* and its derivatives are foreign to Republican and classical Roman jurisprudence and represent a Greek transplant onto Roman legal science.[67] He thus finds *legem ponere* where Greek influence is greatest, such as in the writings of Cicero and the late Romano-Byzantine legal compilations.[68]

Subsequent scholarship forces us substantially to revise Gagnér's claims about Aquinas's contributions both to legal practice and even to legal discourse. Whereas Gagnér sees Boniface VIII as making an innovative claim for plenary legislative powers at the end of the thirteenth century, subsequent historians of the rise of legislative power have emphasized the much earlier *Dictatus Papae* of Gregory VII in 1075.[69] Moreover, even Gratian, who is for Gagnér the embod-

---

66. *Nomos* modified by variants of *tithēmi* means to lay down the law (*theinai nomon*); *keitai* or *keimai* is used as the passive voice of *tithēmi* to refer to law laid down (*keitai nomos*). As some examples of Moerbeke's rendering of Aristotle's Greek expressions for legislation in the *Politics,* Gagnér cites these: *tous nomous keimenous orthos* = *leges recte positas* (1282b 2); *keisthai tous nomous* = *poni leges* (1282b 10); *keisthai nomous* = *ponere leges* (1286a 22); *peri te nomōn theseōs* = *de legum positione* (1298a 17); in the *Ethics, peri tēs nomothesias* = *de legis ponere* (1181b 13). For more evidence of Plato's and Aristotle's very frequent use of these expressions, see the list of citations in Gagnér, *Studien,* pp. 244–49 and 258–59.

67. "Der Ausdruck *legem ponere* taucht in der lateinischen Antike nur dort auf, wo griechisches Gedankengut vorhanden ist." Gagnér, *Studien,* p. 208. The classical Roman jurists preferred such expressions as *condere iura* and *constituere ius,* which connote law being built up rather than, as with *legem ponere,* laid down.

68. Thus in Cicero (*De legibus* I, 12.34): *ius in natura esse positum.* "Im römischen Recht aber macht sich die Redensart *legem ponere* erst in der Kaisergesetzgebung der Spätantike geltend, und zwar im griechischen Kulturmilieu." Thus *legem ponere* is used as a technical expression for legislation in Justinian's *Institutes* (II, 16,1; II, 20, 27; III, 3, 4; III, 9, 5; III, 1, 2; III, 1, 14) and the *Codex* (II, 58, 2). In short, *legem ponere* emerges in the sixth-century context of Byzantine imperial legislation: "Wie sich am byzantinischen Hofe das lateinishe Äquivalent des gr. *tithenai* als Fachwort der Gesetzgebung verwerten liess." Gagnér, *Studien,* p. 209.

69. Armin Wolf, for example, cites Gregory's claim to legislative power: "Während des Investiturstreites beanspruchte Gregorius VII. im *Dictatus papae* dieses Recht für den Papst (1075): '*Quod illi (sc. Papae) soli licet pro temporis necessitate novas leges condere. . . .*'" See Wolf's "Die Gesetzgebung der entstehenden Territorialstaaten," in *Handbuch der Quellen und Literatur der Neueren Europäischen Privatrechtsgeschichte* vol. 1, ed. Helmut Coing (Munich: C. H. Beck'sche, 1973), pp. 517–800, at 528. Cf. Wolf's subsequent

iment of the medieval supremacy of custom, affords considerable scope for leg-islative innovation and authority.[70] Aquinas's emphasis on legislative authority looks less like an innovation that anticipates and contributes to a new concep-tion of legislative supremacy and more like a reflection of a long-standing drive for legislative power by popes, emperors, and kings beginning at least with Gregory VII.

Just as Aquinas's emphasis on the supremacy of imposed law is not as inno-vative as Gagnér supposes, neither is Aquinas's discourse of imposed law. In his review of Gagnér's *Studien,* Walter Ullmann presents a great deal of evidence for the pervasive deployment of *legem ponere* throughout medieval legal cul-ture: in the statutes of the feudal kings, in the edicts of popes and, perhaps most salient for Aquinas, in the Vulgate Bible.[71] Ullmann agrees with Gagnér that this expression is closely tied to the theory of legislative supremacy; but Ull-mann insists that this "descending" theory of law imposed by imperial author-ity had always coexisted with the "ascending" theory of law emerging from cus-tom.[72]

Ullmann argues that *legem ponere* grew out of the expression *legem dare.* The old Roman law, he says, sharply distinguished between *legem ferre* or *legislatio,* the law-making act of the Roman people, and *legem dare* or *legisdatio,* the act of imposing Roman law upon dependent communities by a sovereign power.[73] In

---

Gesetzgebung in Europa 1100–1500: Zur Entstehung der Territorialstaaten (Munich: C. H. Beck'sche, 1996), pp. 18–19. Berman follows Wolf in arguing that the legislative revolu-tion of the Middle Ages "was a revolution declared in 1075 by Pope Gregory VII." Harold Berman, *Law and Revolution: The Formation of the Western Legal Tradition* (Cambridge, MA: Harvard University Press, 1983), p. 50.

70. "Das *Decretum Gratiani* gibt sowohl dem Papst als auch Kaisern und Königen des Geset-zgebungsrecht." Armin Wolf, "Die Gesetzgebung der entstehenden Territorialstaaten," p. 529.

71. Ullmann cites a few examples from the Vulgate: Job 28:26; Ps. 26:11; 77:5; 118:33 and 102; Prov. 8:29; Jer. 33:25; 1 Tim. 1:9 (*lex posita*), etc. Curiously, Ullmann does not cite Gal. 3:19 (*lex posita*). These last two, as Gagnér would predict, render the Greek *nomos* modi-fied by *tithēmi.* See Walter Ullmann, Review of Gagnér, *Studien zur Ideengeschichte der Gesetzgebung, Revue d'histoire du droit* 29 (1961): 118–29, at 124 n. 17.

72. In response to Gagnér's claim that "Einen festen Sprachgebrauch dieser Art kannte das Mittelalter vor Thomas nicht" (*Studien,* 207), Ullmann marshals considerable evidence to the contrary: "Historisch gesehen, war allerdings der Begriff des *legem ponere* durchs ganze Mittelalter in Gebrauch. . . . Mit der Erstarkung der monarchischen Gewalt gewinnt der Begriff des *legem ponere* erst recht an Gehalt und Schärfe." Walter Ullmann, Review of Gagnér, p. 124.

73. "Das *legem ponere,* so will es scheinen, hat sich in der weltlichen Gesetzgebung aus dem

his view, *legem ponere* refers to this sovereign act of imposing law (*leges datae*) upon communities whose citizens have no role in the making of that law. Aquinas never explicitly distinguishes between law made by a community for itself (*leges rogatae*) and law imposed upon dependent subjects (*leges datae*), but his language often reflects the imperial view of law, as when he says that law is given (*legem dare*) by a legislator, or when he says that it belongs to the essence of law that it be imposed upon others: "*Lex imponitur aliis.*"

Although Gagnér says nothing about the decisive role of Aquinas's choice of *lex* as his technical term for law, the whole language of law being "imposed" makes sense only as *legem ponere;* the concept of the lawyers' law being imposed by a legislator (*ius ponere*) makes no sense. I emphasize the top-down verbal motion of the act of imposing law (*legem ponere*) and of law as imposed (*ius lege positum*) in my renderings of Aquinas because many translations of these terms use more abstract figures of speech, such as "man-made law" or "posited law." In his analysis of the concept of positivity in Aquinas, Finnis, for example, frequently uses the word *posited* to render what has been imposed. By using such an abstract and vague term as "posited," Finnis can claim that "custom, legislation, and judgments" are all "posited" and, hence, positive law.[74] The abstract "posited" only weakly conveys the verbal action of laying down law and of law laid down, which are so prominent in the Greek and Latin.[75] By positive law,

---

legem dare entwickelt, einem Begriff, der deutlich anzeigt, dass der Recht empfangende Teil mit der Formulierung des Rechtsinhaltes nichts zu tun hatte. Das alte römische Recht schied sehr scharf zwischen dem *legem ferre* und dem *legem dare:* die *legislatio* bezieht sich auf die rechtschaffende Tätigkeit des römischen Volkes, wahrend die *legisdatio* dort gebraucht wird, wo die römischen Gesetze den *municipia* oder *coloniae* kraft Machtvollkommenheit einfach gegeben wurden." Ullmann, Review of Gagnér, p. 124.

74. See Finnis, "The Truth in Legal Positivism," pp. 200–03, 212. "And since the whole of a human community's existing law, however completely just and decent, is positive, somehow humanly posited, why deny that the facts which are referred to as 'human positing'—custom, legislation, judgments" (p. 204). In his subsequent correspondence to the author, however, Finnis uses the expression *laid down.*

75. One of the first uses of a variant of *tithēmi* in relation to law is *thesmos* (statute)—a word with a strong sense of downward motion: "In the earliest occurrences of *thesmos* that have come down to us the 'imposition' is taken in a very concrete and literal sense and refers to an object placed in some significant location." Martin Ostwald, "Ancient Greek Ideas of Law," in *Dictionary of the History of Ideas,* ed. Philip Wiener (New York: Scribner, 1973). According to the *Liddell-Scott-Jones Lexicon,* tithesthai and thesthai mean "to lay down" arms or laws. According to the *Oxford Latin Dictionary,* pono has several uses to convey imposition: to lay down arms, to lay eggs, to lay down (rest), to impose a name, to lay down a law, etc. According to the *Thesaurus Linguae Latinae,* s.v. *positus,* we

Aquinas means statutes imposed or laid down by the governing authorities on their subjects; the law that emerges from custom or from the decisions of judges is arguably not properly described as imposed.[76] True, a judge lays down the law on the parties before him, but not in the same way on subsequent litigants: put simply, common law rules have authority not so much because they were once "laid down" (*legem ponere*) as because they are continually "taken up" by subsequent judges. It is not clear that any single concept could encompass both the deliberate imposition of law in legislation and the process whereby law emerges from custom, judicial decisions, and commentary without being "imposed" by anyone. What is, I think, clear is that precise thought and speech about the sources of law would benefit from the more precise language of enactment, custom, commentary, and precedents, rather than the vagaries of "posited" or positive law.

Positive Law as Contingently Moral

For Aquinas, law is positive because it is authoritatively imposed (*legem ponere*); yet he also tells us that law is positive because its content lacks moral necessity and has moral force only (if at all) because of the contingent facts surrounding its enactment (*ius positivum*). It is difficult to generalize about the content of positive laws, because Aquinas's examples of such laws range from those that are radically unjust (ST, II-II, 60.5 ad 2) to those that have only a very contingent relation to justice (ST, I-II, 102.1 ad 3) and to those that are virtually moral ne-

---

read: "Respicitur potius actio ponendi, quae fit: imponendo vel efficiendo." As an example of this action of imposition, a passage from Aulus Gellius is cited: "Nomina verbaque non positu fortuito (nouns and verbs are not imposed by chance)." In the *Thomas-Lexikon* of Ludwig Schutz (Paderborn: Ferdinand Schoning, 1895), s.v. *positio*, we read: "Setzung, Hinsetzung"; s.v. *positive:* "nach Weise einer Hinsetzung." Finally, recall that the *OED* began its definition of "positive" with "formally laid down or imposed."

76. Even Austin rejected Bentham's concept of "judge-made law" because it blurs the important "distinction between law made *obliquely* in the way of judicial decision, and that made *directly* in the way of legislation." Austin, *Lectures on Jurisprudence,* lect. 29 *ad finem* (emphasis his). According to Austin, judges impose law directly only on the parties before them. More recently, A. W. B. Simpson has also rejected the idea that judges lay down or posit law: "Their actions create precedents, but creating a precedent is not the same thing as laying down the law. . . . To express an authoritative opinion is not the same thing as to legislate . . . and it is merely misleading to speak of judicial legislation." See Simpson, "The Common Law and Legal Theory," in *Oxford Essays in Jurisprudence,* 2nd series (Oxford: Clarendon Press, 1973): 77–99, at 86. Of course, I cannot hope to do justice here to the complex and controversial relation of judging (*richtend*) to legislating (*gesetzgebend*).

cessities (ST, I-II, 95.2c). What this reveals is that when "positive" refers to the content of a legal norm, it involves a question of degree: some laws are more positive than others. In such a spectrum, it is not obvious where natural law becomes positive law; this helps to explain Aquinas's difficulties in dealing with kinds of law that seem to be intermediate between natural law and positive law.[77] Of course, when law is positive in the sense of deliberately imposed, there can be no question of degree.

As we have seen, Aquinas developed this sense of law's positivity in the context of his distinction between the natural law precepts (*moralia*) and the positive law precepts (*caeremonialia*) of the Mosaic law. Since the whole of Mosaic law is positive in the first sense of authoritatively imposed, the part of the Mosaic law he identifies as *ius positivum* (e.g., *caeremonialia*) can be positive only by virtue of its content. Moreover, in the context of divine law, the question is how the contingently moral positive precepts of Mosaic law relate to the necessarily moral natural law precepts. Thus, for Aquinas, positive law in this sense chiefly refers to law whose content is not necessarily, but only contingently, moral; positive law gets its moral force not from its content but from the contingent facts of its enactment. Here we think of all the seemingly arbitrary conventions of law that vary so radically over time and place: the procedures, formalities, schedules, deadlines, and so forth. Because, as Aquinas frequently observes, the detailed specifications of positive law cannot be logically deduced from the moral requirements of the natural law, he must consider how to characterize the relation of positive law to natural law.

Just as Aquinas's doctrine of positive law brings together both dimensions of positivity, so his rhetoric brings together two distinct terminologies of legal positivism—each with its own lineage. We saw Gagnér and Ullmann trace Aquinas's statutory language of *legem ponere* to Moerbeke's translation of Aristotle, the Vulgate Bible, late Romano-Byzantine law, and its ultimate Greek roots; now we shall see Dom Lottin, Stephan Kuttner, Damien Van Den Eynde, and Gagnér trace Aquinas's language of morally neutral law (*ius positivum*) to its proximate causes in the early twelfth-century Neoplatonic school of Chartres and ultimately to its Greek roots.

Both of these conceptual and rhetorical lineages stem from the same ancient Greek debates about the origin and significance of names (words). In these Greek debates about language, we earlier found an interweaving of our two

---

77. Thus, the judicial precepts of the Old Law are intermediate between the natural moral precepts and the positive ceremonial precepts (ST, I-II, 104.1c); and the *ius gentium* is intermediate between natural law and positive law (ST, I-II, 95.4c, and II-II, 57.4).

senses of "positive" law: the question of whether names get their meaning from authoritative imposition usually accompanies the question of whether the content (or sounds) of names are adventitious and unmotivated by their meaning. We saw that, according to Proclus, Greek philosophers argued about whether names are by nature (*physei*) or by imposition (*thesei*). What is of great significance for the vocabulary of legal positivity is how Aulus Gellius renders this Greek distinction: he has the Roman Pythagorean philosopher P. Nigidius Figulus argue that names "non positiva esse, sed naturalia." That this first and highly influential use of *positiva* in contrast to *naturalis* stems from the doctrines that Proclus ascribes to Democritus and to Pythagoras is evident when Nigidius goes on to say that nouns and verbs are not made by fortuitous imposition but are made by a certain power and logic of nature.[78] The linguistic context of the emergence of the contrast of natural and positive is important because when *positivus* is deployed in jurisprudence, it retains its close association with the Democritean theory of names as being both adventitious (*fortuito*) and arbitrary (*arbitraria*).

From the research of Lottin, Kuttner, Van Den Eynde, and Gagnér,[79] we know that the term and concept of "positivity" entered the vocabulary of the theologians, first of the school of Chartres and then at Paris, by at least 1125,[80]

78. "Quod P. Nigidius argutissime docuit nomina non positiva esse, sed naturalia. Nomina verbaque non posita fortuito, sed quadam vi et ratione naturae facta esse. . . . Quaeri enim solitum apud philosophos, *physei ta onomata* sint *ē thesei*. In eam rem multa argumenta dicit, cur videri possint verba esse naturalia magis quam arbitraria." Aulus Gellius, *Noctes Atticae,* ed. P. K. Marshall, vol. 1 (Oxford: Clarendon Press, 1990), 10.4, p. 307. Gellius greatly admired the famous Roman philosopher and friend of Cicero, P. Nigidius Figulus, making it quite plausible that Nigidius himself rendered *thesei* as *positiva;* such is the surmise of Max Radin, "Early Statutory Interpretation in England," *University of Illinois Law Review* 38 (1943): 16–40, at 25.

79. See Odon Lottin, *Le droit naturel chez Saint Thomas d'Aquin et ses prédécesseurs* (Bruges: Charles Beyaert, 1931); Stephan Kuttner, "Sur les origines du terme 'droit positif,'" *Revue historique du droit français et étranger* 15 (1936): 728–40, and *Repertorium der Kanonistik (1140–1234)* vol. 1 (Vatican City: Biblioteca Apostolica, 1937), pp. 175–77; Damien Van Den Eynde, "The Terms '*Ius Positivum*' and '*Signum Positivum*' in Twelfth-Century Scholasticism," *Franciscan Studies* (March 1949): 41–49; Gagnér, *Studien,* pp. 218–48.

80. Gagnér's investigations set the standard on this question, and he claims that Chalcidius's distinction first appeared in William of Conches's influential commentary on Chalcidius in about 1125; see *Studien,* p. 226. Stephan Kuttner, who first surmised that the new vocabulary of legal positivism stemmed from Chalcidius, recently acknowledged the plausibility of Gagnér's identification of William of Conches as the first conduit for Chalcidius; see Kuttner, *The History of Ideas and Doctrines of Canon Law in the Middle*

and quickly spread among theologians, philosophers, and jurists to England and Italy early in the thirteenth century. The concept of positivity appears in a variety of verbal forms, but in every case it is developed explicitly in contrast to what is natural.[81] Just as the ancient Greek debates concerned both law and language, so also the concept of positivity was deployed in the twelfth century to organize analyses both of law and of sign systems.

In this discourse among the French theologians and canonists of the twelfth century emerges an emphasis on our second sense of positive as referring to the content of a law that is not intrinsically moral. Kuttner's surmise that Chalcidius was the primary source of the new language of positivity has been borne out by subsequent investigation; Chalcidius's fourth-century commentary on Plato's *Timaeus* was at the center of study among the Christian Platonists of Chartres and Paris. Chalcidius says, "In this book there is no consideration and contemplation of positive justice but of natural justice and equity." He explains this contrast of *iustitia positiva* and *naturalis* by saying that whereas Socrates discussed the justice employed by men in the civil state, Timaeus of Locri, a pupil of Pythagoras, wanted to inquire into the divine justice of the visible cosmos.[82] Here, "natural" and "positive" are set in sharp opposition: natural is the justice discovered in the providential government of the cosmos, and positive is the justice invented for particular communities. Compared to the divinely ordained permanence of natural justice, positive human justice appears as a fleet-

---

Ages (Aldershot: Variorum, 1992), part V, p. 98, and "Retractiones," part 3, p. 4. Walter Ullmann says he admires this part of Gagnér's book; see Ullmann, Review of Gagnér, p. 123.

81. These different forms include: *ius positivum, iustitia positiva, lex* or *constitutio positionis,* and *signa positiva,* in opposition to, respectively, *ius naturale, iustitia naturalis, lex naturae,* and *signa naturalia.* I have culled these from Van Den Eynde, "'*Ius Positivum*' and '*Signum Positivum.*'" The variety of these forms shows the importance of exploring the whole lexical family of *pono* (as does Gagnér) and not merely the variants of the perfect, passive stem, like *positivus.*

82. "Ex quo apparet in hoc libro principaliter illud agi: contemplationem considerationemque institui non positiuae sed naturalis illius iustitiae atque aequitatis, quae inscripta instituendis legibus describendisque formulis tribuit ex genuina moderatione substantiam, perindeque ut Socrates, cum de iustitia dissereret qua homines utuntur, induxit effigiem ciuilis rei publicae, ita Timaeus Locrensis ex Pythagorae magisterio astronomiae quoque disciplinae perfecte peritus, eam iustitiam qua diuinum genus aduersum se utitur in mundi huius sensilis ueluti quadam communi urbe ac re publica uoluit inquiri." Text in *Timaeus: A Calcidio Translatus Commentarioque Instructus,* ed. J. H. Waszink (London: Warburg Institute, 1962), pp. 59–60. Chalcidius (c. A.D. 256–357) may well have drawn the term *positiva* from Aulus Gellius, since he cites the *Noctes Atticae* twice in his commentary on the *Timaeus* (see the *index locorum* of Waszink's edition).

ing and transient affair. Moreover, positive justice is not described in statutory terms as "imposed" or "posited" but merely as that "which men employ or manage [*qua homines utuntur*]"; indeed, natural justice is associated with the institution of laws (*instituendis legibus*).[83]

Gagnér has shown that the first and most influential conduit for Chalcidius's novel language was most likely the celebrated commentary by William of Conches of the cathedral school of Chartres (c. 1125). Here we read: "Positive [justice] is that which is contrived by men, such as the hanging of a thief; the natural is that which is not contrived by men, such as the love of parents, and the like."[84] Again, what makes the justice positive is that it is a transient human contrivance, as opposed to the permanent and universal justice found in the family bond. With the spread of this new language from Chartres to Paris, we find Hugh of St. Victor saying that "out of natural justice arises the discipline of our mores, that is, positive justice."[85] Far from being set in opposition to custom, positive justice is here equated with custom. Similarly, when Peter Abelard distinguishes natural from positive justice, he includes in positive justice both law and custom.[86] In the *Summa Coloniensis* (1169), human law is divided into what is natural and what is positive; positive law is then divided into what is civil and what is the law of nations: "What is natural, which proceeds from natural impulse among all men, such as the union of husband and wife. . . . What is positive, which, if proper to a particular polity, is called civil law, such as the religious cult and the particular ceremonial rites; or, if in diverse nations, is called the law of nations."[87] Here again, what is positive is not what

83. As Gagnér observes: "Wenn Chalcidius die *positiva iustitia* und die *naturalis iustitia* vergleicht, bezeichnet er die erstere eindeutig als bestehendes Recht, das die Menschen anwenden—*iustitia . . . qua homines utuntur*—nicht aber als Tätigkeit, sondern das Erzeugnis eines etwaigen gestezgeberischen Wirkens." *Studien*, p. 244.

84. "Et est positiva que est ab hominibus inventa ut suspensio latronis, etc. Naturalis vero que non est homine inventa ut parentum dilectio et similia." William of Conches, cited in Gagnér, *Studien*, p. 231.

85. Hugh of St. Victor (*Didascalion*, VI, 5 (c. 1130)): "In illa enim [de tropologia, id est, moralitate] naturalis iustitia est, ex qua disciplina morum nostrorum, id est, iustitia positiva nascitur." Cited in Van Den Eynde, "'*Ius Positivum*' and '*Signum Positivum*,'" p. 43.

86. Abelard, *Dialogus inter Philosophum, Judaeum et Christianum* (1141): "Positivae autem iustitiae illud est quod ab hominibus institutum, ad utilitatem scil. vel honestatem tutius muniendam, aut sola consuetudine aut scripti nititur auctoritate." Cited in Kuttner, "Sur les origines," p. 730.

87. *Summa Coloniensis* (1169): "Ius humanum aut est naturale, ut quod instinctu nature apud omnes est, puta maris et femine coniunctio. . . . Aut est positivum; et hoc si cuius civitatis sit proprium, civile dicitur, ut cultus numinum et caeremoniarum ritus specialis.

is imposed by statute (*ius gentium* is not statutory) but what cannot be directly derived from natural morality. Near the end of the twelfth century, Simon of Tournai brings law and linguistics back together in his novel deployments of the idiom of positivity. He says that "there are two laws [*leges*], one by nature and one of position [*positionis*] . . . and natural law is prior to and more worthy than positive law . . . nature judges position"; he also says that "signs are to be divided into natural signs and positive signs." Van Den Eynde surmises that Simon's use of the noun *positio* in relation to positivity reflects the direct influence of Aulus Gellius's discussion of language.[88]

Perhaps the most influential interpretation of the positivity of law is the claim that natural law concerns those things intrinsically evil (*mala in se*), while positive law concerns those things that are evil only because they are prohibited (*mala quia prohibita*). The source of this commonplace seems to be Hugues de Saint-Cher, a Dominican master at Paris, 1230–35. He said that certain acts are intrinsically evil apart from legal prohibitions, such as killing and adultery; they belong to the natural law. Other acts are evil only because they are prohibited by positive law, such as eating of the biblical fruit.[89] Here we find a good

---

Si diversarum sit nationum, ius gentium vocatur." Text from Lottin, *Le droit naturel,* p. 105.

88. Simon of Tournai: "*Sunt* enim due leges: una nature, alia positionis. . . . Quia lex naturae et prior est et dignior lege positionis . . . preiudicet natura positioni"; "Signorum enim alia sunt sacra, alia non. Non sacrorum alia naturalia, alia positiva." The deployment of *signum positivum* in the twelfth century was just as innovative as the deployment of *ius positivum*. See Van Den Eynde, "'*Ius Positivum*' and '*Signum Positivum*,'" pp. 45 and 47. Van Den Eynde (p. 44) sees Aulus Gellius as the most likely source for the pivotal innovations of Simon of Tournai: "Gellius makes the grammarian Nigidius say that the *nomina* are divided into *naturalia* and *positiva,* and that they do not originate *fortuito positu* but *quadam vi et ratione natura.* Such terminology, which opposes the nouns *natura* and *positus* as well as the adjectives *naturalis* and *positivus,* might easily have impressed the theologians and canonists of the twelfth century. It is in any case noteworthy that Simon of Tournai, in one and the same sentence, opposes *lex naturae* to *lex positionis* and also *natura* to *positio.*"

89. Hugues de Saint-Cher poses this problem: "In lege positua nichil [*sic*] est peccatum nisi quia prohibitum; ergo eadem ratione in lege naturali. Set [*sic*] omne peccatum est contra legem positivam vel naturalem. Ergo simpliciter omne peccatum ideo est peccatum quia prohibitum." And as a solution he says: "Alii dicunt et forte melius quod quedam sunt mala quia prohibita, ut fuit comestio pomi; alia mala in se et ideo prohibita, ut occidere hominem et mechari etc., que sunt legis naturalis." This fascinating passage was uncovered by Dom Lottin in *Le droit naturel chez Saint Thomas d'Aquin et ses prédécesseurs,* pp. 116 and 41.

description of the contrast of natural and positive: natural law precepts are intrinsically related to the requirements of true morality, while positive law precepts are not. The act of eating fruit is not intrinsically evil, so its prohibition must concern its extrinsic relation to some other aspect of the common good— perhaps that kind of fruit is only for export.[90] Because the obligatory force of the positive law is not intrinsic to its content, we must look beyond its content to the source of its authority, variously conceived as "the will of the sovereign," or to some intelligible relation to the demands of the common good, namely, the need for myriad detailed regulations to coordinate a complex society, this being but one. In this way, what is not intrinsically related to the requirements of morality can become such a requirement: what has no direct relation to morality thus acquires an indirect relation when we reflect on the need for detailed and specific rules for effective social coordination.

Aquinas devoted a great deal of his scholarly activity to the articulation of the rational grounds for the Mosaic law—a project that forced him to confront the question of the authority of positive law in a rather pointed way. Recall that the author of the *Summa Coloniensis* cited the ceremonial rites of the divine cult as examples of positive law; and indeed, many of the ceremonial precepts of the Mosaic law seem paradigmatic examples of sheer positivity, that is, having no intrinsic connection to morality. In the early *Commentary on the Sentences of Peter Lombard,* Aquinas often uses the expression *positive law* in connection with ceremonial precepts of the Mosaic law. More than any other kind of legal rules, the ceremonial precepts appear to be brute facts impenetrable to reason except as signs of the unfathomable will of God. Having established that the Decalogue embodies natural law precepts, Aquinas considers whether all of the precepts of the Mosaic law could be led back to (*reducantur,* that is, find their moral rationale in) the Decalogue.[91] In the fourth objection, Julian (D, 1.3.20) is cited to argue that there are legal rules for which no rationale was obvious.[92] Aquinas basically concedes the objection: the content of the ceremonial precepts is not grounded in true morality. Nonetheless, he says, these precepts may have an indirect connection to the requirements of the common good: "The ceremonial precepts or the precepts of positive law cannot be led back to the natural precepts as if they had the force of obligation from nature itself; but

---

90. Hugues, of course, is referring to the forbidden fruit of Eden.

91. CS, vol. 3, d. 37, q. 1, a. 3.

92. Julian: "Non omnium, quae a maioribus constituta sunt, ratio reddi potest"; cited in CS, vol. 3, d. 37, q. 1, a. 3 obj. 4.

they have this from the will of the institutor, who in instituting uses natural reason, if rightly instituted."[93]

Aquinas here recognizes that the authority of positive law (where it has authority) stems not from its intrinsic relation to morality but from its extrinsic relation to an authoritative scheme of social coordination. Jumping ahead to the treatise on law in the *Prima Secundae,* Aquinas says: "The observances of the Old Law may be said to have no reason in their very nature, for instance, that no garment should be made of wool and linen. They could, however, have had a reason in relation to something else, as signifying or excluding something. . . . The moral precepts have rational causes of their very nature; as, for instance, 'thou shalt not kill, thou shalt not steal.' But the ceremonial precepts have rational causes in relation to something else" (ST, I-II, 102.2 ad 1 and 3). Aquinas seems to distinguish between the moral and the ceremonial precepts of the Mosaic law when he says that divine law (*ius divinum*), like human law, may be distinguished into two parts: "Certain things are enjoined because good, and prohibited because evil, while others are good because enjoined and evil because prohibited" (ST, II-II, 57.2 ad 3). What could have less intrinsic relation to morality than something evil because it is prohibited? Even Aristotle, when he seeks to illustrate the morally contingent nature of legal justice, mainly cites examples of ceremonial precepts: "That a goat and not two sheep shall be sacrificed . . . that sacrifice shall be made in honor of Barsidas."[94]

Law's positivity is also apparent, says Aquinas, when we consider that many matters are morally indifferent until legally prohibited or enjoined: "It is here that positive law [*ius positivum*] has its place" (ST, II-II, 57.2 ad 2). Here Aquinas is interpreting Aristotle's discussion of legal justice in the *Nicomachean Ethics* (1134b 20), in which Aristotle says that legal justice concerns matters in principle indifferent [*ex archēs . . . ouden diapherei*] but not indifferent once determined by law, such as "that a prisoner's ransom shall be a mina, or that a goat and not two sheep shall be sacrificed." If we grant that there could be human affairs genuinely indifferent *in concreto,* the authoritative choice between them would seem to be groundless. Faced with matters truly indifferent, what role could reason play in such a choice? The determination of the precise specification of such a rule would seem to stem either from arbitrary willfulness or from

93. "Praecepta caeremonialia vel juris positivi non reducantur ad naturalia quasi ex ipsa natura vim obligandi habeant; sed hoc habent ex voluntate instituentis, quae in institutione naturali ratione utitur, si recte instituit." CS, vol. 3, d. 37, q. 1, a. 3, ad 2.

94. Aristotle, *Nicomachean Ethics* (1134b 21). That Aristotle uses ceremonial laws to illustrate the conventionality of law is noted by Harry A. Wolfson, *Philo,* vol. 2, p. 175.

random accident. As we shall see, although Aquinas says that "matters indifferent" are subject to determination by positive law, he also seems to deny that any concrete legislative choice could actually be indifferent.

The Ambiguity of Positivity

Thus Aquinas inherited two distinct concepts of the positivity of law: law is positive in the sense that its source is an authoritative imposition by a legislator, and law is positive in the sense that its content lacks necessary moral force. His frequent deployment of the new discourse of "positive" law in both of these senses makes him the first major theorist of positive law. Recall that just as the English word *positive* yokes together two quite different meanings, so do its Latin and Greek counterparts. Unfortunately, the conceptual distinction is not marked by any consistent verbal distinction. In general, the sense of statutory imposition and of law laid down is associated with the active and passive voices of the verbs *pono* and *tithēmi, ponitur* and *keitai;* while the sense of what is morally contingent is usually conveyed by adjectival and participial forms of the same verbs: *positive* and *thesei, positivus* and *thetikos.* These are only rough generalizations, though; virtually any of these forms can be found to encompass both meanings. Because of the intimate relations of the lexical family of "positive" (*tithēmi, pono*), it is all too easy to move verbally from the act of imposing law (*legem ponere*) to the law as imposed *(lex posita)* to the positivity of the content of law (*lex positiva, ius positivum*) without noticing the shift of concepts.

We can follow precisely this evolution of discourse in Aquinas's analysis of human law in the *Prima Secundae* (Q. 95). The first article begins with the question of "whether it is useful that laws be imposed [*leges poni*] by men." As the verb indicates, the issue here is the source of law in the act of legislation, not the content of the laws imposed; it is the authoritative source of imposed law that marks its superiority over both paternal discipline and the unfettered arbitration of judges. Anticipating his review of the fatal defects of the alternative sources of law, Aquinas concludes: "Therefore, it was necessary to impose human laws [*ponere leges humanas*]." Now that he has discussed the necessity of the act of authoritative imposing of laws, he can proceed to speak of laws as imposed (*lex posita*), as he does in the second article: "Is every imposed human law [*lex posita*] derived from natural law?" Here the issue would seem to be not the source of human law but the morality of its content; yet his language suggests a focus not on that content but on the statutory source—indeed, the first objection concludes: "Therefore, not all the statutes of human law are derived from natural law." Thus, even when positive human law is being contrasted with natural law, the expressions used refer to the contrast of statutory with nonstatutory law.

The third article also concerns the proper content of law, and here the discourse shifts again from the imposed law (*lex posita*) to the positive law (*lex positiva*). The reason for this otherwise inexplicable shift seems to be that, in the fourth article, Aquinas takes up the issue of how positive law (*ius positivum*), here taken to include the law of nations (*ius gentium*) and the civil law (*ius civile*), relates to natural law (*lex naturae*). In short, *lex positiva* serves as a halfway house between a focus on the statutory form of *lex posita* in the second article and a focus on the morally contingent content of *ius positivum* in the fourth article. The crucial discussion of *ius positivum* in the corpus of the fourth article takes place in the context of a focus on the content rather than on the source of law: "First, it is of the essence of human law to be derived from the natural law . . . and according to this [derivation], positive law is divided into the law of nations and civil law."[95] By using the relation to natural law as the standard for judging what is included in positive law, Aquinas seems to say that what is necessary for law to be positive is merely that its content not be identical to the requirements of true morality.[96] The content of the law of nations is derivable (as conclusions from premises) from the natural law and, therefore, has few elements that are morally contingent; the content of the civil law, by contrast, cannot be derived from the natural law as conclusions from premises and has, therefore, many morally contingent elements.[97] Thus, through a brief tour of this short and remarkable Question, we are lulled by the almost imperceptible shifts of terminology into thinking that the object of inquiry remained the same; yet in fact the object of inquiry has shifted from human law as imposed to human law as morally contingent in content. Recall that the *Oxford English Dictionary* begins its first definition of "positive" with "formally laid down or imposed" and ends with "conventional; opp. to natural." Remarkably, in this Question, Aquinas covers exactly the same ground.

95. Positive law is derived from natural on the basis of its content here; later in the article, Aquinas turns to the formal source of law: "Thirdly, it is of the essence of human law to be instituted by the governor of the political community."

96. At the same time, the law of nations seems to be a part of the natural law, so direct is its derivation from principles of natural law; see ST, I-II, 95.2c and 95.4c.

97. So deep is the ambiguity of law's positivity that, as we shall see, this same discussion can reasonably be interpreted to mean "of human positive laws laid down, some are morally motivated in content while others are morally neutral in content."

If Aquinas was led by the close lexical relation of *legem ponere* to *ius positivum* sometimes to conflate the conceptual distinction between them, so were his commentators. Even Kuttner, who has shed the most light on the lineages of the expression *ius positivum,* seems not to have fully understood what he had uncovered. He says that the canonists of the Middle Ages deploy the term *ius positivum* "to establish a distinction between the natural law, on the one hand, and on the other hand, all the laws (*lois*) whose origin stems from a legislative act, as for example the commandments that God gives to the Jewish people by the mouth of Moses, or the civil laws and the 'canons.' "[98]

Because he is the leading authority on the medieval canonists, Kuttner's interpretation has been highly influential. J.-M. Aubert seems to follow Kuttner by equating *ius positivum* with *lex posita* when he defines *ius positivum* as "*lex, constitutio positionis.*"[99] Perhaps most surprising of all, Gagnér, the only scholar systematically to analyze the deployment of the whole lexical family of *pono,* almost always interprets the term *ius positivum* in statutory terms. Because *positivus* is formed from the perfect passive stem of *ponere,* he insists that it has the same meaning, namely, "having been imposed."[100] Ullmann is the most forceful in advocating the statutory interpretation of positive law: he boldly insists that the distinction between enacted law (*lex posita*) and positive law (*ius positivum*) rests merely on a spelling mistake: "The *lex posita* or the *ius posit[iv]um*—the law laid down—was what through a mistaken copying much later (in the twelfth century) became 'positive' law which should be corrected to be called posited law. The opposite to 'positive' law was (and is) customary law

98. Kuttner: "On le chercherait en vain dans le vocabulaire des philosophes et des juristes romains, et ce ne sont que les canonistes du Moyen âge qui se servent du mot '*ius positivum*' pour établir une distinction entre la loi naturelle, d'une part, et d'autre part toutes les lois dont l'origine remonte à un acte législatif, comme par exemple les commandements que Dieu donna au peuple juif par la bouche de Moïse, ou les lois civile et les 'canones.'" See Kuttner, "Sur les origines," p. 728.

99. It is not clear how precisely to render "*constitutio positionis,*" but he seems to mean "law created by imposition." See Jean-Marie Aubert, *Le droit romain dans l'oeuvre de sainte Thomas,* p. 106n. (Paris: J. Vrin, 1955).

100. "Der Ausdruck *positiva iustitia* wäre demnach als 'gesetztes Recht' . . . oder, möglicherweise ebenso wie *positio iustitiae* als 'Setzen des Rechts' . . . oder schliesslich als 'Recht, das gesetzt wird,' 'Recht, das man setzen kann.'" Gagnér goes on to suggest that *iustitia positiva* be seen as the Latin equivalent of the Greek expression for enacted laws, *nomoi keimenoi;* yet *keitai,* unlike other variants of *tithēmi,* really only means "laid down" and not "arbitrary." See Gagnér, *Studien,* 243. Michel Villey, in turn, explicitly follows Gagnér by rendering *positivus* as "*qui a été posé;* see Villey, *La formation,* p. 131.

which was a rule that became binding as a result of usages and practices by a group of people through a more or less well-defined stretch of time."[101]

In the end, Aquinas is much less positive about the meaning of "positivity" than are his commentators. Only in the dialectical unfolding of his analysis of positivity contained in both the treatise on law and in the treatise on justice of the *Summa Theologiae* do we discover the essential ambiguity and ultimate indeterminacy of the question: What makes law positive? The basic philosophical question here is: Are the two dimensions of positivity coextensive or are they logically independent? Typically, as we have seen, statutory source and morally contingent content are treated as if they were coextensive. When what is imposed is also morally contingent we do not hesitate to describe it as positive. The ceremonial precepts of Mosaic law are thus exemplars of positivity in both senses. But what if we hold the statutory source constant and vary the content: some statutes are morally contingent, while others are morally necessary precepts. Is natural law positive if enacted? Here the answer is not so clear: the moral precepts of the Mosaic law are positive in the first sense but not in the second. Or, what if we hold the content constant and vary the source: some morally contingent laws are imposed, while others are customary. Is a customary law positive if morally contingent? Such an analysis produces an indeterminate answer to the question of positivity where the two dimensions do not coincide.

In many places, Aristotle and Aquinas seem to assume that the two dimensions of positivity are coextensive; at the same time, however, we find intimations of a recognition that they might vary independently. For example, in the *Nicomachean Ethics* (1134b 18f), Aristotle famously says of the politically just (*dikaion politikon*) that some of it is natural (*dikaion physikon*) and some of it is legal (*dikaion nomikon*). On the one hand, the legally just is radically relative and changeable; in this sense, it contrasts with what is natural and universal (though the natural, he says, is also changeable). On the other hand, the legally just is also emphatically legislative, illustrated by laws enacted on matters originally indifferent (*thōntai*), by laws enacted for particular cases (*nomothetousin*), and by provisions of decrees (*ta psēphismatōdē*). Here legal justice means what is deliberately enacted; in this sense, forming a contrast with the spontaneous, tacit, and organic processes of custom. As a kind of afterthought, Aristotle also says of the legally just that it is human (*anthrōpina*, 1135a 4) and con-

---

101. Walter Ullmann, *Law and Politics in the Middle Ages* (Ithaca: Cornell University Press, 1975), p. 62.

ventional (*synthēkē*, 1134b 32), suggesting that the domain of the morally contingent might be wider than the domain of the statutory.

In Aquinas's commentary on this passage we find the same two faces of positivism. He says that Aristotle divides the just into natural and legal; the jurists, he adds, divide law into natural and positive. Since Aquinas here uses the expression *positivum*, we might assume that he is speaking of what is morally contingent; instead, he is speaking of what is statutory: he says that when Aristotle speaks of the legally just, he means what is enacted by statute (*lege positivum*) or what the jurists call positive (*positivum*). Aquinas goes on to underscore the statutory character of the legally just when he says, "The citizens use justice, both what is implanted in the human mind by nature and that which is imposed by law [*positum lege*]." When Aquinas discusses Aristotle's examples of the legally just, he makes extensive use of technical terms for legislation: "When something is universally or generally imposed by statute (*lege imponitur*), that is the legally just; Aristotle says that the just is called legal which, in principle, before it was enacted by statute (*statuitur lege*), is indifferent whether done thus or so; but, when it is enacted (*ponitur*), that is, enacted by statute (*statuitur lege*), then a difference arises because observing it is just, disregarding it is unjust."[102]

One wants to inquire here of both Aristotle and Aquinas: Why is this account of positive law so focused on statutes? Are there not other sources of positive legal determination of matters in principle indifferent, such as juristic commentary, precedents, and legal custom (*usus fori*)?[103] Such a question would be unfairly anachronistic if posed to Aristotle, who lived in a polity without a professional class of jurists, and, therefore, without an established body of nonstatutory lawyers' law. In the case of Aquinas, though, who was familiar with the essential role of juristic commentary in the formation of Roman law, the neglect of nonstatutory sources of law is difficult to explain.[104]

---

102. Aquinas, *In Ethicorum*, V, 12, sec. 1017 and 1020. On Aquinas's combination of *statuere* and *lex* as technical expressions for legislation, see Adolf Berger, *Encyclopedic Dictionary of Roman Law* (Philadelphia: American Philosophical Society, 1953), where we read under *statuere*: "To ordain, to enact (e.g., *lex, imperator statuit*)."

103. True, Aquinas goes on to include the sentences passed by judges as a part of the legally just (sec. 1022); but he does not describe them as positive, nor, as we shall see, does he treat such sentences as a source of law for the adjudication of future cases.

104. As noted above, when Julian says (D. 1.3.20) that "we cannot find a rationale for every legal rule created by our revered [juristic] forefathers (*a maioribus constituta*)," Aquinas revealingly misquotes this twice: in the *Commentary on the Sentences* (CS, vol. 3, d. 37, q. 1, a. 3, obj. 4) juristic commentary becomes "the enacted law" (*in lege posita*); in the

The indeterminacy of law's positivity only emerges where the two dimensions of positivity are not coextensive; this indeterminacy fully reveals itself when we contrast two major uses of positivity in the treatise on law of the *Prima Secundae* and in the treatise on justice of the *Secunda Secundae*. In the treatise on law (for example, I-II, 95), Aquinas explicitly identifies human law and positive law by frequently using the expression *human positive law* (*lex humana posita*). He then divides the law "laid down" into two classes based its content: "Positive law [*ius positivum*] is divided into the law of nations [*ius gentium*] and the civil law [*ius civile*]" (ST, I-II, 95.4c). In the context of this question, what is decisive for law's positivity is that it be authoritatively imposed; as such, positive human law may include precepts of widely varying content, from the intrinsically moral *ius gentium* to the relatively nonmoral *ius civile*.

In the treatise on justice, by contrast, in considering whether judges should always pass judgment according to the written laws (*leges scriptae*), Aquinas uses the concept of positivity in a very different way (ST, II-II, 60.5c). He says that the lawful or just is twofold: "first, from the very nature of a thing, which is called natural law (*ius naturale*); and second, from some agreement among men which is called positive law (*ius positivum*)." He then proceeds on the assumption that all human law is statutory and considers the varying content of those laws: "Laws are written to declare each one of these kinds of law, though in its own fashion. For written law contains natural law but does not establish it, for it [natural law] has its force not from statute [*lex*], but from nature. Positive law, however, is both instituted and contained in written law, which gives it [positive law] the force of authority." Positivity here refers not to the formal source of law but to its content: within formally enacted law, we find natural law and positive law.

Such divergent uses of the same expression (*ius positivum*) is quite puzzling; perhaps our analysis of the deep ambiguity of the very concept of positivity will help to illuminate this puzzle. If we define positivity mainly in terms of its source in the authoritative act of legislation (as does I-II, 95), then we can expand positive law to include precepts of widely varying content: in this sense,

---

Prima Secundae (95.2 obj. 4) juristic commentary becomes "statutory law established by the authorities" (*a maioribus lege statuta*). Aubert points out the first misquotation in *Le droit romain*, p. 107. Yet Aquinas undoubtedly knew Pomponius's famous history of the Roman law in which pride of place is given to the activity of the private jurists (D. 1.2.2). That such law is so totally eclipsed by legislation in Aquinas's account of human law is rather astonishing.

precepts of the law of nations and of the civil law could all be encompassed by the act of legislation into the positive law. In the treatise on justice, however, by focusing on the content of law, Aquinas must confine positivity to the contingently moral precepts of human law. Of course, there is no change in Aquinas's underlying account of human law across the two treatises; in both cases, human law is legislatively imposed with a content that varies in degree of connection to morality. All that varies is Aquinas's use of the concept of positivity, in one case expansively to include all of human law, in the other case narrowly to include only the contingently moral precepts.

The contrast of these two passages beautifully reveals the ultimate indeterminacy of positivity because in neither case do the two dimensions of positivity coincide. In the treatise on law, positive law includes the fairly natural precepts of *ius gentium,* which are not positive in content; in the treatise on justice, positive law excludes natural law precepts imposed by statute, which are positive by authoritative source.

Finnis, however, who does not cite the passage from the treatise on justice, insists that the deployment in the treatise on laws is decisive:[105] "In the *Summa* [read: *Prima Secundae*!] he treats the division between natural [read: *ius gentium*] and civil as a distinction *within positive law.*"[106] If we take this passage as decisive, then we must privilege the formal source of law in authoritative enactment over the content of law, as Finnis does.[107] Why does Finnis privilege the formal source of law as the key to positivity? (Though he often uses "positive"

---

105. Finnis seems to counsel setting aside the complications of the *Secunda Secundae;* he says that whereas the *Prima Secundae* is focused on law (*lex*), the *Secunda Secundae* is focused on the just (*ius*): "In *Summa Theologiae* II-II, q. 57 aa. 2 and 3, where Aquinas is discussing *ius* not so much in the sense of 'law' as of 'right' (what is just), he restates the distinctions between *ius naturale, ius gentium,* and *ius positivum* in a manner designed primarily to reconcile the differing Roman juristic treatments (Ulpian v. Gaius) of natural right with each other and with Aristotle." See Finnis, "The Truth in Legal Positivism," p. 213 n.43. But in our passage (II-II, 60.5c), the subject is the enacted law, not "what is just" more broadly, and our passage ignores the problematic *ius gentium* of the Roman jurists. It is puzzling that Finnis does not discuss here this (admittedly inconvenient) passage.

106. Finnis, "The Truth in Legal Positivism," p. 202. Thus, says Finnis, Aquinas (I-II, 95.3) "settles down to talking of *lex positiva* as synonymous with *lex humana*" (p. 212 n. 38).

107. The positivity of law is decisively linked to "the fact (where it is the fact) that they [positive laws] have been posited humanly, by human will." Finnis, "The Truth in Legal Positivism," pp. 202–03.

in the sense of "contingently moral in content," despite his very strong claim that "what makes law positive is that it is laid down. Period.")[108] Since he does not explicitly consider the relations between the two dimensions of positivity, he does not develop an argument for why the formal source should trump the content of law. Finnis says that Aquinas's doctrine of positive law as law laid down, and Aquinas's equation of human law and positive law, means that "positive law is at last, in its own right, a complete subject or object of study."[109] But does Aquinas's account of positive law really delimit such a science of human legal systems? To begin with, as we have seen, there is nothing about Aquinas's account of positive law that makes it essentially human, even though Aquinas usually, though not always, uses the term *positive* to refer to human law. On his view, God also lays down law of morally contingent content. So a science of positive law would have to include, at a minimum, both divine and human positive law. Moreover, Aquinas's account of positive law lays the basis for at least two very different kinds of legal science. The study of positive law in terms of its deliberate enactment would bring the study of law into relation with other kinds of deliberate stipulations in clubs, grammar, logic, and military commands; and the study of law in terms of concrete determinations of general moral principles would bring the study of law into relation with the many other kinds of social conventions (largely tacit manners and mores) that (when good) give our general moral principles their concrete instantiations.

108. For example, Finnis frequently uses the expression *purely positive law.* "Law made by *determinatio* is purely positive law." See *Aquinas,* p. 268, and correspondence to author of 22 September 1997. To speak of degrees of positivity strongly implies a reference to the moral content of law, since laws vary in the degree to which they reflect the basic requirements of practical reason. Finnis says nothing to suggest that whether or not law is "laid down" could admit of degree; and we normally say that a law is either enacted or not. Of course, a law could be both customary and enacted, but even here whether it was "laid down" does not admit of degree. So when Finnis speaks of "purely" positive law, he means that the content of law may be more or less morally contingent. Or, again, he says: "Positive law (when just) is always somehow derived from the basic moral principles he calls natural law." Here, again, "positive" refers to the content of law, since his concern is how the content of a law can be derived from the natural law. To see that derivation from natural law applies to the content rather than to the enactment, substitute "custom" for "positive law": "custom (when just) is always somehow derived from the basic moral principles he calls natural law." See "The Truth in Legal Positivism," p. 199. Despite his attempt to stipulate a single meaning for "positive," Finnis's uses of the word, not surprisingly, oscillate unstably between our two concepts.

109. Finnis, "The Truth in Legal Positivism," p. 202; cf. 195 and 203.

POSITIVE LAW AND NATURAL LAW

Two Facets of the Relation of Natural Law
to Positive Law

Recall that natural law has a distinct relation to positive law according to each of our senses of positive.[110] Natural law justifies the duty to obey positive law as imposed, even apart from the issues presented by the content of that law; and natural law justifies the right (and sometimes the duty) to disobey positive law by establishing limits to what is permissible in that content. These two justifications are distinct though interlocking: the first could be said to ground a prima facie obligation to obey every law, apart from its content, simply because of its source in an authoritative scheme of coordination.[111] However, these prima facie reasons for obeying any particular law may be defeated if the content of that law is sufficiently at odds with the requirements of practical reason.

What accounts for the moral force of law simply as enacted? In most cases, we have independent moral reasons for conforming to the requirements of law, so we are not aware of the distinctive moral force of the law as enacted. We routinely conform to vast numbers of legal regulations without even knowing that we are obeying the law. Nonetheless, even in cases in which we accept independent moral reasons for general conformity to various laws (such as paying taxes, honoring debts, and the like), we may question whether we have to conform in the way the law specifically requires—for example, by paying our taxes in advance through withholding, by paying at a particular rate, by having contracts notarized, and so forth. We might believe that these specific requirements are unnecessary, inefficient, burdensome, and so on, and yet still be under a moral obligation to obey them because of our duty to our fellow citizens to respect the

---

110. The questions of just what Aquinas means by natural law and whether his ethics can be adequately characterized as a natural law ethics are much controverted; for a survey of, and contribution to, some of these controversies, see Pamela Hall, *Narrative and the Natural Law* (Notre Dame: Notre Dame University Press, 1994). My concern here is not with natural law per se but only with Aquinas's account of the relation of natural law to positive law; in this limited context, I shall assume that by natural law Aquinas means at least "the basic principles and precepts of practical reason," especially the moral precepts governing human choices.

111. On law as a system for social coordination, see Gerald J. Postema, "Coordination and Convention at the Foundations of Law," *Journal of Legal Studies* 11 (January 1982): 165–203.

integrity of the system of legal justice from which we all benefit.[112] Indeed, these irritating legal niceties remind us that we are not just conforming to the law for independent moral reasons but also obeying a law in all its particulars because it is the law.

Although Aquinas does not develop a systematic natural law justification of the obligation to obey the law as enacted, he does suggest how such an account might proceed.[113] First, every human person and even every human family is radically incomplete and depends upon the wider community for enjoyment of the goods of human fulfillment.[114] Since there are many kinds of goods to be pursued in many different ways by many different people, we need a way to co-ordinate the complex "traffic" of individual and communal pursuits. And, since we all benefit from the common good of effective social coordination, we all have a moral obligation to contribute to it. Law is a uniquely effective instrument in securing this coordination, for several reasons. First, in many cases justice and efficiency require a single, shared rule. Because consensus on this rule is unlikely—there are almost always several equally serviceable possibilities, and conscientious people will often disagree—we need an authoritative imposition. Second, law, unlike counsel or even parental discipline, has the coercive power of punishment to foster compliance in the face of recalcitrance. Third, law, unlike the unfettered arbitration of judges, is less subject to corruption and the sway of passion (ST, I-II, 95.1). Thus, if we all have moral duties to secure certain public goods, and if law is uniquely qualified to effect that coordination, then we have a moral obligation to obey the law.

This at least prima facie moral obligation to obey the law as enacted is most evident in the absence of independent moral reasons for conformity. In his early *Commentary on the Sentences,* Aquinas considered the source of obligation to laws not intrinsically moral in content. In a passage cited above, he concedes that the precepts of the ceremonial law and of the positive law do not have in-trinsic moral force "but they do have this from the will of the institutor, who in

---

112. For an exposition and critique of this argument from "fair play," see A. John Simmons, *Moral Principles and Political Obligations* (Princeton: Princeton University Press, 1979), pp. 101–42.

113. In this paragraph I draw freely on Finnis's development of Aquinas's account. See Finnis, "The Authority of Law in the Predicament of Contemporary Social Theory," in *Natural Law,* vol. 2 (New York: New York University Press, 1991), pp. 259–81, especially at 261.

114. On individuals as incomplete, see ST, I-II, 90.2c; on families as incomplete, see ST, I-II, 90.3 ad 3.

instituting uses natural reason, if rightly instituted."[115] In his mature writings, Aquinas places the obligatory force less in the will of the legislator and more in the rational requirements of the common good. Many legal requirements, especially procedural ones, seem to lack intrinsic moral content; nonetheless, they can be morally obligatory in relation to the common good of the rule of law, which may well require that we not pick and choose which morally permissible legal obligations to respect.

Still, this moral obligation to obey the law as enacted is not conclusive and may be overridden if a particular law is radically unjust.[116] Yet even in the face of unjust laws we may be obliged to yield to them because our disobedience could cause scandal and undermine respect for the law generally.[117] Aquinas's view that there may be a moral obligation to yield to even a clearly unjust law in some circumstances reveals how seriously he takes the claims of law merely as enacted.

In short, we cannot know whether our prima facie obligation to obey a particular law is conclusive or not unless we can discern whether the content of that law is consistent with the demands of the natural moral law. That is, natural law justifies not only the existence of positive law, and its authoritative enactment, but also the content of every particular law. Thus Aquinas famously says that "every law laid down by men has the character of law inasmuch as it is derived from the law of nature."[118] Because the context here is his discussion of the way in which laws varying in degree of connection to morality are derived from the natural law, we see that this statement concerns the moral justification not just of the existence of law but also of its content.

One way to interpret what Aquinas means here is captured in the words of Christopher St. German: "In every law positive well made is somewhat of the law of reason and of the law of God: and to discern the law of God and the law of reason from the law positive is very hard. And though it be hard, yet it is much necessary in every moral doctrine, and in all laws made for the commonwealth." Rather than set the natural law of reason and human positive law in

---

115. CS, vol. 3, d. 37, q. 1, a. 3, ad 2.
116. A law may be radically unjust not only because of its content but also because the legislator is acting beyond his authority or because the law imposes a disproportionate burden on one part of the community. ST, I-II, 95.4c.
117. ST, I-II, 95.4c. Aquinas does not consider the harm to the common good caused by our being seen to obey unjust laws.
118. "Omnis lex humanitus posita . . . habet de ratione legis inquantum a lege naturae derivatur." ST, I-II, 95.2c.

opposition, St. German suggests that within every positive law "well made," no matter how seemingly nonmoral, we ought to be able to discern a moral rationale. Such a rationale will often be fairly well obscured by the detailed positive specifications, but "though it be hard," we ought to be able to find it. Human law is neither wholly positive nor wholly natural, but a mixture. Finnis says that St. German here expresses "the fundamental concern of any sound 'natural law theory' of law: to understand the relationship(s) between the particular laws of particular societies and the permanently relevant principles of practical reasonableness."[119]

St. German and Finnis articulate a notion of human law as a mixture of natural and positive elements, of morally neutral externals animated by an intrinsic moral purpose. We can discern this moral purpose even if only through a glass darkly. The point of such a moral justification of the content of law is not to attempt to determine if a particular law uniquely fulfills the requirements of practical reason, but to make the much more modest attempt to see if the content of a legal regulation is at least tolerably ordered to those requirements.[120] By such a procedure, a citizen can determine whether his or her prima facie obligation to obey the law is a conclusive one.

In short, human laws normally have two kinds of interlocking moral force, answering to the twofold requirements of the common good: the content of a law has a generic moral force from its rational connection to some principle of morality, while the fact that the law was enacted gives it a specifically legal moral force stemming from the need for an authoritative and unique coordination scheme.[121] Legal enactment ensures that the good of a law will be genuinely common to the political community, and a rational content ensures that what is common serves the good. Although this generic moral force ("con-

---

119. St. German, *Doctor and Student,* ed. T. F. T. Plucknett and J. L. Barton (London: Selden Society, 1974), I, c. 4. Finnis cites this passage (*Natural Law and Natural Rights,* p. 281) but omits the two references to divine law.

120. As Finnis puts it: "To be, itself, authoritative in the eyes of a reasonable man, a *determinatio* must be consistent with the basic requirements of practical reasonableness, though it need not necessarily or even usually be the *determinatio* he would himself have made had he the opportunity; it need not even be one he would regard as 'sensible.'" *Natural Law and Natural Rights,* p. 290.

121. Finnis notes that both the enactment of a law and its content have a distinctive and normally concomitant moral force: once "a law has been made, its directiveness derives not only from the fact of its creation by some recognized source of law (legislation, judicial decision, custom, etc.), but also from its rational connection with some principle or precept of morality." Finnis, *Aquinas,* p. 267.

tribute to the common good") and this specifically legal moral force ("by paying an income tax of 33.65 percent") are normally concomitant in legal rules, in
some laws either the specific or the generic moral force might be especially
salient. The contrast of these two kinds of moral force is especially clear in the
contrast of the moral and the ceremonial precepts of the Mosaic law: the more
"natural" a law in content, the more salient its generic moral force ("you may
not kill"); the more "positive" a law in content, the more salient its specifically
legal moral force ("you may not wear garments of wool and linen"). As we shall
see, Aquinas tends to divide human law on the model of Mosaic law into precepts with mainly generic moral force (*moralia* or *ius gentium*) and precepts
with merely legal moral force (*caeremonialia* or *ius civile*). However, can we separate human laws into those with mainly generic moral force and those with
merely legal moral force? Or do both these kinds of moral force blend in virtually every human law?

On the Derivation of Positive Law
from Natural

Since Cicero, many philosophers of law have claimed that the civil law grows
out of, proceeds from, the natural law.[122] We might distinguish a weak from a
strong version of this claim. The weak version would merely hold that all positive law proceeds from the natural law simply because the authoritative imposition of law itself is a requirement of the natural law; on this view, natural law
justifies the institution of positive law. Aquinas seems to defend the strong version, however, which includes the claim that the content of the law imposed
must in some way be justified and rationally grounded in the natural law. It
turns out to be quite difficult, though, to characterize precisely the relation of
the highly specific, and often seemingly arbitrary, content of positive law to the
permanent and universal requirements of practical reason. Aquinas's distinctive
contribution to this tradition of reflection was to specify and describe two distinct modes of "derivation" whereby human positive law proceeds from natural
law. Yet when we examine Aquinas's discussion of these two modes of "derivation" we find some puzzles that raise questions of how to understand the rela-

122. Indeed, Aquinas cites (I-II, 95.2c) from Cicero's famous statement in the *De inventione*
(II, 53; cf. II, 22). "The first principles [of justice] proceed from nature; then certain
ones, by reason of their usefulness, come into custom; afterwards both the things proceeding from nature and those approved by custom are sanctioned by religion and the
fear of the law." Hugh of St. Victor, recall, said that positive justice arises out of natural
justice.

tion of positive law to natural. While promising to show us how to discover the natural law within the positive law, how particular human laws are grounded in the universal requirements of practical reason, Aquinas's account sometimes leaves us wondering if ever the twain shall meet.

In his commentary on the *Nicomachean Ethics* of Aristotle,[123] Aquinas says that legal or positive right "arises" (*oritur*) from natural: "The just, legal or positive, always arises from the natural. . . . Origin from the natural law can occur in two ways: in one way as a conclusion from a premise." Yet, to our surprise, he then tells us that "in such a manner, positive or legal right cannot arise from natural right." Despite having been told that positive right or law arises from the natural in two ways, we now discover that the first way does not count. Why not? Aquinas tells us that "once the premises are stated, the conclusion follows by necessity." What he means is that in a formal syllogism, the conclusion is implicit in the set of major and minor premises, so that if we begin with premises taken only from the natural law, our conclusion merely makes explicit what is already implicit and thus cannot introduce anything new.

In short, from natural law premises alone you cannot draw positive law conclusions. Aquinas provides an example: "Thus, from the fact that no one should be injured unjustly, it follows that one must not steal, which pertains to natural justice." But from the normative claim that "no one should be injured unjustly" it does not immediately follow that "one must not steal." Other partly empirical premises must be added, such as "where there is property" and "where there is such a scarcity of property that stealing constitutes harm," before we can derive the conclusion that "one must not steal." In other words, even what Aquinas considers purely natural law derivations include empirically contingent premises. Of course, these empirical contingencies are nearly universal and thus, for practical purposes, all but necessary. But they reveal that reasoning to either natural law or positive law conclusions differs not in kind but in degree of empirical contingency.

We then turn to the second (and only!) mode whereby positive law arises from natural, the mode of determination: "And thus all positive or legal justice arises from natural justice."[124] Aquinas uses his familiar example: "That a thief is to be punished is natural justice, that he be punished by such and such a penalty, this is positive justice." Here again we see a difference of degree rather

123. Aquinas, *In Ethicorum*, V, 12, sec. 1023.
124. Despite explicitly stating here that legal or positive justice arises from natural justice exclusively in the mode of determination, Aquinas begins the next section (1024) by referring to the *two* modes whereby legal justice arises from natural!

than of kind between natural and positive justice: natural justice is more nearly universal than is positive justice, but both rest upon empirically contingent premises. A sharp distinction between them fails to capture the complex interplay of moral principle and contingent determination in any legal system. To begin with, positivity descends much further into natural law reasoning than Aquinas admits: "That a thief be punished," he says, is natural justice. But societies vary widely in their determination of what counts as theft: Is gleaning theft? Hunting or poaching on other's lands? Nonriparian water rights? Stealing through stress of need? Copying books or videos? Positive law reaches much deeper than the schedule of punishments; it must determine what precise set of circumstances constitutes a crime (or tort). Conversely, natural law reaches higher than Aquinas allows: the schedule of punishments for a crime is not purely a matter for contingent determination. By Aquinas's account, morality would seem to provide no guidance whatever in the determination of appropriate punishments for crimes, yet natural law jurisprudence has always maintained that there must be some proportionality between the severity of the crime and the severity of the punishment.[125] Certainly, moral reason cannot deduce one universally valid schedule of punishments; the nature and severity of punishments must be largely determined according to contingent circumstances. But the scope of contingent determination is much narrower than Aquinas suggests. In any positive schedule of punishments, we should be able to see the moral requirements of proportionality: in short, we should be able to discern the natural law within the positive human law.[126]

Aquinas sometimes seems to assume that if we find variation in an institution, then it must be wholly the product of positive determination. He says, for example: "Since natural justice exists always and everywhere . . . this cannot correspond to legal or positive justice" (sec. 1023). Here he is sharply contrasting the universality of natural law precepts with the particularity of positive law precepts; to see why this sharp contrast may be misleading, consider this passage (sec. 1030): Aquinas cites Aristotle's statement that legal justice is like measures of corn and wheat, which are not the same everywhere but are larger in wholesale markets and smaller in retail markets. To this Aquinas adds his favorite example of positive law—namely, that the same punishment is not in-

125. For a contemporary natural law theory of punishment, see Finnis, *Natural Law and Natural Rights,* pp. 261–66.
126. Aquinas himself in other places recognizes the moral principle of proportionality of penalties: "The death penalty is to be exacted only for crimes which involve dire injury to others." ST, II-II, 108.3 ad 2.

flicted everywhere for theft.[127] Perhaps we may better interpret these two examples not as illustrations of positive as opposed to natural justice but rather as illustrations of the complex interplay of natural reason and contingent choice. In Aristotle's example, measures do indeed vary; still, everywhere they are larger in wholesale than in retail markets. The observed variation is not wholly contingent; it is structured by natural reason. In Aquinas's example, punishments for theft do indeed vary, but (almost) everywhere they are less severe than punishments for murder. Whether we reason to what he calls natural law or to positive law conclusions, our inferences are always partly natural and partly positive, partly logical and partly empirical.[128]

This tendency sharply to contrast the natural with the positive is evident in the treatise on law (I-II, 95.2). It is here that Aquinas characterizes the relation of positive to natural as one of "derivation" (*derivatio*). He lays down the general principle that "every law laid down by men [*lex humanitus posita*] has the character of law inasmuch as it is derived from the natural law." Again he describes two modes of derivation: "Both modes are to be found in human law laid down." Yet here again the first mode of derivation, by conclusion from premises, fails to reach law positive in content. He illustrates this mode of derivation by saying that the precept "you must not kill" may be concluded from the precept "you must do evil to no one"—a conclusion that strictly belongs to the natural law. He then describes the mode of determination with the example of the schedule of punishments.

Why does Aquinas, both in the commentary on the *Ethics* and in the *Summa,* first present the claim that positive law arises in two modes from natural law and then proceed to show us that the first mode (conclusions drawn from premises) generates only natural law? The answer may lie in the ambiguity of "positive" law: if by positive law Aquinas means "law laid down by statute" (*lex humanitus posita*), then indeed positive law includes both precepts whose content is largely natural and precepts whose content is largely positive. Positive law in this sense is not at all opposed to natural law. In other words, positive law as laid down is derived from natural law in two modes, only one of which generates law positive in content. So the precept "you must not kill,"

---

127. Aquinas, *In Ethicorum,* V, 12, sec. 1030.

128. Kevin Flannery observes that Aquinas's "two" ways of deriving positive law from natural are actually quite similar in structure: "Both ways are positings—just as both are in some sense derivations," because both involve a "combination of positive and logical factors." See his *Acts amid Precepts,* p. 75.

though positive in the sense of "laid down by law," is not positive in content; this ambiguity generates the puzzle noticed by Ralph McInerny.[129]

Aquinas explicitly acknowledges the interlocking nature of generic moral force and of specifically legal moral force only in the case of human law derived as conclusions from natural law premises—that is, in the case of law that is essentially nonpositive in content. Thus he tells us (ST, I-II, 95.2c) that precepts derived from the natural law by the first mode of derivation "have force not only from being laid down but also in part from the natural law"; in other words, these laws have moral force not just because they were imposed but also because their content answers a requirement of the common good. By contrast, when it comes to the second mode of derivation, what he calls "determination," he says that these precepts "have their force only by human law."

What are we to make of this last statement, which seems to suggest that the determinations of positive law (what Aquinas will later call "civil law" at I-II, 95.4c) have only the specifically legal moral force of enactment and lack the generic moral force of a content rationally related to the common good? Laws that "have their force only by human law" are derived from the natural law only in the weak sense that the institution of positive law is itself grounded in the permanent requirements of the common good; yet Aquinas's thesis in this article is the stronger claim that "every law has the character of law inasmuch as it is derived from the law of nature"—that not only the imposition of law but also its content must be somehow derivable from those permanent requirements. We might ascribe this statement that the determinations of positive law "have force only from human law" (I-II, 95.3c) to mere inadvertence, except that Aquinas says the exact same thing about the positive precepts of the Mosaic law.[130] Aquinas explicitly asserts that both human and divine positive law have force only from their enactment; yet his overall theory of law commits him to the view that the content of all genuine law must be reasonably ordered to the moral requirements of the common good. Although Aquinas says that the judicial and ceremonial precepts have force solely from their institution, he devotes much of his vast treatise on the Old Law precisely to showing how the content of the judicial and ceremonial precepts were indeed ordered either to

129. McInerny observes: "We are faced with the peculiarity that the example St. Thomas gives of deriving human law from natural law is actually a conclusion which pertains absolutely to natural law" (citing I-II, 100.1). See Ralph McInerny, "The Basis and Purpose of Positive Law," in *Lex et Libertas, Studi Tomistici,* vol. 30, p. 143.

130. "The judicial and ceremonial precepts have force solely from institution" ST, I-II, 100.11c and ad 2.

the historically contingent common good of ancient Israel or (figuratively) to the good of the Christian revelation.

Is there a way to interpret these curious passages to avoid separating the specifically legal moral force of law as enacted from its generic moral force?[131] Finnis is troubled by Aquinas's expression "have their force only by human law";[132] he says, "More accurate is another of Aquinas's descriptions: 'such laws have their binding force not only from reason, but [also] from their having been laid down'" (ST, I-II, 104.1c). No doubt this latter expression much more effectively conveys the interlocking nature of the two kinds of moral force of positive law, but before we decide what Aquinas should have said, let us consider more closely what he did say and why. Are there grounds for supposing that Aquinas intended to say what he seems to say, namely, that human civil laws, derived in the mode of determinations, have only the legal moral force of enactment and lack the generic moral force of a content rationally related to the common good?

One such ground seems to be furnished by Aquinas's rather puzzling reply to the first objection in this article. Recall that this article (I-II, 95.2) affirms the claim that "every human positive law is derived from the natural law." The first objection cites Aristotle's authority for a direct denial of this claim: "For the Philosopher says, in the *Ethics,* that 'in principle it makes no difference to what is legally just whether it be thus or otherwise.' Now these things that arise [*oriuntur*] from natural law are not matters of indifference. Therefore not all statutes of human law are derived from natural law." Aquinas replies: "Aristotle speaks of those things which are enacted by law through the determination and specification of the precepts of the natural law." By referring here to his view that determination is one way in which human law is derived from natural law, Aquinas is implicitly asserting his own thesis against the objector's denial. But Aquinas seems to concede to the objector that the determinations of positive law are matters of indifference.

131. Martin Golding remarks: "I think he [Aquinas] comes perilously close to a degree of legal positivism in his consideration of whether all positive laws are derived from the natural law. Though he answers this affirmatively, he nonetheless allows that some laws have their force 'only from human law.' Does this admit the existence of an arbitrary element in positive law, and would this be inconsistent?" See Golding, "Aquinas and Some Contemporary Natural Law Theories," *Proceedings of the American Catholic Philosophical Association* 48 (1974): 238–47, at 243.

132. Of the "ex sola lege humana vigorem habent" Finnis says: "This last statement really goes further than the analysis itself warrants." See Finnis, *Aquinas,* p. 267. He does not mention the parallel "ex sola institutione vim habent" of I-II, 100.11c.

In other words, Aquinas, while upholding his thesis that every human law is derived from the natural law, concedes that laws derived from the natural law by the mode of determination have a content that is a matter of intrinsic indifference. If the determinations of positive law are matters of indifference, then they would seem to have only the moral force of their legal enactment (*ex sola lege humana vigorem habent*)—that is, only a very weak connection to the natural law. Perhaps Aquinas should have said that, although there are elements of the determinations of a given positive law that (within some narrow range) could have equally well been otherwise, nonetheless, on the whole, the determinate contents of positive law are not matters of indifference but are more or less rationally constrained by the requirements of the common good.

Another reason for supposing that Aquinas meant to deny that the content of a law derived by the mode of determination has moral force is to consider what he says about the mode of determination in the context of divine law. As we shall see in more detail below, in his discussion of the difference between the moral and the ceremonial precepts of the Mosaic law, Aquinas directly compares the "determinations" of the ceremonial law to the determinations of human positive law (*ius positivum*). These determinations, he says, whether of human or of divine law, have the force of obligation only from their enactment:[133] "The precepts of the natural law are general and in need of determination. They are so determined both through human law and through divine law. And those determinations which are made through human law are said to be not from natural law but from positive law [*iure positivo*]" (ST, I-II, 99.3 ad 2). Thus, repeatedly throughout the treatise on law, Aquinas asserts that when laws are derived from the natural law by the mode of determination, they somehow lose their generically moral force in the process of acquiring their specifically legal moral force. It is as if once they descend into particularity they cannot find their way back to general principles: they have lost their original moral identity and have become wholly positive. This is all the more odd since

133. For the comparison of the mode of determination in both the Mosaic and the positive human law, see ST, I-II, 99.3 ad 2 and I-II, 99.4c. On the disjunction between generically moral and specifically legal moral force in the Mosaic law: "Of the precepts of whatever law, some have the force of obligation from reason itself, since natural reason dictates that a thing ought to be done or avoided. These precepts are called moral, since human morals (*mores*) are said to be from reason. There are other precepts which do not have the force of obligation from the dictate of reason, since, considered in themselves, they have no reason of duty, positive or negative; but they have the force of obligation from the divine institution. Of this kind are certain determinations [*determinationes*] of the moral precepts." ST, I-II, 104.1c.

Aquinas admits that a basic requirement of practical reason is that laws descend into particularity: how else could they serve the common good by coordinating a vast array of competing human pursuits?[134]

Perhaps we can avoid these apparent antinomies if we interpret Aquinas's statement that the determinations of positive law "have their force from human law alone" to mean not "have their force from human law alone excluding any generic moral force" but "have generic moral force only if enacted into law." On this view, the content of these positive laws has no generic moral force until they are enacted, at which time they acquire both their specifically legal moral force and their generic moral force.[135] This interpretation seems to reaffirm the interlocking quality of the two kinds of moral force of positive law required by Aquinas's strong version of the derivation thesis. But does it? Is it true that a positive law requiring a tax to be paid at 33.65 percent or requiring a speed limit of 65 m.p.h. has no generic moral force unless enacted? True, the exact specification might not have moral force before enactment, but then again, the exact specification does not acquire generic moral force after enactment; the exact specification has precisely the specifically legal moral force based on the natural law requirement that the common good sometimes demands an exact and unique coordination rule. The tax law and the speed limit have exactly the same generic moral force, if any, before and after enactment, depending upon whether, in the precise circumstances, they are ordered to the common good.

A precept has generic moral force to the extent that we regard it as obligatory, whether or not we are aware of its enactment. We consider "you shall not intentionally kill the innocent" to be obligatory quite apart from its enactment in human and divine law; its moral force is predominantly generic. By contrast, it would never occur to us to "not wear garments made of wool and linen" unless we were aware of this precept's enactment in divine law; its moral force is entirely legal. Our tax law and speed limits are somewhere between: even if we were totally unaware of their enactment, we would still regard it as obligatory to contribute some proportion of our funds to the common good and still regard it as obligatory to drive at a safe speed. True, the enactment of the precise

134. "The precepts of natural law are general and in need of determination [*determinatio*]." ST, I-II, 99.3 ad 2.

135. "The precise requirements imposed in laws made by *determinatio* would indeed have no moral force but for those laws' enactment. . . . But once such a law has been made, its directiveness derives not only from the fact of its creation by some recognized source of law . . . but also from its rational connection with some principle or precept of morality." Finnis, *Aquinas*, p. 267.

determination of these duties into law aids our efforts to perform these generic moral duties by providing us with a clear target, but we see our duties, more or less, in the tax law and speed limits, as they stand, even before their enactment into law. Yet, according to Aquinas, the determinations of positive law "do not bind from the dictate of reason itself, since, considered in themselves, there is no rational duty, positive or negative; their binding force arises from some enactment, divine or human."[136] Although there is no moral duty to drive at precisely 65 m.p.h. or pay precisely 33.65 percent in tax, apart from enactment, the generic moral force of a law includes more than fulfilling its precise letter: it also means acting in good faith to fulfill the moral spirit of the law, which can and should be done even if one is ignorant of the law (say, in a foreign country) or if the law is itself uncertain (a legal interregnum). In short, to say that some elements of a law have no generic moral force until they are enacted is far from saying that the law itself has no generic moral force until it is enacted. So, as Finnis suggests, Aquinas should have said that laws derived from the natural law by the mode of determination have their force not only from the fact of their enactment but also from reason.

In the treatise on justice (II-II, 60.5c), the at least rhetorical disjunction between the two kinds of moral force of laws grows even sharper. Aquinas says, "For written law does indeed contain natural right [*ius naturale*], but it does not institute it, for [natural right] does not get its force from law but from nature. Positive right [*ius positivum*], however, is both contained and instituted by the written law, which gives it [positive right] the force of authority." Although in both treatises the portion of human law described as "positive" or "civil" is considered to have only the specifically legal moral force of its enactment, here we find the parallel assertion that the part of human law described as natural has only generic moral force. Recall that in the treatise on law (95.2c) Aquinas describes those laws derived as conclusions from natural law premises as having both generic and specifically legal moral force. Here Aquinas's language suggests that, by the act of authoritative promulgation, natural law precepts do not assume a new power of imposing specifically legal, in addition to generically moral, obligations. But surely the fact that one of many possible natural law precepts becomes enacted into law gives us a new reason for obeying it—

136. I-II, 104.1c. This strong disjunction of generically moral from specifically legal moral force seems to apply only to the determinations of the ceremonial precepts, for, of the judicial precepts, Aquinas goes on to say: "They have their binding force not from reason alone, but [also] from enactment."

namely, that it has been authoritatively chosen as a part of a scheme of legal regulations. Therefore, violating it is both intrinsically wrong and a violation of our duty to our fellow citizens to respect the integrity of the system of legal justice from which we all benefit. In short, by Aquinas's own account of the (normally) interlocking nature of moral and legal duties, enactment into law should add legal force to the existing moral force of natural law precepts. Aquinas no doubt means merely to contrast the special role of legal enactment in the moral force of positive right as compared to natural right; he seeks to contrast the differing balance of specifically legal and generically moral force in both kinds of laws. However, his language obscures the interlocking nature of both kinds of moral force, in natural as well as in positive legal enactments.

Reasons for These Dichotomies

What might account for Aquinas's tendency to exaggerate the disjunction of the two kinds of moral force in human laws? To what extent do the tensions in his rhetoric—now affirming, now obscuring, the interlocking nature of legal and moral force in human law—reflect deeper conceptual tensions in his understanding of the relation of positive to natural law? There are grounds for supposing that the rhetorical tensions are not due to mere inadvertence but do indeed reflect some underlying tensions in his understanding of law and morality. First, by identifying positive law with "things originally indifferent," Aquinas exaggerated the groundless freedom of the act of determining positive law—thus obscuring the guiding role of prudential reasoning in those determinations. Second, by accepting the seductive contrast of what is prohibited because evil (*malum in se*) and what is evil because prohibited (*malum quia prohibitum*), Aquinas distinguished too sharply generic from specifically legal moral obligations. Third, and perhaps most important of all, is Aquinas's implicit (and sometimes explicit) use of Mosaic law as a model for human law. Because the moral precepts and the ceremonial precepts of Mosaic law form distinct and mutually exclusive classes, Aquinas may well have thought of human law as being similarly analyzable into distinct classes of natural law and positive law precepts.

Let us begin with "things originally indifferent." Aristotle famously comments in the *Nicomachean Ethics* (1134b 20) that legal justice concerns what is "originally indifferent [*ex archēs . . . ouden diapherei*] but when laid down is not indifferent." He gives such examples as "that a prisoner's ransom be a mina, or that a goat and not two sheep shall be sacrificed." These comments are so familiar we easily overlook their disturbing implications. If we take the main contrast to be between nature and statute, then Aristotle seems to be saying that legal enactments determine matters previously indeterminate except insofar as determined by nature. Thus, as Aristotle notes, the relative strength of the right and left hands, in most people, is not a matter originally indifferent, because, by nature, the right hand is stronger. But is it true that, apart from such natural determinations, the matters governed by legislation are otherwise indifferent until determined by law? Does this mean that the only constraint facing the lawgiver is that he not command the physically impossible—for example, that he not try to make everyone left-handed? Obviously, a lawgiver, and especially a good lawgiver, is aware that the matters to be regulated are not indifferent and indeterminate—that the legislative alternatives open to him are already structured, not just by natural justice but also, and more extensively, by custom. The size of a prisoner's ransom is not indeterminate before legislatively settled; custom establishes clear parameters around the choice. From the point of view of the settled expectations of custom, virtually no human activity is indifferent: whatever custom does not command, it forbids.[137]

Even if we concede that the matters subject to legislation are not, in fact, matters of indifference but are highly structured by settled expectations, why should not the legislator simply treat them as indifferent? Laws acquire much of their power effectively to regulate behavior from the support they receive from custom; because of custom, we conform to many laws without being aware that we are obeying them. The customs a legislator faces are of two kinds. If they are fundamentally opposed to the common good, then the legislator should not ignore them but attack them head on and attempt to inculcate new customs. If they are good or merely neutral customs, the legislator should respect them and, where possible, enlist their support.[138] In either case, a legislator who thinks that he faces matters indifferent to whatever determination he will impose is in for a surprise.

Significantly, in most of those places where we find Aquinas describing positive law as having only the moral force of its enactment, we also find him

137. Aristotle says of *nomos* that what it does not command it forbids (*Nicomachean Ethics,* 1138a 7). While clearly not true of law, which is silent on many matters, it is nearly true of custom.

138. As Aquinas, in other places, well knows: he cites Isidore with approval that law must be "fair, possible, according to nature and the customs of the country, and befitting time and place" (ST, I-II, 95.3c).

explicitly citing Aristotle's authority for the view that positive law concerns matters originally indifferent.[139] If positive law determined only matters "originally indifferent," then the nature of that determination would be groundless. Yet, curiously, in two of the key passages where Aquinas affirms that positive law concerns "matters originally indifferent" (ST, I-II, 95.2 ad 1 and 100.11c) he also tells us that wise men can discern the relation of those positive laws to the natural law. But if the wise can discern how the determinations of positive law are ordered to the common good, then the matters to be determined were not "originally indifferent"—if they were, then any determination would do and wisdom would not be helpful.

Finnis is rightly troubled by this notion of "things originally indifferent," which suggests that positive laws have only specifically legal moral force.[140] He argues that we can reconcile Aquinas's two accounts of the relation of law to morality if we strictly subordinate the claim that the determinations of positive law have force only from enactment to the more general claim that every law derives its character from the natural law:

> Consider the rule of the road. There is a sense in which (as the subordinate theorem implies) the rule of the road gets "all its force" from the authoritative custom, enactment, or other determination which laid it down. For until the stipulation "drive on the left, and at less than 70 miles per hour" was posited by one of these means, there was no legal rule of the road; moreover, there was no need for the legislator to have a reason for choosing "left" rather than "right" or "70" rather than "65." But there is also a sense in which (as the general theory claims) the rule of the road gets "all its normative force" ultimately from the permanent principles of practical reason (which require us to respect our own and others' physical safety) in combination with non-posited facts such as that traffic is dangerous and can be made safer by orderly traffic flows and limitations of speed, that braking distances and human reactions times are such-and-such, etc.[141]

This example well illustrates the difficulty, in practice, of finding laws that can be said to have only specifically legal moral force. Driving over the speed limit is, in many instances, wrong not merely because it is prohibited but also because it endangers human life. Finnis comments that Aquinas's language "can

139. *In Ethicorum*, V, 12 n. 5 (1020); ST, I-II, 95.2 ob. 1 and ad 1, 100.11c; ST, II-II, 57.2 ad 2 and 60.5 ad 1.
140. "So Aquinas was not altogether well advised to adopt Aristotle's dictum that in such cases (i.e., where there is what Aquinas calls *determinatio*) it is a matter of 'indifference' which law is adopted." Finnis, *Aquinas*, p. 268 n. 82.
141. Finnis, *Natural Law and Natural Rights*, p. 285.

be misleading" because "in the vast area where the legislator is constructing *determinations,* rather than applying or ratifying determinate principles or rules of reason, there are relatively few points at which his choice can reasonably be regarded as 'unfettered' or 'arbitrary.'"[142]

It is curious that Aquinas did not see that, although many matters of legal determination might be indifferent in the abstract, they are not indifferent in the concrete circumstances of human life, for in his analysis of human acts, Aquinas clearly recognizes this important distinction. Aquinas considers whether an act may be generically indifferent (*indifferens secundum suam speciem*): he affirms that some actions, such as plucking a blade of grass or walking in a field, if abstracted from the concrete circumstances of their performance, including the intention of the agent, can be classified as generically indifferent (*indifferentes*) (ST, I-II, 18.8c). However, in the concrete circumstances of the performance of a deliberate act, every such act is either rationally ordered to a real aspect of human good or it is not: if well ordered, it is good, if badly ordered, it is bad.[143] Walking through a field is generically indifferent, but my decision to walk across this field at this moment is either rightly ordered to a fit end, such as getting exercise, or it is not so ordered, such as poaching my neighbor's wildlife. The only concrete acts that would be truly indifferent would be inadvertent acts like rubbing my beard or shifting my feet. Such an act would be indifferent because it would not belong to the class of deliberate moral action (*actus humanus*); it would merely be an act of man (*actus hominis*).[144] There are numberless ways I may pursue the rational goods of human life; most of these are, in the abstract, indifferent to practical reason. But as a particular person, with particular talents, particular opportunities, and particular commitments,

142. Finnis, *Natural Law and Natural Rights,* p. 286.

143. "It is necessary that each individual act should have some circumstance by which it becomes good or evil, if only from the intention of the end. Since reason orders, the deliberative act proceeding from reason, if it is not ordered to a fitting end, has the note of evil insofar as it is repugnant to reason. If it is ordered to a fitting end, it agrees with the order of reason and thus has the note of good. It is necessary that it either be ordered or not ordered to a fitting end, and thus every act proceeding from man's deliberative reason, taken individually, is either good or bad." ST, I-II, 18.9c. For this translation and a useful exposition, see Ralph McInerny, *Aquinas on Human Action* (Washington, D.C.: Catholic University Press, 1992), pp. 88–89.

144. ST, I-II, 18.9c. "If, however, an act does not proceed from rational deliberation but [proceeds] inadvertently, as when someone rubs his beard or moves hand or foot, such an act is not properly called moral or human, which is such because it proceeds from reason; and so it will be indifferent, as outside the genus of moral acts."

my decision at a particular moment to work late at the office, or to go hiking in the mountains, is good or bad depending upon whether this action, in the context of these circumstances, is well ordered to real human good. The same applies to the act of legislation: while many determinations of law concern matters indifferent in the abstract, in the concrete circumstances of the situation, every particular course of action open to the prudential judgment of the legislator will be either good or bad, either well or badly ordered to the common good.[145] As Aquinas observes in another context, it requires a great deal of wisdom to grasp the bearing of complex factual circumstances on alternative courses of action.[146]

From his reflections on the contrast between things from natural law, which are intrinsically not indifferent, and things from positive law, which are intrinsically indifferent, Aquinas was led to another portentous distinction: between things prohibited because they are evil (*mala in se*) and things that are evil because they are prohibited (*mala quia prohibita*). In a natural law jurisprudence emphasizing the overlapping and mutually reinforcing nature of generically moral and specifically legal moral obligation, this very sharp distinction between acts intrinsically evil and acts extrinsically evil—unless very narrowly hedged by qualifications—is likely to cause problems.

This seductive distinction, which seems to have originated in Hugues de Saint-Cher, has become commonplace largely because it can mean a variety of mutually inconsistent things about the relation of law to morality.[147] To begin with, Aquinas deploys this distinction over different domains of evils: first, all moral and legal evils; and, second, just the moral evils that are also legal evils

---

145. As Finnis says: "The legislative choice between 'drive on the left' and 'drive on the right' is matter of indifference in the abstract, but not in a society where by informal convention people already tend to drive on the left, and have adjusted their habits, their vehicle construction, road design, and street furniture accordingly." *Natural Law and Natural Rights,* p. 287.

146. "There are some human acts whose character is so evident that they can be approved or disapproved through general first principles with little reflection. There are others, however, whose judgment requires much consideration of diverse circumstances, which is not for everyone but for the wise: just as to consider the particular findings of the sciences does not belong to everyone but philosophers alone." ST, I-II, 100.1c.

147. A distinction that can mean all things to all people probably will not contribute to clear thought; at the level of rhetoric, however, Lottin is right to say of Hugues's coinage: "Formule très heureuse qui deviendra bientôt classique." See Lottin, *Le droit naturel,* p. 41.

combined with the specifically legal evils.[148] In the first domain (setting aside, for the moment, divine law), we seem to have four possible classes of evils: intrinsic evils prohibited by natural law, intrinsic evils prohibited by human law, evils because prohibited by natural law, and evils because prohibited by human law.[149] In the second, we have two classes of evils for each system of law, divine or human: things prohibited because they are evil and things evil because they are prohibited.[150]

Moreover, the question of domain is only one source of ambiguity; the other is whether these two kinds of evil form mutually exclusive classes. Can we divide up all prohibited deeds into two exclusive classes—that is, those prohibited because evil or evil because prohibited? Are they distinct, but overlapping, classes? Or are they largely coinciding and mutually reinforcing aspects of legal precepts? Let us begin with "things prohibited because evil." Actions that are legally prohibited because they are intrinsically evil would all seem to be, in addition, evil because prohibited. Why? Human law does not prohibit all actions (not to mention all thoughts) that are intrinsically evil, only those actions most detrimental to the specifically political common good. We have a reason to avoid everything intrinsically evil and, in addition, a further reason to avoid intrinsic evils prohibited by law—namely, our duty to our fellow citizens to uphold the scheme of authoritative coordination from which we all benefit. Physically to assault someone is both intrinsically evil and evil because prohibited: by such battery, I have harmed both an individual person and the whole fabric of public order upon which we all depend; it is a crime against a person and

148. Because Hugues de Saint-Cher discusses positive law, natural law, and divine law, there are many categories of offences possible in his scheme: prohibited by natural law because evil, prohibited by human law because evil, prohibited by divine law because evil; and evil because prohibited by human law, evil because prohibited by divine law. See text in Lottin, *Le droit naturel*, p. 116.

149. In I-II, 71.6, Aquinas considers whether sins ought to be defined as offences against eternal law. It is objected (obj. 4) that, by this definition, something is prohibited because it is contrary to law, whereas certain things are prohibited because they are evil. Aquinas replies by saying that when it is said that "not all sin is evil because prohibited," this is understood to mean "prohibited by positive law (*ius positivum*)." But if "evil because prohibited" refers to natural law (*ius naturale*), then it is true that all sin is evil because prohibited.

150. "Thus divine right, like human right, may be distinguished into two parts: certain things are enjoined because they are good, and prohibited because they are evil while others are good because enjoined and evil because prohibited." ST, II-II, 57.2 ad 3. Cf. I-II, 71.6 ad 4.

a crime against legal justice. By contrast, consider a verbal, backbiting, calumnious—though legal—assault on a person: it might be much more intrinsically evil than a physical assault, but it lacks the added dimension of being evil because prohibited; since we do not all look to the legal system to protect us from calumny, these kinds of assaults do not undermine public order in the same way as does physical battery.

If all things prohibited because evil are also evil because prohibited, does it follow that all things evil because prohibited are also prohibited because evil? Let us examine "evil because prohibited." What does "evil" mean in this context: a violation of a generically moral or only of a specifically legal moral duty? On Aquinas's account, every violation of a (just) law is also a violation of a moral duty, since we all have a moral obligation to obey the law. In this limited sense, doing something that is evil because prohibited is also doing something intrinsically evil. However, our two situations are not symmetrical: in the first case, doing something prohibited because evil compounds the generically moral evil of the act with the specifically legal moral evil of violating the law; the second case of doing something evil merely because prohibited involves only the specifically legal moral evil of violating a just law.

Consider the example of hiring an illegal immigrant. There is nothing intrinsically evil about hiring a foreign national, but it is arguably immoral to do so because laws against such hires are reasonably ordered to a policy of controlling the flow of immigrants—a policy that itself is compatible with the requirements of practical reason. Here, in short, is an act immoral merely because it is prohibited. While this example seems to illustrate the utility of our distinction, at a deeper level it also calls that distinction into question; although hiring an illegal immigrant is not intrinsically immoral, it quickly and almost inevitably becomes an occasion for acts intrinsically immoral. Because illegal immigrants are powerless to assert their rights, they are usually exploited by their employers, who rarely contribute to their pensions or pay them a living wage. Indeed, it is very difficult for such an employer to do justice to an illegal employee, even if so disposed, because there are no obvious ways to protect that worker's moral rights to pension security, workman's compensation, and unemployment insurance outside legally established institutions. In short, acts that are evil merely because prohibited (hiring an illegal immigrant) are so closely linked to acts prohibited because evil (exploiting workers) that in practice the distinction between them may not amount to much.

Thus, it is possible, though not without some difficulty, to interpret the distinction between what is prohibited because evil and what is evil because prohibited in a way consistent with Aquinas's natural law jurisprudence. Nonetheless, this distinction misleadingly suggests a neat segregation of legal precepts into those with only generically moral and those with only specifically legal force and a neat separation of our moral from our legal duties. It seems to have led even Aquinas in this direction. When he says that the determinations of positive law "have only the force of human law" (ST, I-II, 95.2c), we can hear the implicit maxim "evil merely because prohibited"; when he says that "natural law" gets "its force from nature, not from statute" (ST, II-II, 60.5c), we can hear the implicit maxim "prohibited because evil." Rather than emphasize the interlocking nature of the two kinds of moral force, he often describes two separate modes of derivation from natural law, each mode generating a separate kind of human law.[151]

Aquinas's detailed study of the Mosaic law quite probably inclined him to treat the generically moral and the specifically legal as distinct classes of precepts, rather than as interlocking aspects of every law. Aquinas is confident that he can divide the Mosaic law into three mutually exclusive classes of precepts: moral, judicial, and ceremonial.[152] The basis of this division is the content of the precepts: the moral precepts, for example, "you shall not kill" (Ex. 20:13), clearly express direct requirements of practical reason, while the ceremonial precepts, for example, "you must not wear clothing of wool and linen woven together" (Dt. 22:11), do not. Thus, Aquinas frequently refers to the moral precepts as natural law and the ceremonial precepts as positive law.[153] Just as the Mosaic law includes the distinct classes of moral and ceremonial precepts, so, says Aquinas, human law includes the distinct classes of precepts, which Aquinas variously labels *ius gentium* and *ius civile*, or *ius naturale* and *ius positivum*.[154]

151. Aquinas says that derivation as conclusions from premises leads to *ius gentium*, while derivation as determinations leads to *ius civile*. ST, I-II, 95.4c.

152. "It is necessary to divide the precepts of the Old Law into three classes: the moral precepts, arising from the dictates of the natural law, the ceremonial precepts, which are determinations of divine worship, and judicial precepts, which are determinations of the justice observed among men." ST, I-II, 99.4c.

153. On his comparison of the ceremonial precepts to "positive law" (*ius positivum*), see CS, vol. 3, d. 37, q. 1, a. 3, ad 2, and ST, I-II, 99.3 ad 2 (where both ceremonial and judicial precepts are compared to human positive law). It is revealing that when Aquinas refers to the arbitrary content of Mosaic law, he uses the expression *ius positivum*; it would make no sense to describe the ceremonial precepts as *leges positae*, because the whole of the Old Law is statutory.

154. In ST, I-II, 95.4c, *ius positivum* is divided into *ius gentium* and *ius civile*; in ST, II-II, 60.5c, human written law is divided into *ius naturale* and *ius positivum*.

Aquinas frequently contrasts the generic moral force of the moral precepts with the specifically legal moral force of the ceremonial precepts.[155] The moral precepts, he says, oblige from their intrinsic rationality, while the ceremonial precepts oblige only from extrinsic enactment: the moral precepts have "binding force from reason itself," while the ceremonial precepts "do not have the force of obligation from the dictate of reason" and "have no force of obligation save from divine institution."[156] Human positive laws are like the ceremonial precepts: "Human laws . . . taken in the abstract have reason [an authoritative scheme for the common good] but not so far as regards particular conditions, which depend upon the will of the framer [*ex arbitrio instituentium*]; in the same way many particular determinations in the ceremonies of the Old Law have no literal cause, only a figurative one."[157] Certainly, the moral and ceremonial precepts of the Mosaic law represent ideal types of natural and positive laws: the precept "you shall not kill" is transparently natural, while the precept "you shall not wear clothing of wool and linen" seems radically positive.

Yet in human law we generally do not find these ideal types: our law is not a compound of natural law precepts and positive law precepts; rather, virtually every human law combines natural and positive elements. Although Aquinas usually sets the moral and the ceremonial precepts of Mosaic law in sharp opposition, in one place he describes the precept "keep holy the Sabbath" as a mixture of moral and ceremonial elements.[158] Aquinas more often finds a mixture of the natural and the positive in the judicial precepts of Mosaic law; human law indeed resembles the judicial precepts of Mosaic law more than it does the moral or ceremonial precepts. Aquinas says that the judicial precepts (e.g., "In the mouth of two or three witnesses every word shall stand," Dt. 19:15, ST, I-II, 105.2 ob. 8) are more natural than the ceremonial precepts but more positive than the moral precepts.[159] Thus, we immediately see the moral rationale

155. "The moral precepts have rational causes of their very nature . . . but the ceremonial precepts have rational causes in relation to something else [as figures of the New Law]" ST, I-II, 102.1 ad 3; "Since the precepts relating to the worship of God must be figurative . . . the reason for them is not fully evident." ST, I-II, 101.1 ad 4.
156. See ST, I-II, 104.1c and 104.1 ad 3. "Caeremonialia, quae non habent vim obligationis nisi ex institutione divina."
157. ST, I-II, 102.2 ad 3.
158. "The precept of Sabbath observance is, in one way, a moral precept, inasmuch as man is commanded to make time for divine matters. . . . Not, however, as to the time appointed: according to this, it is ceremonial." ST, I-II, 100.3 ad 2.
159. "Thus the judicial precepts have something in common with the moral, inasmuch as they are derived from reason; and they also have something in common with the cere-

of the precept requiring the testimony of more than one witness for a conviction; yet, at the same time, the exact number of witnesses is ultimately a morally contingent determination.

In the case of such a mixture of natural and positive elements, we would expect the judicial precepts of Mosaic law to have both generic and specifically legal moral force. Indeed, Aquinas in at least one place asserts that "they do not have the force of obligation from reason alone but [also] from enactment" (ST, I-II, 104.1c). In this sense, the judicial precepts are an intermediate and mixed case between the pure types of naturally moral and positively ceremonial precepts. As such, the judicial precepts are an excellent model for human legal precepts, which also mix natural and positive elements and thus combine generically moral and specifically legal moral force. At other times, however, Aquinas loses sight of the intermediate status of the judicial precepts and reverts to a sharp contrast of natural law and positive precepts in the Mosaic law. He lumps the judicial and the ceremonial precepts together as positive contingent determinations of the moral natural law.[160] Here the judicial precepts have lost their promising mixture of natural and positive elements and have become wholly positive. As such, Aquinas now describes them as wholly lacking generic moral force: "The judicial and ceremonial precepts have force solely from institution; since, before they were instituted, it seemed a matter of indifference whether they be thus or so. But the moral precepts derive their force from the dictate of natural reason itself, even if they had never been enacted in law."[161] There is thus a curious parallel between Aquinas's account of human law and his account of the judicial precepts of the Mosaic law: in both cases he occasionally recognizes the mixed character of these precepts and their unique combination

---

monial, inasmuch as they are determinations of general precepts." ST, I-II, 99.4 ad 2. The judicial precepts are more rational than the ceremonial because they concern matters of natural reason rather than of infused faith: "Since the order of man to his neighbor is subject to reason more than the order of man to God, we find many more moral precepts in the former than in the latter." ST, I-II, 104.1 ad 3. The judicial precepts were not instituted as figures of the mystery of Christ as were the ceremonial precepts. ST, I-II, 104.2c.

160. "Therefore, just as the determination of the general precept of divine worship is through the ceremonial precepts, so the determination of the general precepts of justice observed among men is through the judicial precepts." ST, I-II, 99.4c.

161. ST, I-II, 100.11c. Aquinas repeats this teaching later in the same article: "The ceremonial and judicial precepts, as determinations of the precepts of the Decalogue, have force from enactment, and not from the force of natural instinct, as do the additional moral precepts." ST, I-II, 100.11 ad 2.

of generic and specifically legal moral force; yet, at the same time, in both cases he also undercuts this mixed character by repeatedly insisting that every legal precept that descends into determinate specificity somehow loses its generic moral force.

To what extent is human law analogous to Mosaic law? In human law, instead of forming distinct classes of precepts, moral rationales and morally contingent specifications are inextricably blended. Moral rationales travel through our law incognito, so to speak—not usually dressed up in precepts, but instead well disguised as schedules, definitions, standards, and other specifications. As an example, let us consider the statute defining capital murder in the state of New Hampshire.[162] Here we find the many positive specifications of the statute animated by compelling, though merely implicit, moral rationales:

> A person is guilty of capital murder if he knowingly causes the death of: a) A law enforcement officer or a judicial officer acting in the line of duty or when the death is caused as a consequence of or in retaliation for such person's actions in the line of duty; b) Another before, after, while engaged in the commission of, or while attempting to commit kidnapping . . .; c) Another by criminally soliciting a person to cause said death or after having been criminally solicited by another for his personal pecuniary gain; d) Another after being sentenced to life imprisonment without parole; e) Another before, after, while engaged in the commission of, or while attempting to commit aggravated felonious sexual assault; f) Another before, after, while engaged in the commission of, or while attempting to commit an offense punishable under RSA 318-B:26, I (a) or (b) [selling drugs].

The subsections add three interesting clarifications: that a person convicted of capital murder may be punished by death, that the meaning of "another" does not include a fetus, and that no one under 17 years may be culpable of a capital murder. This statute further includes equally detailed descriptions of first-degree murder, second-degree murder, manslaughter, negligent homicide, and causing or aiding suicide. What we do not find in the law of murder are natural law precepts side by side with positive determinations; all we find are determi-

---

162. *New Hampshire Revised Statutes Annotated 1955* (1996 Replacement Edition), Title 62 (Chap. 630). This statute, of course, does not represent the whole of the law of capital murder in New Hampshire, which would include parts of the law of criminal procedure, as well as both common and statutory law governing the consequences of capital murder for insurance claims, descent and distribution of property, political rights, and many other matters.

nations, beginning with the very category of "capital murder."[163] These determinations, beginning with the divisions of murder into capital, first-degree, second-degree, and so on, do not seem to follow the moral distinctions of degree of premeditation or of presence of wanton cruelty.[164] No law could have a more transparent moral purpose, and yet virtually every detail of this statute reasonably could be different, has been different, is different somewhere, and will be different in the future. Nonetheless, all those mutable elements do not in any way reduce the moral force of the statute.

Since every actual detail of the statute is the product of a morally contingent determination, we might wonder wherein lies its moral rationale. The statute never actually states that capital murder is wrong! The moral rationale of the statute is what connects the disparate elements into a coherent directive for, mainly, prosecutors and, secondarily, for all citizens; all of these seemingly contingent details are held together as a whole that is far from merely contingent. The moral rationale is the unseen string that holds all the pearls in place; it is not stated but presupposed with such vigor that stating it ("capital murder is wrong") would actually detract from its moral force. In short, the generically moral and the specifically legal moral forces of a human law share an intimacy wholly different from the mere coexistence of moral and ceremonial precepts in the Mosaic law.

Derived From, or Reduced To, Natural Law

Let us return to Aquinas's famous statement (I-II, 95.2c) that "every law laid down has the character of law inasmuch as it is derived [*derivatur*] from the law of nature." According to Aquinas, not only is all human law derived from the natural law, but all just human law is derived from the eternal law, and the whole of the moral, judicial, and ceremonial Mosaic law is derived from the Decalogue.[165] At the same time, though less frequently, he says that positive law can be reduced or "led back" (*reducatur*) to natural law and that the moral

163. Finnis points out that the two modes of derivation are not separate but interlocking: "The central principle of the law of murder, of theft, of marriage, of contract . . . may be a straightforward application of universally valid requirements of reasonableness, but the effort to integrate these subject-matters into the Rule of Law will require of judge and legislator countless elaborations which in most instances partake of the second mode of derivation." See *Natural Law and Natural Rights,* p. 289.

164. Capital murder focuses mainly on murders connected with other crimes and on murders of legal officials.

165. For these claims, respectively, see ST, I-II, 95.2c; 93.3c; 96.4c; 99.4c; 100.11 ad 2.

precepts of the Mosaic law can be reduced to the Decalogue. In other words, sometimes he says that we begin with the natural law and proceed to the positive, while at other times he says that we begin with the positive and work backward to the natural. Are these two distinct modes of legal reasoning, or just two aspects of the same mode? Which approach best reveals the connection of natural to positive law?

Aquinas distinguishes two procedures for deriving the human law from the natural, both of which work forward from natural law to human law. The first procedure, he says, is like the sciences, in which demonstrable conclusions are drawn from principles; the second procedure is like the arts, in which a general idea is determined into a special shape. Here we can already see how Aquinas avoids a natural law rationalism: though the mode of derivation, by means of conclusions from premises, involves a kind of logical necessity, the mode of derivation by determination is highly creative and sensitive to local circumstances. We can predict what laws follow logically as conclusions from the natural law—they are the precepts of the universal law of nations—but we could never predict in advance the determinate civil laws of a given society.

These two procedures of derivation are of relevance mainly to a legislator who wishes to frame new laws consistent with the basic principles of practical reasonableness. Yet for citizens, lawyers, and judges who are concerned not so much with framing new laws as with understanding, evaluating, interpreting, and applying existing laws, the concern is not to derive positive laws from natural but to see if a particular positive law may be reduced, or led back, to natural law. Moreover, since legislation is rarely a matter of generating new laws de novo, and almost always a matter of selecting among concrete alternatives, the legislator needs chiefly to see if various proposals can be reduced to natural law precepts.

As it happens, when Aquinas discusses the relation of various kinds of law (divine and human) to the Mosaic Decalogue, he asks whether the moral, judicial, and ceremonial precepts of the Mosaic law (and even human civil law) might be somehow "led back" or reduced (*reducantur*) to the Decalogue.[166] Is there any difference between deriving positive law from natural and reducing positive law to natural? Perhaps more is involved in the contrast between "derived from" and "led back to" than a mere reversal of metaphor.[167] But we of-

166. On "reducing" laws of various kinds to the decalogue, see CS, vol. 3, d. 37, and ST, I-II, 100.3 ob. 1 and 100.11c.

167. Finnis sees little difference between "led back to" and "derived from" except a reversal of metaphor: "*Reducantur* . . . one of Aquinas' most common and flexible philosophical

ten can and do lead laws back to the principles that justify them even in cases where we could not have performed the much more demanding task of deriving the positive law from the natural. Whether the mode of derivation is as conclusions from premises or as a determination, it is much more difficult to forge a new path from the very general precepts of the natural law to the concrete specifications of the positive law than to find one's way back along the same path.

Aquinas himself often has trouble describing how positive law is derived from natural law. The first mode of derivation never really gets us out of the natural law,[168] while the second mode of derivation generates law so positive that it seems to lose the force of the natural law.[169] Just at the point in the pivotal question on human law (I-II, 95.2) when Aquinas seems to verge on asserting that the determinations of positive law lose all connection to the natural law, the possibility of reducing positive law to the principles of natural law emerges to restore the crucial grounding of positive law in nature. Objection 4 cites the authority of *Digest* for the claim that "a reason cannot be offered for every law enacted by the authorities. Consequently, not all human laws are derived from the natural law." Aquinas's reply to this attack on his central thesis begins with what seems like a concession: "This saying of the Jurist is to be understood of those measures introduced by the authorities as particular determinations of the natural law." At this point we might wonder how the mode of determination counts as a derivation of positive law from natural if we cannot offer reasons for those determinations. But then Aquinas appeals to the possibility that lawyers can lead those determinations back to their fundamental rationales: we should begin, he says, with the judgment of expert and wise jurists inasmuch as they see instantly what is better served by particular determinations of law.[170] Here, Aquinas seems to be referring to a distinctively lawyerly

---

terms; literally 'may be brought back to'; here [3 C.S. d. 37, a. 3c] the meaning is 'may be traced back to' or, reversing the metaphor, 'may be derived/are derived from'—a matter of justification rather than of historical causation." Indeed, Finnis translates *reducantur* as "derived from." See Finnis, "The Truth in Legal Positivism," pp. 209 n. 9 and 210 n. 19.

168. Aquinas explicitly denies that this mode of derivation yields positive law in *In Ethicorum,* V, 12, sec. 1023.

169. Thus, the several places in which Aquinas describes the determinations of positive law as having only specifically legal moral force. ST, I-II, 95.2c; 99.3 ad 2; 104.1c.

170. "Ad quas quidem determinationes se habet expertorum et prudentum judicium sicut ad quaedam principia, inquantum scilicet statim vident quid congruentius sit particulariter determinandum." Aquinas, ST, I-II, 95.2 ad 4.

mode of reasoning: practical jurists do not attempt to derive the determinations of the law from first principles; rather, they begin with those determinations and try to lead them back to underlying legal and moral principles.[171] Positive law retains its intrinsic connection with natural law even if that connection is not here one of ex ante derivation but of post hoc justification. Could Aquinas be suggesting that a lawyer may be better equipped to discern the natural law in the positive law than would a philosopher or even a theologian?[172]

Aquinas has thus been struggling with how to do justice to the bounded freedom of a legislator in framing human law. If we emphasize the logical derivation of human law from natural law, then the legislator loses all creative freedom and is tightly bound by the laws of logic. But if we emphasize the freedom of the legislator's determinations, then human law seems to lose all connection to the requirements of natural law. Aquinas's solution seems to be to say that the legislator does not usually follow any procedure of logical derivation in his free determinations, and that the connection of these determinations to the natural law may well be obscure to all but wise jurists.

171. This contrast of a procedure of reduction and a procedure of derivation seems to be at work in the Roman jurist Paul's famous and cryptic statement of the relation of the underlying principles of law (*regulae iuris*) to the surface rules of law: "The law may not be reached from the principle, but only the principle from the law [*non ex regula ius sumatur, sed ex iure quod est regula fiat*]" (D. 50.17.1).

172. That Aquinas is referring to a lawyerly method of leading law back to principles, rather than to a philosophical method of derivation, is clear when he goes on to cite Aristotle: "In such matters it is as necessary to attend to the indemonstrable maxims and opinions of experienced, older, and wiser people as to their demonstrations." ST, I-II, 95.2 ad 4. Aquinas was not always so generous to lawyers: "It appears ridiculous and unseemly for theologians to appeal to the authority of the jurists' glosses or to enter into debates among them." ("Inconsonum et derisibile videatur quod sacrae doctrinae professores, iuristarum glossulas in auctoritatem inducant, vel de eis discepent," *Opusculum contra retrahentes* 13 ad finem).

Chapter 3 Positive Language
and Positive Law
in Thomas Hobbes

"Nothing is more proverbial than that Laws are like Spiders'
webs, only to hold the smaller Flies."[1]

"For speech is (as was once said about the laws of Solon) something similar to the web of spiders; for tender and delicate minds
stick and are ensnared in words, but strong minds break
through."[2]

LANGUAGE AND LAW

Historians have long pointed out that the discourse of "positive law"
arose from Latin translations of ancient Greek debates about lan-

1. Hobbes, "A Discourse Upon the Beginning of Tacitus," in Thomas Hobbes,
   Three Discourses (1620), edited by Noel B. Reynolds and Arlene W. Saxonhouse (Chicago: University of Chicago Press, 1995), pp. 31–67, at 49.
2. Hobbes, "Computatio sive Logica" (Logic), or part 1 of *De Corpore* (1655),
   Latin text with English translation and commentary by A. P. Martinich,
   edited and with an introductory essay by Isabel C. Hungerland and George R.
   Vick, I, 3, 8 (p. 234): "Habet enim oratio (quod dictum olim est de *Solonis* legibus) simile aliquid telae aranearum; nam haerent in verbis et illaqueantur in-
   genia tenera et fastidiosa, fortia autem perrumpunt." I have corrected Martinich's translation.

guage. Recall that Hermogenes, in Plato's *Cratylus,* argues that names get their correctness from the shared expectations of speaker and listener, that is, from social consensus (*kata synthēkēn*). Aristotle goes further when he tells us that words get their meaning, and laws their validity, from the consensus of the community (*kata synthēkēn*).[3] We saw earlier that Boethius's fateful translation of *kata synthēkēn* as "according to the pleasure [of the name giver]" (*secundum placitum*) radically shifted the understanding of the authority of language and of law throughout the medieval and early modern periods. Where Aristotle's usage emphasizes the spontaneous convergence of social custom as the basis for the validity both of names and of laws, Boethius's translation emphasizes the arbitrary power of the name giver or lawgiver to make authoritative impositions. Because of Boethius's influential translation, even Aquinas interprets Aristotle to say that names get their meaning by deliberate imposition (*ex institutione*). Aquinas also, as we saw, says that names get their meaning, and laws their authority, according to the will and reason of the institutor (*secundum placitum*). When Hobbes uses his scholastic Latin, he consistently describes names being "imposed" on things, using the same variants of *pono* we found in Aquinas's description of positive law.[4]

Thus, from the medieval Scholastics Hobbes has inherited a discourse about language and law that is already quite "positivisitic," in the sense of focusing on the deliberate imposition of meaning and validity. Hobbes often explicitly compares law to language, and legal validity to linguistic meaning. Indeed, Hobbes thinks that legal authority is itself a kind of linguistic authority, in the sense that law making is essentially a matter of sustaining civil order by publicly stipulating the meaning not only of legal terms, such as theft, adultery and murder, but also of all disputed philosophical and theological terms. Since Hobbes says that words get their meaning and laws their validity from the will of the name giver or lawgiver,[5] he seems to be asserting a radical legal and lin-

---

3. On names arising *kata synthēkēn,* see *De interpretatione* (16a 19); on law arising *kata synthēkēn,* see *Ethica Nicomachea* 1134b 35. Of course, Aristotle also describes law as arising from deliberate enactment (*nomothetma*).

4. Of Adam, Hobbes says: "Nam eodem modo rebus aliis alia nomina imponere. . . . imposuisse Adamum . . . nomina . . . imposuisse illum nomina." *Leviathan,* in *Opera Latina,* vol. 3, ed. William Molesworth (London: John Bohn, 1841), pp. 21–22. "Ab arbitrio eorum qui nomina rebus primi imposuerunt, vel ab aliis posita acceperunt . . . illa nomina imponi placuit." Logic, 3.8, p. 234.

5. "For names are not from the essences of things but are constituted by the will of men" (Logic 5.1, p. 270); "all laws, written and unwritten, have their authority and force from

guistic positivism in which all linguistic and legal categories reflect merely the unfettered will of the sovereign.[6]

But Hobbes's deeper understanding of law and of language is not purely positivistic or relativistic or skeptical. In fact, his account of legal and linguistic stipulation rests on his account of natural signs. Because Hobbes's account of law is deeply connected to his account of language, to understand how positive law is structured and constrained by natural signs in Hobbes, we must first examine Hobbes's view of how language is structured and constrained by natural signs. Although it is true that Hobbes's account of name giving and law giving is voluntaristic, in both cases the will of the name giver or lawgiver is structured by natural signs.

Let us examine two puzzles: a small linguistic one and a large legal one. In his discussion of meaning of words and of the validity of law, Hobbes sometimes emphasizes the role of conventions while at other times he emphasizes the role of nature. These differing emphases help explain the endless interpretive controversies about whether Hobbes was a positivist or a natural law theorist. On the one hand, as we noted, Hobbes often asserted that "words . . . have their signification by agreement and constitution of men" (L, 31, 38, p. 242); or "names are not from the essences of things but are constituted by the will of men" (Logic 5.1, p. 270). And because words get their meaning from the deliberate will of men, the sovereign is free to alter or abolish that meaning by law (L, 31, 38, p. 242). Although Hobbes often describes these linguistic conventions in terms of deliberate enactment, in one place he suggests that other, less deliberate, conventions might also be at work: "For that men convened in council to legislate by decree what all words and verbal connections would signify is not to be believed."[7] On the other hand, however, Hobbes says that words get their meaning not from linguistic conventions but from the natural passions of individual men. He says that "the names of such things as affect us"—that is, moral, religious, aesthetic, and legal words—lack any stable or shared signification; these words get their signification from the natural passions and the ac-

---

    the will of the commonwealth." Hobbes, *Leviathan* (L), edited by Edwin Curley (Indianapolis: Hackett, 1994), 175.

6. Of course, legal positivism since Hans Kelsen and H. L. A. Hart no longer claims that all law must have its source in sovereign imposition.

7. Hobbes, *De Homine* (DH), in *Opera Latina,* vol. 2, ed. William Molesworth (London: John Bohn, 1839), 10, 2, p. 89. I have not adopted but I have benefited from the English translation of *De Homine* (chaps. 10–15) in Bernard Gert, ed., *Man and Citizen* (New York: Anchor Books, 1972).

quired interests of private individuals. Normative words "have a signification also of the nature, disposition, and interest of the speaker" (L, 4, 24, pp. 21–22). So now, it seems, many words get their meaning not so much from the public agreement or constitution of men as from the natural and habitual passions and interests of private men.

Similarly, and more familiarly, Hobbes can certainly sound like a thorough-going moral positivist: "One must accept what the legislator enjoins as *good,* and what he forbids as *evil*."[8] And yet he also can sound like a traditional natural law theorist: "The laws of nature are immutable and eternal; for injustice, ingratitude, arrogance, pride, iniquity, acceptation of persons, and the rest can never be made lawful. For it can never be that war shall preserve life, and peace destroy it" (L, 15, 38, pp. 99–100). Many well-known passages in Hobbes might be cited in parry and thrust on this question.

I propose to contribute to the resolution of these puzzles by using Hobbes's own technical distinction between the signification (*significatio*) and the denotation (*denotatio*) of words to show that his understanding of both language and of law was a subtle blend of naturalist and positivist elements. This distinction was developed in Hobbes's Scholastic Latin treatise on logic; unfortunately, Hobbes did not consistently employ his own careful distinction in his humanist Latin and English discussions of language and of law. By signification, Hobbes means the relation between a word and the private thought of a speaker or listener; by denotation, he means the relation between a word and the object it names. Signification is embedded in the whole network of natural signs that constitute mental discourse, belief, and understanding. It is a central tenet of Hobbes's philosophy that signification, belief, and understanding are not subject to direct voluntary control and, hence, cannot be deliberately imposed by law. Denotation is a direct relation between word and object; what a word denotes, says Hobbes, can be deliberately stipulated and, hence, imposed by law. Of course, signification and denotation—what a word means and what a word names—are related; and any coherent theory of language must tell us how they are related. Unfortunately, Hobbes tells us next to nothing about the

8. *De Cive* (DC), 12, 1, p. 132. *De Cive* appeared in Latin in 1642 and then in English in 1651. I have consulted both versions in Howard Warrender's critical editions: *De Cive: The Latin Version* and *De Cive: The English Version* (Oxford: Clarendon Press, 1983). Richard Tuck and Michael Silverthorne have also translated *De Cive* from the original Latin: Hobbes, *On the Citizen* (Cambridge: Cambridge University Press, 1998). I have quoted from this new translation while noting some discrepancies with both the Latin version of 1642 and the English version of 1651.

relation of signification to denotation, leaving his theory of language gravely underdeveloped. I shall try to develop his distinction between signification and denotation so as to illuminate his account of language and of law; but Hobbes's theory of language will forever remain profoundly inadequate.

We can be sure, nonetheless, that, on his view, authoritative denotation is not determined by private signification: there is always considerable freedom in the act of denotation. At the same time, however, the deliberate act of imposing names is constrained and structured by the substrate of natural signification in mental discourse and in moral actions. For example, to name what is inconceivable is an absurdity, so even the sovereign cannot properly name what is inconceivable (DC, 18, 4, p. 238; L, 46, 31, pp. 463–64); and what is inconceivable includes forbidding what conduces to peace or enjoining what promotes war (L, 15, 38, p. 100). So what the sovereign denotes by a word must be at least a possible signification of it. Exploring how denotation relates to signification in Hobbes's theory of language will help to illuminate how positive law relates to natural law. For positive law is not determined by natural law: there is always considerable freedom in the act of imposing positive law; nonetheless, natural law does structure and constrain the range of possible positive law.

For Hobbes the purpose of language is to transfer mental discourse into verbal; but that mental discourse is structured by natural relations of associations of signs, which can be disciplined, but not replaced, by the deliberate imposition of names. What words signify to private individuals is due to natural cognitive processes in which one sign triggers any number of conceptual associations; thus, the conceptual significance of any word, especially moral words connected to our interests, will vary according to the natural temperament and acquired dispositions of the individual (L, 4, 24, p. 21). Because of the naturally varying passions and, hence, conceptions of individuals, each person will have a unique conception of common moral concepts.

Anarchy is generated not by these natural differences of conception but by each individual insisting that he or she may determine the application of his or her conceptions to objects. Anarchy emerges from the clash of mutually inconsistent denotations of words. My unique conception of justice does not conflict with your unique conception until I insist upon deciding unilaterally what objects or actions are denoted by "justice." Hobbes frequently insists that all laws require interpretation; one crucial way to interpret what a law or a word means is to consider what objects it denotes. What words or laws signify to private individuals depends upon natural and customary processes of sign association, which cannot be directly controlled by deliberate stipulation. The private mental discourse of individuals is beyond the direct reach of sovereign power—though he might try to shape mental discourse indirectly through political education; but the public objects and actions denoted by words and by laws can be stipulated by the sovereign.

By using Hobbes's own technical distinction to disambiguate his own imprecisions, we shall find that his view of language and of law is less radically positivist than we might have first thought. For example, he says, "Though words have fixed meanings [*significationem*] defined by decision (*ex constituto*), they are so distorted in popular usage from their proper meanings by a particular passion for ornament or even deception, that it is very difficult to recall to memory the concepts for the sake of which they were attached [*impositae,* that is, imposed on] to things" (DC, 18, 4, pp. 237–38). Here Hobbes ought to have disambiguated the term *meaning* into both "signification" and "denotation"; but what he intends to say is clear enough, namely, that the original act of the deliberate imposition of names on things fixed and established, in the first place, what objects words would denote. True, when the public denotation of words is established, Hobbes expects the private signification of those words also to be indirectly shaped; but the public denotation of words is not determined by their private signification. Indeed, the public establishment of denotation clearly fails to fix private signification, which, he says, evolves in unpredictable and uncontrollable ways.

Similarly, just after Hobbes says that it was not to be believed that all words originally got their meaning (*significatio*) from a single legislative decree, it is clear that, in this context, he means their "denotation," since he goes on to say that "the first man, by his own decision, imposed names on just those animals, most assuredly the ones God led into his view" (DH, 10.2, p. 89). Since Hobbes defines the relation between a word and its object as the relation of denotation, he is clearly saying here that public authority may impose not the significance but the denotation or reference of words. And since the freedom of positive denotation is constrained by natural signification, the act of stipulating the denotation of words is not wholly arbitrary.

Another passage from the 1651 English *De Cive,* often cited as evidence of Hobbes's radical linguistic and legal positivism, reads: "*Theft, Murther, Adultery, and all injuries* are forbid by the Lawes of nature; but what is to be called *Theft,* what *Murther,* what *Adultery,* what *injury* in a Citizen, this is not to be determined by the *naturall,* but by the *civill Law*" (DC, 6, 16, p. 101). By saying that civil law determines "what is called" theft, murder, and adultery, Hobbes creates the impression that civil law can wholly determine the meaning of those key moral terms. But in the original Latin, Hobbes's claim for civil law is much more modest: he says that civil law determines "what is to be denoted by [*appellandum sit*]" theft, murder, and adultery. In Hobbes's Scholastic Latin, to call (*appellare*) an object by a name is to denote it; or to say that an object is called by a name is to say that it is denoted by that name. Words that denote objects are "appellations" in Hobbes's technical usage.[9] The sovereign can determine what words denote, not what they signify: "Now because in every language the use of *Names* or *Appellations* [*Appellationum*] arises from decision, it will also be able to be altered by decision" (DC, 15, 16, p. 181).[10]

Once we grasp Hobbes's linguistics, we see that he is not claiming that "what theft, murder, and adultery" signify is determined by positive civil law, only that what precise actions are denoted by those vague concepts is determined by positive law. These moral terms signify to all men what ought to be forbidden (either by natural or by positive law); but men vary in how they interpret the range of application of these terms, that is, in what they precisely denote. To create anarchy, they need not even vary widely in their interpretations; but, with terms so morally charged, it is crucial that the sovereign offer an authoritative interpretation of what they denote.

Here the new English translation of this passage is quite helpful: it says that "what is to count" as theft, murder, and adultery is to be determined by the civil law. The expression "what is to count" nicely captures Hobbes's implicit reference here to the public objects sorted by these concepts. This translation makes it clearer that civil law determines the objects sorted and denoted by a moral concept, not the significance of that concept in mental discourse.

No doubt the sovereign has considerable freedom in determining what precise objects are denoted in law by those moral terms. He must first decide which actions comprising theft, adultery, and murder ought to be denoted crimes against positive law and which should remain only sins against natural

9. For example, Hobbes says that despite what words might signify to ordinary people, mathematicians call (*appellarent*) the figures they discover parabolas, hyperbolas, and so on (Logic 2, 4, p. 198). For an argument that *appellare* is a technical term for denotation in Hobbes, see Logic, editors's introduction, p. 55. "In the *Computatio sive Logica,* the first part of *De Corpore,* containing Hobbes's most mature work on the philosophy of language, this opposition is displayed by way of a distinction between, on the one side, *nominare, denotare* and *appellare* and, on the other side, *significare.*" Willem R. De Jong, "Did Hobbes Have a Semantic Theory of Truth?" *Journal of the History of Philosophy* 28 (1990): 63–88, at 64.

10. The decisions here are not the decisions of judges in particular cases but the decisions of the sovereign (or his ministers) in drafting the civil law.

law. For, as Aquinas also held, law cannot suppress all vices. Then there are many borderline cases of theft, such as those involving intellectual property, and borderline cases of murder, involving passion or ignorance, that must be clarified by law. Finally, the sovereign may denote actions as "murder" that would not fall under anyone's private conception of that term—actions defined, for example, by felony murder. So Hobbes's sovereign indeed has a very wide range of freedom in determining the denotation of moral terms in law. Still, legislative interpretations of the application of moral terms are not wholly unfettered; they remain interpretations of something, however vague. If sovereign stipulations of the denotation of moral terms were wholly detached from their private significations, moral language would remain in a state of anarchy. For the sovereign to end the violent controversies over the meaning of moral terms, his official interpretations of the denotative reach of those terms must be intelligibly related to the range of natural significations of those terms to the private parties in controversy. To decree that "murder" denotes "felony murder" cannot be expected to resolve disputes about the proper meaning of adultery. Positive denotation is constrained by natural signification, just as positive law is constrained by natural law.

Natural law is the true significance of moral terms in the conscience of virtuous individuals; but since the significance of moral terms is shaped by the differing constitutions and passions of each person, we are not likely to converge spontaneously on a shared understanding of the natural law. For this reason, we need positive law as an authoritative interpretation of the natural law. No doubt "theft, murder, and adultery" mean quite different things in different ages and nations, but: "The laws of nature are immutable and eternal; for injustice, ingratitude, arrogance, pride, iniquity, acceptation of persons, and the rest can never be made lawful. For it can never be that war shall preserve life, and peace destroy it" (L, 15, 38, pp. 99–100). As we have observed, what cannot be properly named is what is inconceivable: Hobbes's sovereign, unlike George Orwell's, cannot define war as peace. The moral objectivity, moral significance, and moral force of these natural concepts are by no means effaced, or even necessarily reduced, by the wide variety of official interpretations of what these concepts denote in positive law. And even though we are sometimes tempted by pride to insist upon our own private interpretations, natural reason teaches us that no one's judgment is infallible, and that it is often more important that, as Justice Brandeis put it, "the law be settled than that it be settled right." As many commentators have pointed out, Hobbes erects many moral standards over positive law: clearly, the distinction between equity and iniquity is antecedent to the institution of sovereignty; and although no positive law can be unjust, on Hobbes's view, he does admit that positive laws can be bad (L, 30, 20, p. 229).[11] No doubt Hobbes's sometimes provocative and even misleading language about the authority of the sovereign creates the impression that he can make black into white, but Hobbes himself seems to take a quite restricted view of the proper latitude of sovereign interpretations of moral concepts at law. For example, he explicitly rejects "felony murder" as a permissible interpretation of "murder" in positive law.[12] Would Thomas Aquinas adopt such a narrow view of the permissible determinations of positive law?

POSITIVE LANGUAGE

Not surprisingly, many twentieth-century interpretations of Hobbes's linguistics read him in terms of the contrast between a semantic and a pragmatic approach to meaning.[13] One influential study argues that Hobbes was a pioneer in the pragmatic approach to meaning.[14] Although these readings of Hobbes in terms of contemporary semantics and pragmatics have been partially illuminating, ultimately, I shall argue, they obscure the essence of Hobbes's account, which is best understood in relation to Augustine and Aquinas. As we shall see, Hobbes's account of language is neither basically semantic nor basically pragmatic (though it has elements of both) but voluntaristic, like his account of law. In this way, Hobbes follows Augustine, who also made a basic distinction between voluntary and involuntary signs. And Hobbes's strong distinction between signification and denotation is best understood against Aquinas's attempt to subordinate denotation to signification.

That Augustine's and Hobbes's account of human language is voluntaristic does not imply that it is positivistic or radically arbitrary; for both of them, the voluntary signs of language rest on a substrate of involuntary and natural signs

11. Compare Hobbes, *The Elements of Law* (1640), hereafter Elements, ed. Ferdinand Tönnies, second edition by M. M. Goldsmith (New York: Barnes and Noble, 1969), 2, 9.1.

12. Hobbes, *A Dialogue Between a Philosopher and a Student of the Common Laws of England* (D), ed. Joseph Cropsey (Chicago: University of Chicago Press, 1971), pp. 171–72, 148.

13. For a small sample of these treatments see: De Jong "Did Hobbes Have a Semantic Theory of Truth?"; R. M. Martin, "On the Semantics of Hobbes," *Philosophy and Phenomenological Research* 14 (1953–54): 205–11; Deborah Hansen Soles, *Strong Wits and Spider Webs: A Study in Hobbes's Philosophy of Language* (Aldershot: Avebury, 1996), pp. 75–81.

14. Isabel Hungerland and George Vick, "Hobbes's Theory of Language, Speech, and Reasoning," the editors' introduction to Hobbes's *Logic.*

of mental discourse and of countenance and gesture. Stipulated names, like stipulated laws, do not arise ex nihilo, they arise from the natural and customary world of mental discourse and visible gesture. Indeed, failure to see how deliberate verbal signs rest upon natural and customary processes of thought and communication has led commentators to accuse Hobbes of falling into a vicious circle, in which language seems to require organized society, while organized society requires language.[15] As Deborah Soles rightly notes: "Hobbes is able to avoid precisely this sort of circle by grounding language use in the recognition of natural signs as he does."[16]

Positive Voluntary Signs and Natural Involuntary Signs

Let us explore the relation between the voluntary signs of language and the involuntary signs upon which they rest. When Hobbes says that "the general use of speech is to transfer our mental discourse into verbal" (L, 4, 3, p. 16), he means that language translates the natural and largely involuntary discourse of conceptions into the artificial and voluntary discourse of names. So we cannot understand the deliberate discourse of language until we first grasp the given mental discourse of concepts. Prudence reasons from the natural or given signs of human experience, while science reasons from the deliberately imposed signs of language (L, 3, 22, pp. 26–27). Hobbes is quite skeptical of the certainty of any reasoning from signs given in nature or in custom; his aspirations for science stem from his view that we can only reason with certainty from signs we deliberately construct. As we shall see, Hobbes's view of the privileged status of

---

15. Language seems to require organized society: "Though words [*voces*] have fixed meanings defined by decision [*ex constituto*] . . . it is very difficult to recall to memory the concepts for the sake of which they were attached [*impositae*, that is, imposed on] to things" (DC, 18, 4, pp. 237–38). Organized society seems to require language: without speech, "neither commonwealth, nor society, nor contract, nor peace" (L, 4, 1, p. 16). John Watkins accuses Hobbes of circular reasoning: Hobbes "made organized society a precondition for the creation of language, and a common language a pre-condition for the creation of organized society." *Hobbes's System of Ideas* (Aldershot: Gower, 1973), p. 100.
16. Soles, *Strong Wits and Spider Webs*, 65. She continues: "Perceived correlations and expectations about the future are thought by Hobbes to be sufficient to account for at least the rudiments of convention-formation, and custom or habit (again, at least for Hobbes, a kind of perception of correlations plus expectation, which is ultimately causally explicable) is supposed to be sufficient to account for the transmission of a verbal language from one generation to the next."

a maker's knowledge of what he has made will deeply shape his commitment to the deliberate and public stipulation of the denotation of words and of laws.

When Hobbes says that language is the translation of mental discourse into verbal, it is clear that he is chiefly interested in the relation of language to thought rather than in the relation of language to the world. This is because Hobbes was convinced that our natural processes of sensation and of conception reflect the nature of the subject more than the nature of the world. Hobbes was very impressed by the arguments of Galileo and others that the "secondary" qualities, of color, shape, and warmth, were not objective qualities of the things themselves but merely by-products of our cognition of them. After arguing that conceptions of image or color, and indeed that conceptions arising from all the senses, are inherent not in the world but in ourselves, he says: "It followeth, that whatsoever accidents or qualities our senses make us think there be in the world, they are not there, but are seemings and apparitions only. The things that really are in the world without us, are those motions by which these seemings are caused" (Elements, I, 2, 10, p. 7).

This sounds like a radical skepticism about perception until Hobbes goes on to say: "And this is the great deception of sense, which also is by sense corrected. For as sense telleth me, when I see directly, that the colour seemeth to be in the object; so also sense telleth me, when I see by reflection, that colour is not in the object." Hobbes here clearly recognizes that although it is true that our conceptions of secondary qualities reflect our relation to real things, this relational fact does not imply that we cannot, upon reflection, refer to these qualities objectively and reliably.[17] That sensory or moral qualities are relative, in the sense of founded upon a relation between subject and object, does not imply that they are merely subjective. That relation might itself become objectively verifiable.

Hobbes's alleged moral skepticism stems from his parallel analysis of moral qualities, which, he says, reflect not objective reality but merely the subjective dispositions and passions of the subject. "Every man, for his own part, calleth that which pleaseth, and is delightful to himself, *good;* and that *evil* which displeaseth him: insomuch that while every man differeth from other in constitution, they differ also one from another concerning the common distinction of good and evil. Nor is there any such thing as *agathon haplōs,* that is to say, sim-

17. As David Boonin-Vail says, "The fact that no object is simply red does not, for Hobbes, imply that the term 'red' cannot be applied correctly and objectively." *Thomas Hobbes and the Science of Moral Virtue* (Cambridge: Cambridge University Press, 1994), p. 61.

ply good" (Elements, I, 7, 3, p. 29). Hobbes seems to be more skeptical about the objectivity of moral terms than about sensory terms because he does not here go on to tell us how we might correct for the distortions in our use of moral terms introduced by our own unique prejudices and passions. Perhaps he thinks that, where our interests and passions are at stake, the reflective detachment required for objectivity is lacking. So he says that moral terms are inevitably of "inconstant signification" and that "such names can never be true grounds of any ratiocination" (L, 4, 24, pp. 21–22). Yet reasoning our way out of the state of nature requires precisely such ratiocination about the moral qualities conducive to peace.

In short, Hobbes's view that both sensory and moral concepts reflect the nature of the agent more than the nature of the external world leads him to focus on the relation of language to our mental discourse. The train of mental discourse is a succession of concepts linked by the natural tendency of the mind to take one thing to be the sign of another. This habit of taking an antecedent conception to be a sign of a subsequent one can be either a free association, idiosyncratic to each individual, or the disciplined inference from cause to effect or from means to end, called prudence. Both kinds of train of conception are natural to humans, and prudence is shared by man and beast (L, 3, 3–5, pp. 12–13).

Of course, that the train of mental discourse is based on the natural semiotics of taking one thing for another does not mean that we can be confident that this mental discourse reflects natural reality. Indeed, Hobbes is quite skeptical about drawing inferences about reality from the nature of mental discourse; but neither is this mental discourse arbitrary. As Hobbes shows, even the free association of signs has its logic, and prudence is the natural cunning of all animals. In the *Elements of Law* (1640), Hobbes defines signs in terms of mental discourse, or "the succession of conceptions in the mind" (I, 4, 1, p. 13). He inquires as to the "cause of the coherence or consequence of one conception to another" and not as to whether a particular conception is, as the Scholastics would say, of a real being or a merely mental being. Hobbes has just told us about the products of memory: "I know no *kritērion* or mark by which he can discern whether it were a dream or not" (Elements, I, 3, 10, p. 12). Indeed, as we shall see, Hobbes is skeptical of the objectivity of the deliverances of mental discourse precisely because it is natural, that is, given in human experience. We can reason prudentially with what is naturally given in human life, but we can reason scientifically only with what we deliberately make or stipulate.

That the natural signs of mental discourse are frequently associated does not imply that we can infer real causation from our experience of their constant conjunction. Through our memory of observing a constant succession of two conceptions, we form a habit of expecting the one when we see the other. This habit leads us to treat the antecedent event as a sign of the consequent and to treat the consequent event as a sign of the antecedent: thus, says Hobbes, "clouds are a sign of rain to come, and rain of clouds past" (Elements, I, 4, 9, p. 15). But the basis of this presumption of a succession need not be any genuine causal relationship in the world. When we think of our ends, we think of the means to those ends. So the coherence of the discourse of the mind does not necessarily tell us anything about the coherence of the world. Prudence, he says, is "nothing else but conjecture from experience, or taking of signs from experience warily" (Elements, I, 4, 10, p. 16). From the whole of our experience, both from sense and from imagination, we learn to expect one thing to precede or to follow from—that is, be a sign of—another, and our capacity to judge the probability of that sequence is prudence.

Because anything could potentially be a natural sign of anything else, the natural sign relation need not have any "real" foundation: so when the word *just* is observed to be correlated with certain conceptions of state of affairs, we can conclude, not that we know what is "really" just, only how the word *just* is generally used. In general, warns Hobbes, it is important that "we conclude not such to be without, that are within us" (Elements, I, 4, 11, p. 17). Prudential reasoning based on given experience and through the natural association of signs will never, for Hobbes, lead to certain knowledge: "Experience concludeth nothing universally" (Elements, I, 4, 10, p. 16).

Although Hobbes often describes deliberate signs as arbitrary, it would be more accurate to say that they are not arbitrary but artificial. Indeed, on his account, natural signs are more arbitrary than conventional signs. Within the given world of experience, anything may be a sign of anything else: "The mind may run almost from any thing to any thing" (Elements, I, 4, 2, p. 13). Nothing is intrinsically a sign of anything else. In other words, the natural-sign relation is symmetrical: as Hobbes says, clouds are a sign of rain and rain a sign of clouds. But when it comes to signs deliberately created by human beings, some things are intrinsically signs, in the sense that now the sign relation becomes asymmetrical: a mark, he says, reminds us of a former conception better than the former conception reminds us of a mark.[18] Thus, he says: "A *Mark* therefore is a sensible object which a man erecteth voluntarily to himself, to the end

---

18. Martinich points out that Hobbes does not contradict himself, at least verbally, because he distinguishes "marks" from "signs" (Logic, p. 348).

to remember thereby somewhat past, when the same is objected to his sense again" (Elements I, 5, 2, p. 18). A buoy is thus a mark to remember dangerous rocks at sea. A buoy is a mark of dangerous rocks, but one would not set out dangerous rocks to remind one of a buoy; so this relation is not like that between clouds and rain. A buoy is intrinsically a sign, because it is more perspicuous to the mind than what it signifies. So artificial signs are not purely arbitrary but must be perspicuous to the mind if they are to function as signs in the natural processes of cognition. For this reason, Hobbes tells us that a good law must be perspicuous if it is to be an effective sign of the will of the sovereign (L, 30, 20, p. 229).

Hobbes's discussion of a "mark" clearly reveals his debt to Augustine. Hobbes's definition of a "mark" as a "sensible object" is drawn from Augustine's definition of a sign: "A thing which, in addition to the impression it makes on the senses, also through itself brings something else to mind."[19] Hobbes's Latin word for "mark" (nota), however, stems not from Augustine but from Boethius, who used notae to render Aristotle's sēmeia and symbola.[20] Hobbes also follows Augustine in assuming that all signs are what Hobbes's contemporary John Poinsot (1589–1644) calls "instrumental signs": that is, every sign can refer the mind to something else only after it has first been cognized as an object; an instrumental sign cannot function as a sign until it first functions as an object of cognition. By contrast, a "formal sign," says Poinsot, such as a percept or a concept, refers the mind to its object without first being cognized, though a formal sign may also be made into an object of reflection.[21] In Poinsot's late Scholastic logic, concepts and percepts are not mental objects, as are Hobbes's phantasms and ideas; instead of being objects of cognition, Poinsot's concepts and percepts are more like lenses or windows that serve only to bring things to our attention. Hobbes is not aware of the Scholastic distinction between instrumental and formal signs, perhaps preventing him from developing a semiotics of cognition. Richard Tuck attributes the semiotic interpretation of perception to the anti-Aristotelian Epicureanism of Mersenne, Descartes, Gassendi, and Hobbes.[22] Yet even a casual glance at the work of Poinsot will reveal that the

19. Augustine, De Doctrina Christiana, in Patrologia Latina, ed. J.-P. Migne, vol. 34, II, 1, 1, col. 35.
20. See John Magee's Boethius on Signification and Mind (Leiden: E. J. Brill, 1989), pp. 56–57.
21. See John Poinsot (John of St. Thomas), Tractatus de Signis, ed. in bilingual format by John N. Deely (Berkeley: University of California Press, 1985), p. 27.6.
22. "At the center of his [Gassendi's] version of Epicureanism was the argument that science

semiotic treatment of perception and cognition is, by Hobbes's time, already traditional Aristotelianism. Hobbes says that one phantasm often refers the mind to another phantasm; to my knowledge, he does not say that a phantasm is a sign of a real thing. So Hobbes's treatment of cognition is not fully semiotic: he says that words are signs of conceptions and that one conception might be a sign of another conception but he does not say that conceptions are themselves signs of things. By not developing an account of how conceptions relate to things, Hobbes makes it difficult to understand how words can both signify concepts and denote things.

A name is a mnemonic device for remembering a conception: "A *Name* or *Appellation* therefore is the voice of a man, arbitrarily imposed, for a mark to bring to mind some conception" (Elements, I, 5, 2, p. 18). This conception of language is astonishingly subjectivist as well as solipsistic: language here marks only our concepts, but not things in the world, and language is not here a medium of communication among men. True, Hobbes does go on to say that "things named" include "the objects themselves" (Elements, I, 5, 3, p. 18), but this seems inconsistent with his explicit definitions of names as marks and of marks as reminders of conceptions. Clearly, Hobbes has not yet distinguished how names signify concepts from how they denote objects.

What is key to Hobbes's account of language is how he contrasts marks with natural signs by observing that marks have a logical necessity lacking in signs. Science begins with the disciplined use of marks, while prudence must get by with natural signs. The reason seems to be that, since signs are merely based on observed probabilities of sequences, we cannot ever conclude anything universal from conjectures of those probabilities. By contrast, we have "maker's knowledge" of marks, since we impose them ourselves: "We cannot from experience conclude . . . any proposition universal whatsoever, except it be from re-

---

depends on an analysis of *signs*—that is, observations or sense-perceptions are the signs of the real natural events, standing in the same relationship to them as the conventional sign for a word stands for the word, or as words themselves may signify objects. . . . In general, one might say that quite a lot of the new philosophical view espoused by Gassendi, Descartes and Hobbes can be captured by viewing it as the application to *perception* of a long-standing set of concerns with the fit between *language* and the world." Richard Tuck, *Philosophy and Government, 1571–1651* (Cambridge: Cambridge University Press, 1993), pp. 289 and 292. Tuck further argues that what is new in neo-Epicurean semiotics is the view that percepts have a nonrepresentational relation to their objects (*Philosophy and Government*, pp. 289–92); but Poinsot had already carefully distinguished signification from representation (*Tractatus de Signis*, pp. 26.39 to 27.6).

membrance of the use of names imposed arbitrarily by men" (Elements, I, 4, 11, pp. 16–17). In Hobbes's example, by merely observing how the signs "just" and "unjust" happen to correlate with states of affairs, we cannot draw any necessary conclusions about what is just; but by deciding arbitrarily what is to be counted as just, we can know with certainty what states of affairs are just.

Hobbes's next major foray into the philosophy of signs and language comes in *Leviathan* (1651). Here, following the *Elements,* he introduces "signs" in the context of exploring the coherence of our "train of imaginations." As we order our imaginings into relations of antecedent and consequent, we come to treat each as a sign of the other (L, 3, 8, p. 14). The prudent man is he with the greatest experience and memory of these signs; he can make the best estimates of the likely probability of the sign/signified sequence because "he hath the most *signs* to guess by" (L, 3, 4, p. 14). But the prudential interpretation of signs is necessarily unreliable and common to man and beasts. What distinguishes human beings is the "invention" of speech—an invention Hobbes compares to the invention of letters and of printing. Hobbes emphasizes the artificiality of language because, on his account, the essence of language is that it is voluntary: we always use language deliberately to mark or to signify our thoughts. Linguistic meaning, like legal validity, is rooted in the human will. The general point of language is not to assist man in the grasp of real things but rather to fix and to communicate his own mental discourse. As such, speech has two purposes: as a mnemonic to recall our conceptions and as a medium for conveying our conceptions to others. Hobbes says that the first use of "names" is as "marks" or "notes" of remembrance; another use of speech is as signs to communicate our thought to others (L, 4, 3, pp. 16–17). So the account here shares the subjectivism but not the solipsism of his earlier account of language.

Indeed, between the *Elements* and *Leviathan* we find a shift in the unit of analysis. Before, the unit of analysis was the individual mark, such as a buoy; a word was defined as a kind of mark. Now the unit of analysis is speech, which consists of words and their connection (L, 4, p. 15). Words are no longer kinds of marks; rather, words can be used as either mnemonic marks or communicative signs—but with this crucial distinction. An individual word may serve as a mark or mnemonic; but, says Hobbes, individual words cannot serve as communicative signs. Words can signify in communication only "by their connexion and order one to another" (L, 4, 3, p. 17). In short, the unit of linguistic communication is not the word at all but an act of speech.

To some extent, it is helpful to interpret Hobbes here as moving, *avant la lettre,* from a semantic model of language, in which the unit of analysis is a linguistic unit (morpheme, word, or sentence), to a pragmatic model of language, in which the unit of analysis is a communication unit (a speech act).[23] The semantic model of language, ultimately originating in logic, asks: What does a word or proposition mean?; the pragmatic model of language, ultimately originating in rhetoric, asks: What did the speaker mean by that speech act? The semantic model of language sees language in the context of all other kinds of signs: linguistic signs are thought to signify their objects, just as smoke signifies fire, or an irregular pulse signifies heart trouble. The pragmatic model of language looks at speech not in the context of other signs but in the context of other voluntary acts: we ask what he meant by that assertion, just as we ask what he meant by slamming the door. Semantics is mainly concerned with the representation of truth, whereas pragmatics is mainly concerned with the communication of intentions.

Because Hobbes never settles upon either a linguistic or a communicative unit of analysis, the basic distinction between semantic and pragmatic approaches is foreign to his thought. There are, of course, what we would call both semantic and pragmatic elements in his account of language, but it is anachronistic and misleading to attempt to squeeze him into our distinctions. What unifies Hobbes's account of language is that both marks and signs are deliberately deployed at will: his philosophy of language is neither semantic nor pragmatic but is, like his philosophy of law, voluntaristic. In *Leviathan,* Hobbes strongly emphasizes the gulf between the signs interpreted by both animals and men and the uniquely human linguistic signs we deliberately deploy. In *De Cive,* he distinguishes "two kinds of signs: *Natural* signs and *Conventional* signs" (DC, 15, 16, p. 181). But all of his distinctions, whether between signs and marks in the *Elements,* or between natural and conventional signs in *De Cive,* or between nonlinguistic and linguistic signs in *Leviathan*—all these distinctions really come down to the distinction between signs we merely interpret and signs we deploy by will.

In this sense, Hobbes's semiotics does not look forward to Paul Grice as much as it looks backward to St. Augustine—for Augustine divided signs into two kinds, based upon whether the sign expressed a will to communicate. Natural signs (*signa naturalia*) he defined as those that refer the mind to an object apart from any will to communicate, such as smoke, tracks, and symptoms; given signs (*signa data*), by contrast, are signs deliberately deployed in order to

---

23. Hungerland and Vick, in their introductory essay to Marinich's translation of Hobbes's *Logic,* make the strongest case for the Gricean reading of Hobbes.

communicate mental discourse.[24] For Augustine, this distinction between signs merely interpreted and signs willfully deployed is logically basic and cannot be confused with other, more familiar distinctions. It is not, for example, the distinction between natural and conventional signs: Augustine says that animals may use given signs to communicate their thoughts; nor is it the distinction between nonlinguistic and linguistic signs: Augustine says that we signal our thoughts not only through words but also through gestures.[25]

In the *Elements* (1640), Hobbes defines the uniqueness of human reason not in terms of language but in terms of the deliberate use of marks as mnemonic devices: he said that animals, lacking such marks, forget where they hid food (Elements, I, 5, 1, p. 18). But by *De Homine* (1658), Hobbes says that while animals can interpret and use signs, they cannot interpret or use words. Animals, he says, interpret our words as signs of our desires but not as words, because they are not aware that words have their significance by the decision of men; animals interpret our words as symptoms of our desires, not as arbitrary symbols (DH, 10, 1, p. 88). Here, Hobbes seems to recognize that speakers intend not only to communicate but also to communicate by a system of conventional representation; in other words, that speakers have both communicative and representational intentions in the act of speaking. Moreover, speakers intend that their listeners recognize both kinds of intentions; yet animals do not recognize the human intention to represent. Hobbes argues that animals do not deliberately communicate but use their voices purely from natural necessity. Moreover, he says, animals do not represent their thoughts by an arbitrary system of signs; their voices are natural and vary by species.

Hobbes's most detailed and comprehensive treatment of signs and language is in his *Logic* (1655). Just as Aristotle's logic moves from the analysis of words, to propositions, and then to syllogisms, so does Hobbes's logic. The second

24. Augustine, *De Doctrina Christiana*, II, 1, 2, and II, 2, 3, cols. 36–37. I emphasize Hobbes's debt to Augustine because the editors of his *Logic* make a very misleading claim: "No medieval or earlier version of Hobbes's theory of signifying was found. In Hobbes's technical use of *significare*, the notion of acts of signifying on the part of speakers, not, as is usual, that of the signification of words and sentences, is logically basic. Moreover, Hobbes uses *significare* in a wide enough sense to include the signaling of animals to one another, in the concept." See "Editors' Foreword," by Isabel C. Hungerland and George R. Vick, to Hobbes's *Logic*, p. 11.

25. Augustine says that "beasts use certain signs for manifesting the desires of their minds to each other," but he hesitates to call them "*signa data*" because, like the cry of a man in grief, they might be involuntary (*De Doctrina Christiana*, II, 2, 3, col. 37). For nonverbal given signs among humans, see *De Doctrina Christiana*, II, 3, 4, col. 37.

chapter of his *Logic* is entitled "On Words" (*De Vocabulis*), but it actually begins with an account of signs in general. Hobbes repeats his distinction between natural signs (*naturalia*) that we interpret but do not deploy and deliberate signs (*arbitraria*) (Logic, 2, 2, p. 196) that we deploy at will. Among these deliberate signs are marks we use to recall our thoughts and signs proper we use to convey those thoughts to others (Logic, 2, 1–2, p. 195). Deliberate signs, both marks and true signs, need not be linguistic: Hobbes cites "a bush hung, to signify the sale of wine and a stone, to signify the boundaries of a field." The difference between a mark and a sign proper is that we deploy a mark for ourselves but a sign for others (Logic, 2, 2, p. 196).

Hobbes goes on to claim that names serve both as marks and as signs—which is not quite accurate (Logic, 2, 3, p. 196). Recall that in *Leviathan* Hobbes asserted that words signify only through their order and connection in speech. So words severally may serve as marks, but only words jointly may serve as signs: "Single names in themselves are marks . . . they are not signs unless they are arranged in speech" (Logic, 2, 3, p. 196). Hobbes insists that words have arisen from the deliberate decision of men; they clearly do not reflect the nature of things, so they must stem from deliberate invention and decision (Logic, 2, 4, p. 198).

To the extent that Hobbes emphasizes speech or discourse, that is, a connected string of words as the unit of signification, he has made the speaker's intention to communicate his basic semantic concept; but if Hobbes were truly committed to the thesis that all meaning derives from the speaker's intention to communicate, then why does he persist in emphasizing the importance of words as marks?[26] "The nature, therefore, of a *name* consists primarily in this, that it is a *mark,* deployed for the sake of memory" (Logic, 2, 3, p. 196). Hobbes retains two fundamental units of linguistic analysis: the word as mark for memory and speech as sign for communication. He neither subordinates the representational function of marks to the intention to communicate (as in pragmatics) nor subordinates communication to the semantics of representation (as in semantics). What unifies his account of both marks and signs is their basis in the deliberate will of the user.

But language is a mixed blessing for Hobbes. For even if the deliberate stipulation of names makes possible scientific thought, it also makes possible deception, betrayal, and sedition. Animals, who interpret natural signs, thus have a more reliable guide to the passions of other animals than do people, who in-

26. This question is posed by Soles in *Strong Wits and Spider Webs,* p. 80.

terpret words and are thus more vulnerable to the deceptions of language. Here Hobbes reveals a still deeper debt to Augustine in his view that the natural signs of countenance, gesture, and deed more accurately reveal our true passions than do the deliberate signs of words.[27] "The best signs of passions present are in the countenance, motions of the body, actions, and ends or aims which we otherwise know the man to have" (L, 6, 56, p. 34).[28] In his discussion of how God ought to be honored, Hobbes says that there are no words that by nature honor or scorn God, but there are, he says, actions that by nature honor or scorn God (DC, 15, 16, pp. 181–82; L, 31, 10, p. 238). We shall return to Hobbes's doctrine of actions as natural signs to show how it radically constrains the arbitrary scope of positive law and how it undermines his explicit view that "all actions are indifferent."

Signification versus Denotation

In showing how positive signs emerge from natural ones, we have seen how language emerges from thought and from gesture, how science emerges from prudence, and, in general, how what is voluntary emerges from what is involuntary. I think it clear that Hobbes's understanding of what is voluntary in positive law and language is grounded in, and structured by, what is involuntary in natural law and natural signs. Natural mental discourse is marked and signified by voluntary discourse, just as natural prudential reasoning is sharpened and corrected by deliberate scientific discourse. Moreover, voluntary signs are not wholly arbitrary in content but are structured by the natural cognitive requirement for perspicuity. The final and, for our purposes, most salient aspect of the emergence of positive language is the emergence of deliberate denotation from the involuntary signification of words. For we cannot deliberately control what our words signify to those who hear them; each individual, through the natural and customary processes of sign association, will interpret our words quite differently; but we can, by deliberate stipulation, in science and in law, control which objects are denoted by our words. How language is conceptualized in thought is largely an involuntary process, related to the natural and customary dispositions of the individual; but how language names and

27. Hobbes: "These forms of speech, I say, are expressions, or voluntary significations, of our passions; but certain signs they be not, because they may be used arbitrarily, whether they that use them have such passions or not" (L, 6, 56, p. 34).

28. Augustine says that the countenance of a man is a natural sign because it betrays his emotion, quite apart from any intention he might have of making it known (*De Doctrina Christiana*, II, 1, 2, cols. 36–37).

sorts particular objects in the world can be deliberately instituted. Language and law are positive for Hobbes, chiefly in how they publicly denote objects in the world—either for the purposes of precise scientific reasoning or for the purpose of clear standards of conduct at law.

The best way to understand Hobbes's distinction between signification and denotation is in relation not to Augustine but to Aristotle and Aquinas. Aristotle's *On Interpretation* (*Peri hermēneias*) contains a few brief lines in which he asserts, among other things, that "spoken words are symbols of the passions of the soul" and that the "passions of the soul are likenesses of real things."[29] These few lines are so tantalizingly cryptic that they have become the most influential text in the history of philosophical semantics by inspiring a vast tradition of commentary. Because Aristotle's treatment of the interplay among language, mind, and the world is so elliptical and underdeveloped, it has generated a vast range of incompatible views about how words relate to concepts (passions) and to things. Aquinas and Hobbes have quite different views of this common set of semantic relations, and this difference has profound implications for their understandings of law. Aquinas attempts a unified understanding of words, concepts, and things in which words denote things only through the mediation of concepts: words signify immediately concepts of the mind but also ultimately the things themselves. In this view, signification determines denotation. Hobbes rejects this unified account and strongly contrasts two quite distinct relations whereby words "signify" only concepts but also directly "denote" things.

Since Hobbes has defined words as either marks or signs of thoughts, it is not surprising that he says "words are not signs of things but of thoughts" (Logic, 2, 1, p. 192). Hobbes wonders how the word *stone* could be a sign of a stone except in the sense that if we heard it, we would assume the speaker has thought of a stone (Logic, 2, 5, p. 200). Once we approach language as a form of deliberate human action, words are taken to manipulate and to communicate thought more than merely to represent reality. Still, on Hobbes's account, language does not lack all connection to the world: in addition to signifying thoughts, words also name things (Logic, 2, 6, p. 200). But what of names that do not name things but name mere phantasms, such as chimeras? Here Hobbes follows stan-

---

29. "Esti men oun ta en tēi phōnēi tōn en tēi psychēi pathēmatōn symbola, kai . . . tauta . . . pathēmata tēs psychēs . . . tauta homoiōmata pragmata" (16a 3–8). Text from Norman Kretzmann, "Aristotle on Spoken Sound Significant by Convention," in *Ancient Logic and Its Modern Interpretations,* ed. John Corcoran (Dordrecht: D. Reidel, 1974): 3–21, at 3–4. Kretzmann calls these lines "the most influential text in the history of semantics" at p. 3.

dard Scholastic logic by distinguishing real things from fictive things, in which case every name names something (Logic, 2, 6, p. 202).

So words signify concepts as well as denote things: by sharply distinguishing signification (*significare*) from denotation or reference (*denotare*), Hobbes here departs from many Scholastic theories that either subordinate signification to reference or subordinate reference to signification. Aquinas, for example, says that "words refer to the things signified by means of a concept of the intellect."[30] Aquinas thinks that we name as we know: that is, we name or refer to things only in accordance with what they signify to us; reference is always mediated through signification: "Vocal sounds signify the conceptions of the intellect immediately and things by means of them." He says that words could not immediately signify things, because general words, such as "man," signify the abstract conception of human being rather than particular men.[31] For Aquinas, to refer to something without the mediation of a concept would be to name unknowingly, as does a parrot.

In the Aristotelian tradition, the reference of words can be reliably guided by concepts because Aristotle and Aquinas believe that, although written and spoken words are not the same for all men, concepts of the intellect and the things themselves are the same for all men.[32] What Aristotle literally says here is that the "passions" (*pathēmata*) of the soul are the same for all men. But, according to Hobbes, it is precisely our passions that radically individuate our concepts and make spontaneous conceptual concord impossible: "For seeing all names are imposed to signify our conceptions, and all our affections are but conceptions, when we conceive the same things differently, we can hardly avoid the different naming of them. For though the nature of what we conceive be the same, yet the diversity of our reception of it, in respect of different constitutions of body and prejudices of opinion, gives everything a tincture of our different passions" (L, 4, 24, p. 21; cf. DC, 3, 31, p. 55). So Hobbes agrees with Aristotle and Aquinas that the things themselves are the same for all men, but he argues that our concepts of those things (especially when they affect our interests) will be as divergent as our differing passions.

So linguistic anarchy is rooted in the prior conceptual anarchy whereby the differing passions of men lead to differing conceptions of the same things. How is communication even possible in the face of this conceptual anarchy? One

---

30. "Voces referuntur ad res significandas mediante conceptione intellectus." ST, I, 13.1c.

31. *In 1 Perihermeneias*, lect. 2.5.

32. Aristotle, *Peri Hermēneias*, 16a 6–7; Aquinas, *In 1 Perihermeneias*, lect. 2, 9.

purely conventionalist solution to this conceptual anarchy would be for everyone simply to agree that the sovereign's conception of moral concepts shall be authoritative. In this way, the sovereign's private understanding of moral concepts is simply enacted into law. But I do not think that this is Hobbes's solution. To begin with, since the processes of belief formation are natural and customary, no one can simply decide to adopt a new understanding of "murder" or "adultery"; our beliefs about these matters just are what they are. We cannot choose to substitute the sovereign's beliefs for our beliefs, nor can he coerce our process of belief formation. Moreover, our private moral concepts and beliefs are inherently vague and do not pick out any unique set of objects to be forbidden or enjoined by law. This is true as much of a sovereign's private moral concepts as of anyone else's. For Hobbes, the denotation of a moral term is always underdetermined by its signification; for any private conception of "murder" or "adultery" there are any number of possible sets of objects that might be forbidden or enjoined by law. After all, not everything immoral ought to be made illegal, so some key questions are: Of the things that are immoral, what is to be illegal? And who will decide?

So Hobbes's solution to the problem of conceptual anarchy is to emancipate the public denomination of words from their controversial private significations. Laws pick out particular objects to be forbidden or enjoined without attempting to determine what is signified by moral words. I think this is the political and legal function of Hobbes's notion that words can directly denote their objects. Law is the positive denotation of moral concepts; morality is the true natural significance of moral concepts in conscience. Law is to morality as public denotation is to private signification. Recall our earlier discussion of the word *murder*. What this word signifies to private individuals varies considerably in our society. When public authorities stipulate that "murder" denotes, among other things, accidental deaths caused in the course of committing a felony, they are not elevating a private understanding of "murder" into a public standard. They are simply presupposing that this public denomination of "murder" is not entailed by any particular understanding of murder but should be compatible with any reasonable understanding. In this way, public denotation is emancipated from private signification. For Aquinas, denotation is determined by signification; for Hobbes it is not. Nor can Hobbes simply be understood to mean that public denotation strives to create a new and shared signification. By denoting "felony murder" as a kind of murder, the sovereign is not necessarily attempting to change the significance of the word *murder* among citizens.

In short, the diversity of private moral understandings and beliefs does not of itself generate a state of war; anarchy arises only when each person claims that he can denote the unique set of actions to be forbidden or enjoined by law. Because no such unique set of actions at law is entailed by any private moral beliefs, it is arrogant for anyone except the sovereign to attempt to denote them. "When private men claim for themselves a knowledge of *good* and *evil,* they are aspiring to be as Kings" (DC, 12, 1, p. 132). Because of Hobbes's view that we only truly know propositions whose denotations we have ourselves stipulated, only the sovereign has true knowledge of good and evil in the sense of knowing precisely what ought to be denoted by them at law. We all have our private beliefs about the significance of moral terms but these beliefs do not determine what might be publicly denominated at law. When Hobbes thus says that we transfer our right of judging controversies to the sovereign, he means only that we transfer our right of deciding which objects at law our moral concepts denote. We do not transfer our right to make moral judgments, which we could not even if we would; we only transfer our right to interpret what precise actions our judgments denote.

Unfortunately, Hobbes tells us very little about how names denote their objects and about how denotation is related to signification. His discussions of signs and of language always begins from within the world of private conceptions, where words serve either to mark or to signify that internal discourse of mind. In these discussions, the world of things almost never makes an appearance—except, for example, in the *Logic,* where Hobbes explicitly reminds us that words signify concepts and not things (Logic, 2, 1, p. 192). The discussion of language in his *De Homine,* however, is a striking change from this pattern. True, the tenth chapter begins familiarly by defining speech in terms of the signification of concepts, but in the second section, despite Hobbes's confusing use of the term *signification* (*significare*) Hobbes launches into a discussion of the imposition of names upon "things," that is, a discussion of reference (*denotare*). He says that at first "there were few names, and of those things that were most familiar" (DH, 10, 2, p. 89). For example, he says, Adam imposed names upon the few animals and other species that God led before him; here names are directly imposed upon things. Because of Adam's authority, "these names, having been accepted, were handed down from fathers to sons." In short, before the chaos after Babel, linguistic anarchy was avoided by Adam's public stipulation of names on things. In this way, what words name is not determined by what they signify to private individuals; because of the riot of private concepts of the same things, references of words could not be mediated by some spontaneous convergence of private signification of concepts. Instead, names are publicly imposed upon things through some deliberate stipulation: this official "dubbing" of a thing is then transmitted through a causal chain that does not depend upon the varying private conceptualizations of men.[33]

Hobbes is clearly not arguing that the human use of names to refer to things ought to bypass all conceptual signification: we should not be parrots. Indeed, Hobbes scathingly attacks philosophers who use words to refer to things that are "inconceivable" (DC, 18, 4, p. 238). The things referred to by words need not be real, but they do need to be at least conceivable. For example, in the same section of *De Homine,* Hobbes asks how Adam could have understood the serpent's reference to death when Adam had no concept (*idea*) of death. Hobbes says that God must have supernaturally infused Adam's mind with the concept signified by the word *death.* The point of these tales of official "dubbings," whether by God or by Adam, is that our private conceptions do not determine the public reference of words; rather, the official imposition of words fixes their public signification and reference. Of course, it is very difficult to preserve the integrity of the transmission of the original imposition of names; the vulgar customary use of words tends to corrupt their original signification through the mediation of private concepts. We should look for the proper meaning of words not in the distortions introduced by custom but by trying "to recall to memory the concepts for the sake of which they were attached [*impositae*] to things" (DC, 18, 4, p. 238). This "public dubbing" theory of reference helps to explain why Hobbes goes on to say that, of all the wonderful advantages of language, the greatest is the capacity to command and to understand commands (DH, 10, 3, p. 91). For by commanding the public reference for moral names, such as good and evil, just and unjust, we subordinate the anarchy of private moral significations to the objective denominations of what Hobbes calls "public good" and "public evil" (DH, 10, 5, p. 94). By so subordinating private signification to public reference, not only do we make way for all the fruits of peace, we also make possible a demonstrative science of politics

33. Here I follow Soles's view that Hobbes develops a public "dubbing" origin to a causal chain determining the reference of names: "These [private] conceptions do not have a role in the causal history which is relevant to determining the denotation of a name. The latter history is, if you will, public history, linking particulars to utterances. The individual causal histories also link particulars to utterances, but do it by very different routes, which are peculiar to individual persons. The individual's causal history may overlap the public history, but they will not be identical." *Strong Wits and Spider Webs,* p. 94.

and ethics, since we have a maker's knowledge of deliberate, public denomination.

POSITIVE LAW

Hobbes's strong mind broke through many verbal webs only to become hopelessly ensnared by the positivity of law. To begin with, Hobbes, like Aquinas, devoted most of his legal analysis to biblical law and to the question of how to distinguish natural biblical law that is binding upon Christian sovereigns from positive biblical law that is not. As we saw, Aquinas distinguishes natural from positive biblical law on the basis of its content: natural biblical law has the intrinsic moral necessity and universality lacking in merely positive biblical law. During the Reformation, Aquinas's efforts neatly to distinguish the natural Mosaic law binding on Christians from the positive Mosaic law not binding on Christians was challenged. Some reformers, such as Johannes Karlstadt, argued that the whole of Mosaic law was binding on Christians; other reformers, including Luther, rejected this view.[34] Thus, in the wake of the Reformation Hobbes was anxious to avoid such a disputable normative analysis; he sought a more objective way to distinguish natural from positive divine law.

Because of Hobbes's view that positive law stems from the will of the sovereign and must be backed by civil sanction, Hobbes attempts to distinguish natural from positive biblical law not by reference to the content but by reference to the authoritative source of law. Of biblical laws he asks: Was this law enacted by God as sovereign of mankind, or as sovereign of Israel? Who is the civil sovereign who enforces God's authority? Unfortunately, none of these criteria enables Hobbes consistently to distinguish natural from positive divine law. Indeed, we shall find him resorting to precisely the normative analysis of content he sought to avoid. Second, in Hobbes's account of positive law, it is often difficult to tell if he means to assert that all human law actually is positive or that all human law ought to be positive: Does Hobbes see law's positivity as a description of law or as a norm of law? Hobbes's strong normative commitment to positive law seems to make it difficult for him accurately to describe English law. Third, Hobbes's discourse of positive law leads him to assert that all human actions are morally indifferent until regulated by law—even though, in other contexts, he denies that all human actions are indifferent. Ultimately, as we

---

34. On Luther's debate with Karlstadt, see W. D. J. Cargill Thompson, *The Political Thought of Martin Luther* (Totowa, NJ: Barnes and Noble, 1984), p. 85.

shall see, Hobbes's sharp contrasts between positive denotation and natural signification will lead him to assert that a civil sovereign may rightfully require a devout Christian subject verbally to deny his faith; Aquinas's integration of denotation and signification, by contrast, prevents him from permitting even verbal apostasy.

I have frequently compared Hobbes's view of language and of law to that of Thomas Aquinas. Hobbes's relation to Aquinas, however, is not a mere artifact of my argument but is internal to Hobbes's own philosophical development. For if, as most scholars now think, the "Discourse of Laws" (1620) is by Hobbes, then his early understanding of law was deeply Thomistic. Indeed, as we shall see, he captures not only Aquinas's understanding of the relation of natural to positive law but also shares Aquinas's equivocations about the meaning of "positive" law. Other scholars have pointed to the broad similarities of Aquinas's and Hobbes's understanding of the relation of natural to positive law, but none has explored the similarities of their specific understandings of positive law.[35]

Given Hobbes's Scholastic education at Magdalen Hall, he could hardly have avoided the influence of broadly Thomistic thought, which is especially evident in the early "Discourse of Laws"—if that work is indeed by Hobbes.[36]

35. Timothy Fuller, "Compatibilities on the Idea of Law in Thomas Aquinas and Thomas Hobbes," *Hobbes Studies* 3 (1990): 112–34. Mark C. Murphy, "Was Hobbes a Legal Positivist?" *Ethics* 105 (July 1995): 846–73. A. P. Martinich, *The Two Gods of* Leviathan (Cambridge: Cambridge University Press, 1992), p. 113. No one to my knowledge has yet commented upon a related similarity, namely, that between the debate among Hobbes scholars about whether natural law is really "law" and the parallel debate among Aquinas scholars. Given that both Hobbes and Aquinas describe the essence of law in statutory (positive) terms, natural "law" will always pose a problem.

36. For an argument and stylometric evidence that the Three Discourses of 1620 are by Hobbes, see Noel B. Reynolds and Arlene W. Saxonhouse, "Hobbes and the *Horae Subsecivae*," in Thomas Hobbes, *Three Discourses,* pp. 3–19. For a vigorous critique of Reynold's and Saxonhouse's claims, especially in regard to the "Discourse of Laws," see John C. Fortier, "Hobbes and 'A Discourse of Laws': The Perils of Wordprint Analysis," and the ensuing exchange in the *Review of Politics* 59 (Fall 1997): 861–914. Tuck says that Hobbes's authorship of these Discourses "is now quite convincingly established" in his introduction to Hobbes's *On the Citizen* (p. x). Martinich claims about the Discourses, perhaps prematurely: "The standard scholarly view now is that Hobbes is their author." *Hobbes: A Biography* (Cambridge: Cambridge University Press, 1999), p. 44. My argument is that this Discourse embodies the same ambiguity about the nature of "positive" law that we have already seen in Aquinas and shall see in the mature Hobbes; if the "Discourse of Laws" turns out not to be by Hobbes, this development would only strengthen

In this essay, Hobbes follows traditional Thomism by describing civil or human law as being a concrete specification of the broad moral principles of the natural law: "If men were not limited within certain rules, such confusion would follow in government, that the differences of Right and wrong, Just and unlawful, could never be distinguished."[37] Legal rules must be specific enough to guide conduct and to settle disputes; they ought to be clear enough not to generate competing interpretations. Laws, he says, are "nothing else but virtue, and good order of life, reduced unto certain rules" (DL, p. 109). Again, following Aquinas (and ultimately Ulpian), Hobbes hierarchizes three fundamental kinds of law according to their degree of specificity: The law of nature, he says, is the ground or foundation of the other laws; it governs marriage, procreation and education, in humans and other animals as well. The law of nations is "those rules which reason has prescribed to all men in general" and to all nations in their mutual relations. Finally there are the civil or municipal laws, which he calls the "Peculiar Laws of every Country." (DL, p. 110). The thought here is that the law of nations and the municipal law derive their legal and moral force from their relation to the law of nature: The natural law establishes the principle of making and keeping promises, for example, while the law of nations specifies this principle in terms of defining the legal validity of contractual promises, and the municipal law further specifies the terms and conditions governing the legal enforcement of contracts.

Through this hierarchy of generality and specificity, we can "see" a connection between the "peculiar" laws of each city and the general moral principles of the natural law: in the image of Christopher St. German, we can see the law of reason in each civil law. Hobbes here develops the familiar classical image of the sources of law (*fontes iuris*) to convey the relation of natural to civil law: "There are certain fountains of natural Justice and equity, out of which has been taken and derived that infinite variety of Laws which several people have apted to themselves: and as several veins and currents of water, have several qualities and tastes, in respect of the nature of that ground and soil, through which they flow and run: so these Laws and the virtue of them, which be fetched from an original fountain, receive a new kind of application, and tincture, in respect of the situation of the Country" (DL, p. 112). Here the natural law, as it flows through each community, takes on the unique flavor and color of the particular epoch and locale, yet with-

---

my overall argument about the fundamental ambiguities of all discourse about "positive" law.

37. "A Discourse of Laws" (DL), in Hobbes, *Three Discourses,* pp. 105–18, at 106.

out losing its connection to the original fountain of Justice. "For Law is nothing but reason dilated and applied upon several occasions, and accidents" (DL, p. 115). The Thomistic understanding of law could hardly be more vividly captured. Through the progressive specifications of natural law, law becomes more precise, more clear, and more determinate; thus Hobbes says that laws ought to be changed only when they can be "made more perfect, more clear, more positive, more profitable" (DL, p. 113). Here the term *positive* refers to the specificity and clarity of the content of a law rather than to its source in legislation.

Hobbes even follows the classical Roman view that statute law (*lex*) is only one kind of law (*ius*); Hobbes lifts the list of the *fontes iuris* from Gaius and provides what he takes to be the English equivalents (DL, pp. 117–18).[38] Later, when Hobbes wishes to privilege statute law (*lex*), he will explicitly strip *ius* of its legal office and make it a moral term for right or liberty (DC, 14, 3; L, 14, 3). Hobbes says in the "Discourse of Laws" that the ancient Romans had an unwritten customary law or *mos Maiorum* as well as a written statutory law; he says that those customs not repealed by statute ("a Positive Law") have the same power and authority as statutory law. Here, by contrast, "positive" refers to the source of law in deliberate legislation. He then compares the ancient Roman customary law to the English common law, which is, he says, "of equal power and authority with our Statutes" (DL, pp. 118–19). Of course, one reason why Hobbes can countenance here the equality of common law and statutes is that he thinks them not so different: first, he notes that much of common law is written in the judgments and opinions found in the reports and cases expounded by judges (DL, pp. 117–18); second, Hobbes argues that many customs are but ancient statutes "without any known Author" (DL, p. 118). In sum, in this Discourse, Hobbes describes the civil law as "positive" in two senses: positive in content, meaning determinate rather than vague like the natural law; and positive in source, meaning imposed by statute rather than emerging from custom.

The Quest for Divine Positive Law

The first duty of any sovereign, says Hobbes, is to secure the well-being of his people: "The safety of the people is the supreme law." And, says Hobbes, "the

38. For Gaius's list, see *The Institutes of Gaius,* translated by W. M. Gordon and O. F. Robinson with the Latin text of Seckel and Kuebler (Ithaca: Cornell University Press, 1988), 18–23. Hobbes found Gaius's list in Justinian's *Institutes.* The same list and English equivalents are found in *Leviathan,* chap. 26.

safety of the people" means, in the first place, the eternal salvation of the people by the proper opinions and worship of God (DC, 13, 2 and 5, pp. 143–44). So the first duty of any sovereign, according to Hobbes, is to interpret natural divine law in order properly to regulate the public cult (DC, 15, 15–17).[39] In addition, a Christian sovereign must interpret the law of Christ (DC, 17, 27, p. 232), which Hobbes says includes the Decalogue, the moral law, and the law of Abraham (DC, 17, 8, p. 212). So a Christian sovereign must interpret biblical law in order to distinguish the natural divine law binding on Christians from the positive divine law not binding. As we shall see, Hobbes's own efforts so to distinguish natural from positive biblical law were a conspicuous failure, undermining his aspirations for Christian sovereignty.

We saw that Aquinas developed his conception of *ius positivum* through his lengthy analysis of divine law, by which he means the 613 commands of the Mosaic law. Since all of Mosaic law is positive in the sense of imposed by statute, when Aquinas distinguishes divine law into natural and positive precepts, by "positive" he clearly means morally contingent in content. Ambiguity emerges, however, because to be positive in content is a matter of degree: Does positive law mean law partially or wholly positive? Aquinas is inconsistent in this regard: sometimes, for example, he says that the judicial precepts are mixedly positive and sometimes he lumps them with the ceremonial precepts as simply positive.

Still, Aquinas is confident that he can classify the Mosaic precepts according to the degree of their moral contingency and distinguish those precepts morally necessary even for Christians from those precepts morally contingent on God's covenant with Israel through Moses. But the Reformation created immense controversies precisely on the question of what parts of Mosaic law are still binding on Christians. In the wake of these controversies, Hobbes seeks to find a way to distinguish natural from positive divine law without recourse to a controversial analysis of the moral content of those laws. As we shall see, instead of such a normative analysis of the content of divine law, Hobbes will mount a historical and empirical investigation of the pedigree of those laws. His criteria will be: Does this law issue from God as sovereign of mankind or from God as sovereign of Israel? Who is the civil sovereign who vouches for God's authorship? Is this law enforceable by a civil sovereign? How is the law promulgated? None of these criteria enables Hobbes consistently to distinguish natural from

---

39. "The *interpretation* of *natural laws,* both *sacred* and *secular,* where God reigns through nature alone, depends on the authority of the commonwealth" (DC, 15, 17, p. 183).

positive divine law; indeed, he cannot even do so for the precepts of the Decalogue. Moreover, we shall find Hobbes implicitly relying on the normative analysis of content in order to distinguish natural from positive divine law.

In the early "Discourse on Laws," Hobbes had not yet developed his command theory of law; he thus admitted a wide range of legal norms, from statutes to customs, to precedents. But by the time of the *Elements of Law* (1640), however, Hobbes had a much more exacting definition of law. Since law is now a command, and since reason, for Hobbes, cannot issue commands, then commands must stem from a commander. So the first division of law must be according to the differences of the "authors or lawmakers" (Elements, II, 10, 6, p. 187); by this logic, then, all law must be either divine or civil law, since there are only two rightful lawgivers, God and the human sovereign.

Yet Hobbes then asserts that "[f]rom the difference of the authors, or lawmakers, cometh the division of law into divine, natural, and civil" (Elements, II, 10, 6, p. 187). But how can three kinds of law stem from a distinction of only two lawmakers? Hobbes must find a way to collapse natural law into divine and/or civil law. As we shall see, he will do both. But, in order to effect this reductive collapse, Hobbes must distinguish the content of natural law from its source, even though his whole account and classification of law is an attempt precisely to avoid any distinction among commands on the basis of disputable content. By content, natural law is the "dictates of natural reason" (Elements, I, 18, 1, p. 95) and not properly law; but by source, these dictates are commands of God and so are properly law (Elements, I, 17, 12, p. 93). Having thus collapsed natural law into divine, he then proceeds to say of the first division of law into divine, natural, and civil that "the first two branches are one and the same law" (Elements, II, 10, 7, p. 187; cf. II, 6, 10, p. 155). But divine law and natural law cannot be one and the same law, even on Hobbes's account, for some parts of divine law are in content the dictates of natural reason, such as "thou shalt not kill," while other parts of divine law are in content morally contingent, such as "do not wear garments of wool and linen sewn together." Hobbes recognizes this Thomistic distinction within divine law between natural and positive precepts when he says of the lawfulness of man's dominion over the beasts, "And this dominion is therefore of the law of nature, and not of divine law positive" (Elements, II, 3, 9, p. 130). Here, not only is Hobbes implicitly distinguishing natural from positive precepts within divine law, he is doing so precisely, it seems, on the basis of the content of those norms. Natural divine law would mean precepts whose content has intrinsic moral force; and positive divine law would mean precepts whose content lacks intrinsic moral force. Hobbes claims that it is evident to natural reason that we human beings are permitted to make use of other living beings for our own survival and that we do not depend upon positive divine revelation for this permission.

But Hobbes's official classification of law seeks to avoid reference to the disputed moral content of legal norms; he seeks criteria to identify law that do not depend upon moral argument about the content of those norms, criteria that are public and unassailable. The first of these criteria, as we have seen, is the distinction of lawgivers; but this distinction will not suffice, as we just saw, to distinguish the varieties of divine law. The second of these criteria is the difference of mode of promulgation: "From the difference of promulgation, proceedeth the division of laws into written and unwritten" (Elements, II, 10, 6, p. 187). Civil law, he says, is written, while natural law is unwritten (Elements, II, 10, 10, p. 190). Might we say, then, that natural divine law is unwritten, while positive divine law is written? Hobbes may well have something like this in mind: in one place he says that natural law is "written only in the heart" (L, appendix 2, p. 528). But, as Hobbes himself admits, much of the Decalogue consists of written natural law; so if the Bible contains both natural and positive written law, then how will the mode of promulgation distinguish them? Hobbes may well argue that divine natural law, unlike divine positive law, is also written in the heart; but how would we know what is written in the heart without a normative analysis of the kind Hobbes seeks to avoid? Hobbes's final criterion for the division of laws is in terms of their intended audience: he says that simple laws are addressed to everyone, while penal laws are addressed to judges, who set the penalty. Perhaps he thinks that natural divine law is addressed to all human beings, while positive divine law is addressed only to ancient Israel. But again, neither God nor his prophets consistently distinguish divine law into those precepts for Israel and those precepts for mankind; and every biblical faith interprets this distinction in radically different ways.

When we turn to Hobbes's *De Cive* (1642) we find even more extensive use of the concept of "positive" law. Instead of asserting, as he did in the *Elements,* that natural law and divine law are one and the same law, Hobbes now says more accurately that "the natural and moral law is divine law" (DC, 4, 1)[40]—thus making room for positive divine law. Like Aquinas, Hobbes develops his notion of

---

40. Here Tuck's and Silverthrone's translation is misleading: they say that the natural and moral law is *the* divine law (DC, 4, 1, p. 58); the 1651 English version captures Hobbes's actual doctrine by saying that the natural and moral law is *a* divine law. The original Latin, of course, lacks definite and indefinite articles.

"positive" law mainly through an analysis of the variety of precepts found in the Mosaic law. After first dividing law according to the diversity of its authors into divine and human, Hobbes then proceeds to divide divine law according to the diversity of its promulgation into "*natural* (or *moral*) and *positive*" (DC, 14, 4, p. 156). Natural divine law is promulgated through natural reason, while positive divine law, he says, is promulgated through prophetic utterance recorded in the Bible. Hobbes also implicitly retains his third division of laws from the *Elements,* division by the intended addressees of law, when he says that positive divine law may be called "*divine civil laws,* because they were particular to the commonwealth of Israel, his own particular people" (DC, 14, 4, p.156). Yet Hobbes knows that these criteria are inadequate for sorting divine law into natural and positive precepts: first, because prophetic law includes natural precepts and, second, because not all positive divine law is prophetic.

Hobbes begins his analysis of divine law by distinguishing three ways in which God's laws are promulgated: first, "*by the silent dictates of right reason*"; second, by direct revelation from divine voice, vision, dream, or inspiration; third, by indirect revelation through a prophet (DC, 15, 3, p. 172). Hobbes proceeds to drop the second mode of promulgation and to distinguish the natural kingdom of God, based on the rational word, from the prophetical kingdom of God, based on the word of prophecy. The natural kingdom of God includes all rational creatures while the prophetical kingdom "is a particular kingdom, because he has not given positive laws to all men, but only to a particular people" (DC, 15, 4, p. 173). Unfortunately, due to the ambiguities of the notion of "positive" law, Hobbes's tidy scheme breaks down as soon as he begins his detailed exposition of divine law in chapter XVI. Hobbes here tells us that, from the beginning, God's rule over Adam and Eve "was not only natural but also by *agreement*" (DC, 16, 2, p. 188). So in addition to our simple distinction between God's natural kingdom ruled by natural law and his prophetic kingdom ruled by positive law, we also have God's rule by agreement. Agreement seems to mediate between what is purely natural and what is fully positive. God's agreement with Adam involves positive law in the sense that God imposes a command upon Adam not to eat of the tree of the knowledge of good and evil; Hobbes insists that the content of this commandment is positive and not a dictate of natural reason: the fruit, he says, is not by nature bad but only bad because prohibited. But in another sense, this commandment is not positive law because it was not imposed upon a particular kingdom and enforced by a civil sovereign. So God's commandment to Adam is positive in its content but not in its political source.

God also governs Abraham not only by nature but also by agreement (DC, 16, 3, p. 188). Like a civil sovereign, Abraham was "also the *interpreter* of all the *laws,* both sacred and secular, for his own people" (DC, 16, 7, p. 190). Hobbes says that God's subjects owed him "only natural obedience and natural worship. . . . For the only *Word of God* that they had received was the natural word of right reason" (DC, 16, 9, p. 191).

Abraham, for Hobbes, becomes the paradigm of the civil sovereign because he is subject to no law other than the law of nature. Indeed, according to Hobbes, this Kingdom of God by agreement is itself a kind of Kingdom of God by nature, because "they had received no *word of God* beside the natural word of right reason" and they owed God "an obedience and worship only natural" (DC, 16, 9, p. 204). To this extent, Abraham is like a civil sovereign who is subject only to natural law, but who might impose whatever positive laws he wishes upon his subjects. But then Hobbes notes that Abraham is subject to one divine positive law: "We do not read of any laws given to *Abraham* by God or by *Abraham* to his family, either then or later, either secular or sacred (with the exception of the one command about *circumcision,* which is in the *Agreement*). It is clear from this that there were no other laws or worship by which *Abraham* was bound, beyond the natural laws, rational worship and circumcision" (DC, 16, 5, p. 190). Hobbes does not expressly call the command of circumcision a "positive law," but he does clearly distinguish it from natural law and from rational worship.

Of course, in terms of its content, the commandment of circumcision is a positive law, so Abraham is not simply subject to God's kingdom by nature; but neither is he, says Hobbes, subject to God's kingdom by prophecy. Only through the prophecy of Moses does God establish the first "kingdom of God by design [*institutivum*]," the prophetical kingdom of God (DC, 16, 9, p. 192). Moses delivers divine law to a particular people, a divine law that includes, for the first time, fully positive divine law.[41] Although Abraham was subject to a divine positive law in content, that law was not binding on a particular people, because Abraham was the father of more than one nation.[42]

41. Hobbes was clearly thinking of Moses when he wrote: "*Positive law* is that law which God has revealed to us through the *prophetic word* . . . such are the laws which he gave to the Jews about their constitution" (DC, 14, 4, p. 156).

42. As Martinich points out: "It is only the Israelites or Jews who are God's chosen people, not all of Abraham's descendants. For Abraham is the ancestor, not only of the Jews through Isaac, but also of the Bedouins, through Ishmael (Gen. 16:11)." See *The Two Gods of* Leviathan, p. 289.

When he turns to the Mosaic law proper, Hobbes adopts Aquinas's division of the 613 precepts into the moral, the judicial, and the ceremonial precepts (DC, 16, 10, p. 192). Yet whereas Aquinas divided these precepts according to the degree of their intrinsic moral content, Hobbes attempts to divide them by the political circumstances of their enactment ("the knowledge of a Kingdom's laws depends on a knowledge of the Kingdom" [DC, 15, 1, p. 172]). The first set of these precepts, he says, "obligate by nature, because they were given by *God* as *God of nature*"; these are the moral precepts that govern the kingdom of God by nature. The second set of these precepts "derive their obligation from the *agreement* made with *Abraham,* because they were given by God as the *God of Abraham.*" The third set "derive their obligation solely from the *agreement* which was made later with the people itself, because they were given by *God specifically as King of the Israelites*" (DC, 16, 10, p. 192). Here we have three kinds of law and two kinds of kingdom: but if Hobbes is right that genuine law flows only from a genuine kingdom, then only the third set of Mosaic laws are truly law and, in particular, truly positive law.

Of the new divine law, Hobbes says that the law of Christ is wholly "nature's teaching" (DC, 4, 24, p. 65). Thus every Christian sovereign is in the position of Abraham, and subject only to natural divine law. If a Christian sovereign were subject to positive divine law, then he would not be truly sovereign. For to be subject to divine positive law would be akin to being subject to positive constitutional law; in both cases, these higher laws are either dead letters or the true sovereigns. Unfortunately for Hobbes's tidy schemes, just as Abraham was found to be subject to at least one positive divine law, that enjoining circumcision, so Hobbes's Jesus lays down at least one positive divine law, that forbidding divorce.[43]

In general, however, Hobbes is clear that sovereigns are subject only to natural divine law and that it is of the essence of sovereignty that sovereigns have sole right to interpret natural divine law. Hobbes is quite clear that by "natural" he does not mean "secular": natural law includes the "*sacred laws*" dictating that, and how, God must be publicly worshipped and privately honored (DC, 15, 8, p. 175). Hobbes is equally clear that by "civil" he does not mean "secular": the civil laws, he says, are divided into "sacred and secular" (DC, 14, 5, p. 157).

---

43. In the case of Jesus, Hobbes attempts to eliminate this awkward exception by arguing that in laying down the precept against divorce, Jesus was merely explicating "the divine positive law against the Jews who were interpreting *the law of Moses* incorrectly" (DC, 4, 24, p. 65).

Indeed, he says that how religion is taught and how God is worshipped "are not prescribed by any divine positive law" but are prescribed by "*sacred civil laws*," which are the human interpretations of natural divine law. So the civil sovereign must translate the sacred as well as the secular natural divine law into a sacred as well as a secular civil human law (DC, 14, 5, p. 157).

In *Leviathan*, as soon as Hobbes introduces positive law, he turns, like Aquinas, to divine law. For "of positive laws some are *human,* some *divine*" (L, 26, 39, p. 185). "*Divine positive laws* (for natural laws, being eternal and universal, are all divine) are those which, being the commandments of God (not from all eternity, nor universally addressed to all men, but only to a certain people, or to certain persons) are declared for such by those whom God hath authorized to declare them" (L, 26, 40, p. 186). By this broad definition, however, not only Abraham and Moses but also Adam and Noah were subject to divine positive law.

Hobbes begins his account of God's government in *Leviathan* by distinguishing three ways in which God declares his law: "By *natural reason,* by *revelation,* and by the *voice* of some man" (L, 31, 3, p. 235). By revelation, God speaks direct to particular persons; by voice, God speaks to a peculiar people. Thus, because revelation is binding only upon those persons to whom it is addressed, Hobbes attributes to God a twofold kingdom, natural and prophetic. The natural kingdom of God is governed by the dictates of natural reason while the prophetic kingdom of God is governed "not only by natural reason, but by positive laws" (L, 31, 4, p. 235). This definition of divine positive law is already narrower by linking positive law to the prophetic Kingdom of God.

In the English version of *Leviathan,* Hobbes follows his earlier views and explicitly limits the kingdom of God by prophecy to the Jews, because the Jews alone, according to Hobbes, are subject to divine positive law.[44] It is therefore startling to discover that in the Latin version of *Leviathan* (1668), Hobbes explicitly extends the prophetical Kingdom of God and divine positive law to Christians.[45] Yet, throughout *Leviathan,* Hobbes emphatically and repeatedly

44. Hobbes is here emphatic about the uniqueness of the Jews: "wherein, having chosen out one peculiar nation (the Jews) for his subjects, he governed them, and none but them, not only by natural reason, but by positive laws" (L, 31, 4, p. 235). Curley notes the discrepancy with the Latin text in his note to this passage.

45. In the Latin version, speaking of God's rule over his prophetical kingdom, Hobbes says: "Especially of his chosen people, namely, at first the Israelites and then the Christians, whom he rules not only by the dictates of natural reason, but also by positive laws" Hobbes, *Opera Latina,* vol. 3, p. 256.

restates his earlier views that Christians are subject to no divine positive law, that Jesus's teaching is either natural law or mere counsel of perfection, that the Christian kingdom of God is not of this world (L, 41, 5, p. 330; 42, 5, p. 336; 42, 43, p. 355).

Hobbes turns out to be as uncertain about the origin of divine positive law as he is about its scope. Indeed, perhaps the uncertain scope of the prophetic kingdom of God stems from its uncertain origin. In *De Cive,* Hobbes distinguishes three kingdoms of God: by nature, by agreement, and by prophecy (DC, 16, 2 and 9, pp. 188 and 191); he also describes the kingdom of God by agreement as a kind of kingdom of God by nature, because Abraham received only "the natural word of right reason" (DC, 16, 9, p. 191). On this account, the covenant establishing Abraham's sovereignty belonged to natural law, just as does the covenant establishing any civil sovereign. In *De Cive,* positive divine law arrives only with the prophecy of Moses; yet Hobbes concedes there that Abraham was subject to at least one positive law, that of circumcision (DC, 16, 5, p. 190). Perhaps this awkward exception to Hobbes's account in *De Cive* led to his revised account in *Leviathan.* There, Hobbes explicitly says that God's prophetic kingdom begins with the agreement with Abraham, who "obligeth himself and his posterity, in a peculiar manner, to be subject to God's positive law" (L, 35, 4, p. 273; cf. 40, 1, p. 317). Hobbes says that, although God is not expressly called king nor Abraham's posterity called a kingdom, this agreement is nonetheless "an institution by pact of God's peculiar sovereignty over the seed of Abraham" (L, 35, 4, p. 273). In *De Cive,* by contrast, Moses establishes the first "instituted" kingdom of God.

As we noted above, the difficulty with having Abraham found the prophetic kingdom of God is that he did not found a kingdom, and his posterity do not form a peculiar people. Nor is it clear on Hobbes's account why Abraham is special: Hobbes admits that God had "peculiar subjects" to whom he gave commandments, long before Abraham (L, 35, 3, p. 272). If there was divine positive law before the agreement with Abraham, then why should the prophetic kingdom wait for Abraham? No doubt the agreement God establishes with Abraham appeals to Hobbes as the origin of an instituted prophetic kingdom complete with divine positive law. But Hobbes knows that God had earlier established an agreement with Noah, his posterity, and all living things; this Noachite agreement includes both natural and positive divine law.[46] Of course,

---

46. Hobbes plausibly claims, in the *Elements* (II, 3, 9) that God's grant of dominion over living creatures to Noah is by natural law, but this grant of dominion is subject to one clear

Noah and his posterity do not form a "peculiar people"; but then again neither do Abraham and his posterity.

What seems to make Abraham special to Hobbes is his prophetic role as a mediator between God and a "peculiar people": "They to whom God hath not spoken immediately are to receive the positive commandments of God from their sovereign, as the family and seed of Abraham did from Abraham their father, and Lord, and civil sovereign" (L, 40, 2, p. 317). So Abraham is special because he is the first civil sovereign with the right to interpret and to enforce God's natural and positive law upon a nation. Moses, however, who had not only the right but also the might to enforce divine law upon his nation, seems more like a civil sovereign than does Abraham. Hobbes appears to agree: "In short, the kingdom of God is a civil kingdom, which consisted first in the obligation of the people of Israel to those laws which Moses should bring unto them from Mount Sinai" (L, 35, 13, p. 276). So although Abraham is the first "civil sovereign," Moses founded the first "civil kingdom."

Perhaps because of Hobbes's view that a civil kingdom is logically prior to positive law, later in *Leviathan,* Hobbes returns to the view of *De Cive* that not Abraham but Moses is the first bringer of divine positive law. If "positive" law means "posited" in writing, then Mosaic law would seem to be the first divine positive law: "That part of the Scripture which was first [positive] law was the Ten Commandments, written in two tables of stone. . . . Before that time there was no written law of God, who, as yet having not chosen any people to be his peculiar kingdom, had given no law to men but the law of nature" (L, 42, 37, p. 351). Of course, this passage directly contradicts Hobbes's earlier attribution of both a "peculiar kingdom" and "positive law" to the Abrahamic covenant (L, 35, 4, p. 273; L, 40, 2, p. 317). Ultimately, what makes law positive, it seems, is the existence of a civil sovereign in a civil kingdom who has not only the right (as did Abraham) but also the might (as did Moses) effectively to enforce the law: Hobbes asks, "Who it was that gave to these written tables the obligatory force of laws?" (L, 42, 37, p. 352). Hobbes answers: "It was, therefore, only Moses then . . . that had on earth the power to make this short Scripture of the Decalogue to be law in the commonwealth of Israel." So divine positive law is only truly positive when it has become civil positive law enforced by a civil sovereign in a civil kingdom.

---

exception based on positive law: "You must not eat flesh with life, that is to say blood, on it" (Gen. 9:4). So, according to Scripture, all human beings are subject to divine positive law.

Unfortunately, not every written statute enforced by the civil sovereign is positive law: Hobbes tells us that the entire second table of the Decalogue is natural law. So we cannot escape from controversial moral analysis and argument about the content of legal precepts to see whether they are positive or natural. Not only do theologians from the different branches of Christianity disagree about the moral content of the Decalogue, Hobbes's own views change dramatically over time. In *De Cive,* for example, Hobbes claims that not only the second table but also much of the first table belongs to natural law (DC, 16, 10, p. 192); in *Leviathan,* however, the entire first table is said to be "peculiar to the Israelites" (L, 42, 37, p. 352). No wonder Hobbes strives so mightily to avoid an analysis of the content of divine law!

As for the other 603 precepts of the Mosaic law, which he divides into judicial and Levitical law, Hobbes tells us summarily that "they were all positive laws" (L, 42, 38, p. 352). Without descending into an analysis of the content of these precepts, Hobbes says only that the judicial law and the Levitical law were delivered to the judges and priests of Israel by Moses alone, and that they become laws by the promise of obedience to Moses as civil sovereign. Of course, the same could be said of the second table of the Decalogue. If Hobbes had analyzed the content of the judicial precepts, for example, he would have found many that belong to the natural law: "You must appoint judges and scribes in each of the towns. . . . You must not pervert the law; you must be impartial; you will take no bribes" (Dt. 16:18). These precepts are "positive" only in the sense that they were written into statute and enforced by a civil sovereign; if all the judicial precepts are positive, then so is the second table of the Decalogue.

Ultimately, what makes law "positive" remains ambiguous in Hobbes. For example, he tells us that "amongst the Israelites it was a positive law of God their sovereign that he that was convicted of a capital crime should be stoned to death by the people" (L, Conclusion, 10, p. 492). It is not clear, even in the context, what makes this precept "positive": that it is enacted in statute by the sovereign (in which case it might also be natural) or that its content is not dictated by natural reason but is morally contingent (in which case it cannot simply be natural). In short, Hobbes is uncertain about the origins of divine positive law, about how to identify it, and about its scope.

Hobbes's account of divine positive law helps us to understand why John Austin will avoid using the term *positive* law in reference to divine law. If positive law is law imposed by the sovereign authority, then there can only be one kind of positive law. For if there are two kinds of positive law, divine and human, then there are two sovereigns; but sovereignty is a jealous God. If God can impose positive law on a human sovereign, then the human sovereign is no longer sovereign, and if the human sovereign is fully sovereign, then there is no room for divine sovereignty. Hobbes has not yet worked out a complete theory of sovereignty, as will Austin, but sovereignty is essentially indivisible. Aquinas, who is not saddled with a theory of sovereignty, can countenance a division of temporal and spiritual authority, in which the temporal sovereign interprets natural law into civil positive law, while the pope interprets both natural and positive divine law into ecclesiastical positive law. Because Aquinas is not committed to a theory of sovereignty, he can accommodate divine positive law and a division of authority, but Hobbes and Austin, who define positive law in terms of sovereign command, cannot.

Hobbes's Analysis of Positive Law:
Descriptive or Normative?

Any attempt to describe all of human law as "positive" in the sense of deliberately stipulated will confront difficulties with the existence of customary law—either specific lay customs (such as the customs of merchants) or the customs of legal institutions (such as the custom of following precedents or of following leading juristic doctrines). These legal norms were never deliberately stipulated by a lawgiver, and they enjoy their legal status not by virtue of being "laid down" but by virtue of being "taken up" by generations of judges. To say that all human law is positive is not just to attempt to describe it but also to set forth statutory law as the norm of human law. In Hobbes's discourse of positive law, it is often unclear whether he means that all civil law really is positive or just ought to be. Is his clear normative preference for statutory law leading him to describe all existing law as positive? Or is his descriptive analysis of law as command leading him to prefer law that is the express rather than the merely tacit will of the sovereign?

Hobbes's descriptive analysis of human law is so internally inconsistent and misleading that one suspects that his description is being driven by his normative commitment to statutory law. Hobbes cannot decide whether all civil law is positive or not: sometimes he describes all civil law as "made" or "written" by the sovereign; other times he says that civil law includes both positive and natural law. In the *Elements,* he says that the sovereign "hath the making of all the laws civil" (II, 8.6, p. 172), implying that all civil law is made by sovereign enactment. He strongly contrasts civil law here with natural law (Elements, II, 10.5, p. 186); but he also says that when a case arises that is not covered by the civil statutes, the judges should have recourse to natural reason, in which case natural law becomes a part of civil law. He says that when a judge passes sentence by his natural reason, that sentence "may attain to the vigour of a law . . . because the sovereign power is supposed tacitly to have approved such sentence . . . and thereby it cometh to be a law, and numbered amongst the written laws of the commonwealth" (Elements, II, 10.10, p. 190). So, through adjudication, natural law becomes incorporated into civil law.

Hobbes's description of civil law as some combination of statutory law and natural equity cannot accommodate common law. "Custom of itself maketh no law . . . if custom were sufficient to introduce a law, then it would be in the power of every one that is deputed to hear a cause, to make his errors law" (Elements II, 10.10, p. 190). Curiously, instead of saying that the custom of following precedents (where it is a custom) can create law because it reflects the tacit will of the sovereign, Hobbes denies that precedents might create law. After all, he goes on to say that when judges make their sentences according to the opinions of learned jurists, those judges thereby make laws "because they are admitted by the sovereign." But if the sovereign can tacitly approve the custom of following the opinions of learned jurists, why cannot the sovereign tacitly approve the custom of following precedents?

In *De Cive,* Hobbes revises his earlier account of the sources of law. He explicitly says that civil law includes both written statutory and unwritten natural law (DC, 14, 14, p. 161). This dichotomy, of course, leaves no room for a customary or common law. He goes on to say that the "writings of the jurists" are not law "for lack of sovereign authority" even though in the *Elements* he said that they were law. Then, in a puzzling passage, he says: "Nor the *responses of jurists,* i.e., of the *judges,* except in so far as their responses have attained customary authority with the consent of the sovereign" (DC, 14, 15, p. 161). Here Hobbes seems to have confused the writings of the jurists, that is, the *responsa prudentium,* with the decisions of judges; but in *Leviathan* we learn that he considers the real judges of English adjudication to be the jury members who consult the jurists (that is, the judges on the bench) on points of law. So when he now says that the "responses of jurists" are law, he is describing common law precedents as the tacit "will of the sovereign, which is declared in the fact that he has allowed the opinion to become customary." So Hobbes has moved from denying that common law is law in the *Elements* to admitting that common law is law in *De Cive.*

But in *Leviathan,* Hobbes's normative preference for statutory law causes him to describe adjudication in terms that exclude the common law from the kinds of human law. Still, so intertwined are Hobbes's descriptive and normative agendas that it is never quite clear whether Hobbes thinks that common law is not actually law in England or whether he simply hopes that it become replaced by statutory codification. This elimination of common law reasoning from the permissible kinds of civil law is curious because Hobbes certainly has the resources within his theory to redescribe common law as the tacit will of the sovereign—even if this redescription is implausible.

For civil law is the will of the sovereign, and that will is made manifest to those who must obey the law by some sign: "For the will of another cannot be understood but by his own word, or act, or by conjecture taken from his scope and purpose, which in the person of the commonwealth is to be supposed always consonant to equity and reason" (L, 26, 15, p. 178). So although law is essentially the will of the sovereign, it is essential to the moral force of law that it be promulgated: "The command of the commonwealth is law only to those that have means to take notice of it" (L, 26, 12, p. 177). Indeed, not only must the content of the legal norm be made known to those subject to it, its source in the will of the sovereign must also be made known (L, 26, 16, p. 178).

The moral salience of promulgation is at the center of Hobbes's normative arguments for the superiority of statutory law, since these laws are much more perspicuous than is common law. The will of the sovereign, however, cannot be known except through signs: Hobbes distinguishes "express signs" from "signs by inference." Express signs "are words spoken with understanding of what they signify" and signs by inference are "sometimes the consequence of words, sometimes the consequences of silence; sometimes the consequence of actions, sometimes the consequence of forbearing an action" (L, 14, 13–14, pp. 82–83). Among the "signs by inference" are the actions of the sovereign, which Hobbes calls "natural signs" of his will (L, 19, 21, p. 126). Although Hobbes believed that the natural signs of countenance and deeds are more reliable guides to the thoughts and passions than are words, in the case of law he says that we should resort to natural signs only where express signs are wanting (L, 19, 21, p. 126). Custom is such a tacit sign, since "whatsoever custom a man may by word control, and does not, it is a natural sign he would have the custom stand" (L, 19, 21, p. 126). Of course, this argument that what "the sovereign permits, he commands" depends upon some highly questionable assumptions, such as that the sovereign knows all the relevant customs, that he knows he might revoke them at will, and that he deliberately decides to permit them to stand.

Custom, in particular the custom of following precedents, seems to vanish from Hobbes's account of adjudication. So Hobbes says of a judge, "If the sovereign employ a public minister, without written instructions what to do, he is obliged to take for instructions the dictates of reason" (L, 26, 14, p. 177). In other words, either if the codified statutes do not cover a case or if the statutes themselves are unclear, the judge must infer that the will of the sovereign is natural equity. "Now the intention of the legislator is always supposed to be equity" (L, 26, 26, p. 183). But, at common law, where statutes are lacking, judges are required to seek guidance from precedents rather than from their own judgment about the dictates of reason.

Because law is essentially the will of the sovereign, and because that will can be known only indirectly through signs, "all laws, written and unwritten, have need of interpretation" (L, 26, 21, p. 180). Even where a code of laws provides for a particular case, that code must be interpreted because "not the letter . . . but that which is according to the intention of the legislator, is the law" (L, 26, 11, p. 176). And the intention of the legislator is, by hypothesis, natural equity. In short, where a judge must interpret a statute, or where he must simply decide without express guidance, his duty is to do what he thinks natural justice requires: "The interpretation of the law of nature is the sentence of the judge. . . . For in the act of judicature the judge doth no more but consider, whether the demand of the party be consonant to natural reason and equity" (L, 26, 23, p. 181).

What the judge must not do is follow the precedent set by another judge, since "no man's error becomes his own law, nor obliges him to persist in it" (L, 26, 24, p. 181). Hobbes is right that the custom of following precedents serves precisely to prevent each judge from deciding by his own lights what natural equity demands. Hobbes's judge takes his law not from precedents but "from nothing but the statutes and constitutions of the sovereign" (L, 26, 27, p. 183). Of course, without a custom of following precedents, each judge's ruling is law only for the parties before them. Hobbes obviously believes that justice is better served by allowing each judge to determine what natural equity demands in each case, rather than by constraining the discretion of judges by the practice of following precedents. What is remarkable is that Hobbes allows this normative argument to lead him to deny that the custom of following precedents has valid legal force in England. Yet if any custom could be plausibly interpreted as the tacit will of the sovereign, it would be the custom of following precedents: that the sovereign could but has not revoked it makes it, by Hobbes's account, a natural sign of the sovereign will.

Once we see the distinction between what is positive by source and what is positive by content, we can appreciate the irony of Hobbes's *Dialogue Between a Philosopher and a Student of the Common Laws of England*. Where we might expect Hobbes to be the advocate of positive law and the common lawyer to be the advocate of natural law, actually, as Martin Kreile notes, "Hobbes was the advocate of natural law, the English jurists were the legal positivists, not the other way round."[47] It would be more precise to say that, in this dialogue, Hobbes champions law that is positive by source but natural in content, while the common lawyer champions law that is positive in content but not in source. We shall see how Hobbes's normative case for statutory law leads him both to misdescribe common law and to deny that it is law.

We saw that Hobbes told us in *Leviathan* that he would not tell us "what is law here and there, but what is law" (L, 26, 1, p. 173); nonetheless, in the *Dialogue* Hobbes ventures to tell us what is law in England, even though, by his own theory, "[i]t is not Wisdom, but Authority that makes a Law" (D, 3, p. 55). Hobbes clearly thought that his own wisdom could identify English law more accurately than could the legal authorities of his day. We saw that in *Leviathan* the civil law comprised positive statutes and natural equity, with no place for common law; we shall find this same argument in the *Dialogue:* "Statutes are not Philosophy, as is the Common-Law, and other disputable Arts, but are Commands or Prohibitions . . . so that the Positive Laws of all Places are Statutes" (D, 30, p. 69). Yet Hobbes also offers arguments for why common law might be understood as an indirect command of the sovereign: "In *England* it is the King that makes the Laws, whosover Pens them" (D, 11, p. 59). Like a good lawyer, Hobbes thus will simultaneously argue that statutory law is superior to common law, that common law ultimately is a kind of statutory law, and that common law is not even law.

Hobbes begins his normative case for statutory law by having the philosopher ask a very provocative question: Why do we need statutes at all, if judges are to settle all disputes according to the light of natural reason (D, 7, p. 57)? Hobbes here entertains the possibility of a legal system without any law—that is, a system of mandatory jurisdiction for the settling of disputes, not on the basis of fixed legal rules and principles but simply on the basis of each judge's sense of justice. This radical question ironically provokes the common lawyer to set forth the Hobbesian case for statutory law. The lawyer begins by asserting that without "Humane Law" all things would be common in the war of all against all (D, 9, p. 58). From this premise about the necessity for some kind of human

47. Martin Kriele, "Notes on the Controversy between Hobbes and English Jurists," in *Hobbes-Forschungen,* ed. Reinhart Koselleck and Roman Schnur (Berlin: Dunker und Humblot, 1969), pp. 211–22, at 215.

law, the lawyer then concludes that "you may see the great Necessity there was of Statute Laws, for the preservation of all Mankind" (D, 10, p. 58). Indeed, Hobbes goes so far as to have the common lawyer say: "It is also a dictate of the Law of Reason, that Statute Laws are a necessary means of the safety and well being of Man in the present World" (D, 10, p. 58).

It falls to the philosopher to fill in the missing steps of this defense of the rational necessity of statutory law: "The King cannot make his Laws effectual, nor defend his People against their Enemies, without a Power to Leavy Souldiers" (D, 11, p. 59). So the necessity for the use of public authority to establish courts, enforce their judgments, and defend the nation from its enemies all speak to the necessity for statutory law. In addition to these plausible public-policy grounds for executive statutory authority, Hobbes insists that only statutes meet the criteria defining the rational essence of law: "A Law is the Command of him, or them that have the Soveraign Power, given to those that be his or their Subjects, declaring Publickly, and plainly what every of them may do, and what they must forbear to do" (D, 32, p. 71). With his doctrines that it is "the King that makes the Laws, whosoever Pens them" (D, 11, p. 59) and that custom and common law reflect the tacit will of the sovereign (D, 27, p. 67), Hobbes can bring common law within his definition of law as sovereign command. But common law seems utterly to fail the requirement that law must declare our duties publicly and plainly; indeed, the philosopher and the lawyer agree that even statutes are not sufficiently promulgated. The philosopher argues that justice requires that the book of penal statutes be as common in every home as the Bible (D, 35, p. 72). Of course, the common law cannot be publicly and plainly promulgated, since it is buried in a vast library of law reports, digests, and commentaries.

No doubt the case for statutory law, because of the importance of clear promulgation, is strongest for the criminal law. As for private law, the lawyer takes Hobbes's view that "a Just Action is that which is not against the Law" (D, 36, p. 72); the philosopher then continues that thus, "before there was a Law, there could be no Injustice . . . and before there could be laws, there must be a law-maker (D, 36, pp. 72–73). Here Hobbes lays out the essential underpinnings of his defense of statutory law: natural reason cannot establish stable conventions of justice, since there are as many natural reasons as there are judges (D, 157, p. 140); custom cannot establish stable conventions of justice—not even courts of justice, due to "the variety and repugnancy of Judgments of Common-Law" (D, 56, p. 84; cf. 30, p. 69; 67, p. 89). Only a sovereign law-giver can establish a stable, enforceable convention for deciding what is just and unjust. The lawyer then concludes where he began: "Without Statute-Laws, all Men have Right to all things" (D, 36, p. 73).

Hobbes's case for statutory law rests on premises about the unity of sovereignty, about the nature of reason, and about interpretation that make it very difficult for him to understand, describe, or acknowledge common law. The English bar and bench have over time expressed many incompatible views of the relation between common law and statutory law. But most jurists, I think, would agree that England has, in the main, two independent sources of law: Parliamentary statute and common law. These two sources are independent in the sense that statutes do not derive their authority from common law and common law does not derive its authority from statutes. Now the independence of these two sources of law undermines the unity of legal command required by Hobbes's theory of sovereignty. By Hobbes's logic, either common law must be subordinated to statute (perhaps by statutory codification of common law or explicit statutory authorization of common law jurisdiction) or statutory law must be subordinated to common law (perhaps giving common law judges the right to interpret, control, or even nullify statutes).[48] If we assume, with Hobbes, that the sovereign in England is the king in Parliament (L, 26, 10, p. 176), then common law must be subordinated to statutory law, because statutes reflect the express, while common law reflects at best only the tacit, will of the sovereign. Hobbes must deny that common law is an independent source of law because his theory of sovereignty cannot permit two independent sources of law.

Hobbes often argues that common law is law only insofar as it is the law of reason. But Hobbes's understanding of reason is so different from that of a common lawyer that he misdescribes the role of reason in the common law. English jurists had claimed that reason is the life of the common law: they meant that generations of learned judges and jurists had built up and refined a body of law whose comprehensiveness and subtlety surpasses the wisdom of any one man. As a product of artificial or artful reasoning upon distinctively English customs, institutions, and cases, the common law is rational in the sense that its unique rules and doctrines are, at best, merely compatible with, but not derivable from, natural reason.[49] The most that could be said about the common

48. To prove that common law is not law, Hobbes thus says: "Nor will you find in any Statute the word Common-Law" (D, 80, p. 97).

49. Though Hobbes ascribes the strong claim that "Common Law it self is nothing else but Reason" to Coke (D, 3, p. 54).

law as a whole is that it is rationally permitted, not that it is rationally required. The "lawyer" in Hobbes's dialogue, though he occasionally expresses the views of Sir Edward Coke, just as often expresses Hobbes's own views. But his description of law as an "artificial perfection of Reason gotten by long Study, Observation and Experience, and not of every Mans natural Reason" (D, 3, p. 55) is from Coke. English judges are not supposed to decide cases by the light of their own natural reason or conscience; they are supposed to decide cases according to rules established by earlier and similar cases. But there cannot always be rules for determining how to identify and to apply rules; indeed, the search for such rules quickly generates a logical regress. So common law reasoning is not just the application of general moral and legal principles to the material of the cases; rather, long experience in studying both legal rules and case materials leads to a capacity for recognizing how new cases fit into existing lines of cases. Common law reasoning is a matter less of deduction or algorithm and more of pattern recognition.

Moreover, because the development and shape of the common law reflects the historical accidents of the various legal controversies that generate new law, in common law reasoning there can be no substitute for mastering the brute historical materials. These materials include the factual contexts of earlier controversies as well as various and sundry rules, categories, and principles of widely varying degrees of rational generality. It is tempting to suppose that one might simply extract the legal rules, categories, and principles from this morass of factual circumstances and then apply the extracted rules to the facts of new cases; unfortunately, however, these rules, categories, and principles get much of their force, weight, and scope from their factual contexts. Common law is not a fixed system of rules applied to ever-changing facts. Common law, as Edward Levi famously said, is a moving system of classification, in which the rules, categories, and principles evolve as a consequence of the evolving facts. The essence of common law is thus the inseparability of its rational form and its brute factual content.

Of course, Hobbes recognizes no other kind of reason than computation (L, 5, 2, pp. 22–23); the judgments or pattern recognition of common law are for him nothing more than mere prudence. Hobbes accepts Coke's view that reason is the soul of the law, but he interprets it to mean that a judge uses his natural reason to interpret statutory law in accordance with the natural law principles of equity (D, 3, p. 54). Equity, says Hobbes, is in the heart of every man, not in the ancient legal materials (D, 57, p. 84), just as "philosophy, that is, *natural reason,* is innate in every man" (Logic 1, 1, p. 173). To become a good judge or a good philosopher requires, he thinks, not long study of the achievements of the past but merely the mastery of the right algorithmic method. He suggests that two months of study are sufficient for mastery of English law (D, 6, p. 56). All of this supposes that the rules, categories, and principles of common law might be extracted from their factual contexts, codified into statutory provisions, and then applied to new facts as they emerge.

Hobbes's view of reason as a capacity for logical and mathematical reckoning causes him to misunderstand the sense in which customs are judged as rational by common law. "I deny that any Custome of its own Nature, can amount to the authority of a Law: For if the Custom be unreasonable, you must with all other Lawyers confess that it is no Law, but ought to be abolished; and if the Custom be reasonable, it is not the Custom, but the Equity that makes it Law" (D, 80, p. 96; cf. 162, p. 143). But where legal customs have rational authority it is precisely because they are neither unreasonable, in the sense of directly contrary to natural justice, nor simply reasonable, in the sense of required by natural reason. Most legal customs, such as the custom of following precedents, are, at best, rationally permissible, not, as Hobbes seems to demand, rationally required. Indeed, reason requires that the content of law not be itself rationally required: if law is to serve as an effective instrument for guiding and coordinating conduct, then it must establish precise determinations and clear lines; but such precision and clarity must be largely contingent in detail, and custom often effectively establishes such determinations. So common lawyers defend legal custom on the grounds of the utility of its positive content, while Hobbes defends custom only on the grounds of its coincidence with natural reason.

Hobbes recognizes the need for laws that are positive in content, that is, laws whose content can make wrongful what was not previously wrongful. But Hobbes argues that all laws that are positive in content must also be positive in origin (that is, statutory). As we have just observed, he says that customs are lawful only when they coincide with natural reason. So if customs cannot introduce the nonrational and largely arbitrary determinations of civil law, then we must look to statutes. Hobbes is right to say "that which is no Sin in it self, but indifferent, may be made Sin by a positive Law" (D, 47, p. 78). Indifferent actions are often made wrongful by prohibitions that are positive in content, whether statutory or customary. Why does Hobbes seem to assume that such "positive" prohibitions need be statutory? "As when the Statute was in force; that no Man should wear Silk in his Hat, after the Statute, such wearing of Silk was a Sin, which was not so before." Many morally indifferent acts are made wrongful by nonstatutory rules that are positive in content, such as commercial customs and common law rules.

Why does Hobbes argue that what is positive in content must also be positive in origin? Is it because he never explicitly distinguishes these two senses of "positive" and uses the term ambiguously? Obviously, in the *Dialogue* Hobbes often uses "positive" to refer to the source of a law in deliberate enactment. Thus, Hobbes says that "the Positive Laws of all Places are Statutes" (D, 30, p. 69). Here by "positive" Hobbes is clearly referring to the source of a law in deliberate enactment; this is why Joseph Cropsey identifies "positive" law with "statute law" (D, Intro., p. 16). Still, so deep is the ambiguity of the discourse of positive law that this statement, "the Positive Laws of all Places are Statutes," might just as well be read to express Hobbes's view that laws positive in content are always statutes, that is, laws positive in origin. Does Hobbes also use "positive" to refer to the content of a law? Throughout the *Dialogue,* he contrasts statutory law to common law (D, 4, p. 55; 26, p. 67; 30, p. 69; etc.), but in one place the lawyer describes the contrast of common law courts and equitable courts as a contrast of "Positive Laws" and the "Law of Reason" (D, 31, p. 70). Here "positive" clearly refers not to statutory law (which is not at issue) but to the differing content of common law rules and the rules of equity. The rules of the common law are "positive" in the sense of morally contingent; for example, a valid will must be attested by two witnesses. Such contingent rules can frequently lead to grave injustice in particular cases; this is why the sometimes arbitrary harshness of judgments at common law traditionally could be remedied by appeal to equity, or natural justice. With respect to the content of legal norms, there is no doubt that, by comparison with equity, common law is positive law. That Hobbes unknowingly uses the term *positive* to refer sometimes to the source of a law and sometimes to its content might help explain why he should assume that a law that is positive in content must also be positive in origin.

Positive Language and Law in Divine Worship and Verbal Apostasy

We saw that Aquinas's discussion of positive law led him to accept Aristotle's doctrine that positive law governs those matters that are morally indifferent; yet, as we also saw, the notion that there could be morally indifferent matters of legislative choice violates Aquinas's own moral doctrine. Hobbes also asserts that positive law governs matters that are morally indifferent: "That which is no Sin in itself, but indifferent, may be made Sin by a positive Law" (D, 47, p. 78). Hobbes goes much further than Aquinas, of course, when he says that "every action in its own nature is indifferent. What is *just* or *unjust* derives from the right of the ruler" (DC, 12, 1, p. 132). Here he seems to be asserting that external actions are merely arbitrary signs of the mind, that no action has a natural connection to a particular disposition of the will. What this means is that, if commanded by law, one can perform some actions associated with theft, adultery, and murder without violating the natural law forbidding theft, adultery, and murder because virtually all actions are compatible with a virtuous will to seek peace by obeying the law (DC, 14, 10, p. 159). On this view, actions are as arbitrarily related to the will as words are to conceptions.

Yet elsewhere Hobbes argues, to the contrary, that actions have a natural connection to the will. We saw that he follows Augustine in holding that our countenance and actions are better signs of our passions than are words (L, 6, 56, p. 34). And in his discussion of how God ought to be honored, he says that "not all actions are signs by constitution, but some are naturally signs of honour, others of contumely" (L, 31, 39, p. 242). Natural law seems to demand not only that God be worshipped and honored but also that he be worshipped and honored in the naturally right manner (DC, 15, 14, p. 178). In particular, natural sacred law requires that God be worshipped publicly and uniformly (DC, 15, 15, p. 181). Perhaps most significantly, in the case of actions honoring God, Hobbes says that some actions are by nature intrinsically oriented toward honor, such "as to draw near, and discourse decently and humbly, to give way, or to yield in any matter of private benefit," while other actions are by nature oriented toward dishonor, such as the exposure of bodily indecency. Hobbes then asserts that no sovereign may require God to be honored by actions that are by nature scornful (DC, 15, 16, p. 182; L, 31, 39, p. 242); "for no one could take a profusion of insults or total absence of worship as a mode of worship" (DC, 15, 18, p. 184).

In the case, then, of the moral requirement that we honor God, Hobbes does not hold that "all actions are indifferent"; there are natural law limits on what a sovereign can require of his subjects in how they worship God.[50] In *Leviathan*,

---

50. In DC (15, 18, p. 184) Hobbes says that "one must not obey" a sovereign command to scorn God in gesture; in *Leviathan* (31, 39, p. 242) he says that such scorn "cannot be made by human power a part of Divine worship." Thus Martinich goes too far when he says of Hobbes that "he thinks that people should accept the religion of the sovereign because citizens owe him obedience concerning all public behavior, religious ritual included." *The Two Gods of* Leviathan, p. 302.

Hobbes restates his view that there are natural kinds of worship, including gifts, petitions, thanks, submission of body, and so on (L, 12, 10, p. 66; 31, 10, p. 238). As in *De Cive,* these natural signs of honor are dictated by natural reason (DC, 15, 15–16, pp. 179–82; L, 31, 34, p. 241). Hobbes here reiterates the constraint this places upon the civil sovereign: natural signs of contumely "cannot be made by human power a part of Divine worship"; in addition, and even more constraining, natural signs of honor cannot "ever be separated from it" (L, 31, 39, p. 242). Nor are these constraints on sovereign power limited to actions oriented to God: "Injustice, ingratitude, arrogance, pride, iniquity, acceptation of persons, and the rest, can never be made lawful. For it can never be that war shall preserve life, and peace destroy it" (L, 15, 38, p. 100). So what happened to Hobbes's view that "all actions are indifferent" before the laying down of positive law?

Hobbes often argues that words are inherently more arbitrary than actions, that although some actions have an intrinsic relation to honor, no words have an intrinsic relation to honor. Whereas all words "have their signification by agreement and constitution of men . . . not all actions are signs by constitution, but some are naturally signs of honour, others of contumely" (L, 31, 38–39, p. 242). From this distinction, Hobbes concludes that a sovereign may require any verbal utterance in the worship of God (L, 31, 38, p. 242). But is it right that although a sovereign may not require any possible action, he might require any possible words in the public worship of God? Here Hobbes should have said that words have their public reference (*denotatio*) by the constitution of men, but that words get their private significance (*significatio*) from the natural and habitual dispositions and passions of individuals (L, 4, 24, p. 21). Since the public denotation of words is structured and constrained by their private signification, then even on Hobbes's account the sovereign is not absolutely free to require any words in the public worship of God. Just as the sovereign stipulation of a set of actions to honor God is constrained by the natural significance of those actions, so the sovereign stipulation of a set of words to honor God is constrained by the natural significance of those words. The sovereign, no doubt, has a wide range of freedom in determining the exact denotation of the words and actions that might be required in public worship; but this range is nonetheless constrained by the natural private significance of those words— unless we suppose that one could honor God by uttering words whose private significance is to dishonor God.

Hobbes's claim that a sovereign might require any verbal utterance in the worship of God rests upon a radical separation of public denotation from private signification. Because Hobbes never developed his account of the relation of denotation to signification, it is not clear just how separable he thought they might be. Nowhere is this divorce of denotation from signification more dramatically illustrated than in Hobbes's defense of verbal apostasy. For Hobbes, the essence of the Christian religion is the inward belief that Jesus is the Christ; such inward belief, he claims, is perfectly compatible with obedience to a civil law requiring us to deny verbally that Jesus is the Christ.[51] Because denotation involves a direct relation of word to object, my public act of denotation simply bypasses my private act of signification: so my inward act of faith is untouched by my outward apostasy. Because denotation is thus emancipated from signification, our salvation is not held hostage to whatever verbal professions of faith might be required of a civil sovereign. Of course, such a radical disjunction of public denotation from private signification is not required by Hobbes's more modest doctrine that positive denotation is not uniquely determined by natural signification.

By contrast, Aquinas's strong subordination of denotation to signification leads him to a quite different understanding of verbal apostasy. Given his view that words denote objects only through the mediation of concepts of the mind, one cannot knowingly deny an article of faith without conceptualizing that denial. We name things as we know them in thought—meaning that verbal professions are never simply external but always require the collusion of the mind. Of course, one might, for the sake of argument, entertain the hypothesis that "God does not exist" without in any way judging, asserting, or professing that God does not exist. Nonetheless, for Aquinas, verbal apostasy in the sense of a profession is utterly inconsistent with an inward act of faith, since faith is the orientation of the whole person, mind, word, and body to God.[52] Although Aquinas always insists that words get their meaning from the imposition of men, he does not hold that the meaning of words is subject to arbitrary transformation. For a sovereign to declare that we honor God by denying that Jesus is the Christ does not cause those words to lose their customary meaning for individuals.

---

51. True, Hobbes does say that to "renounce" the article of faith that "Jesus is the Christ" is "*Apostasy*" (DC, 18, 11, p. 244). Here, however, by "apostasy" Hobbes seems to mean not verbal but inward renunciation, since in *Leviathan* he explicitly says that a Christian "holding firmly in his heart the faith of Christ" is free verbally to deny that faith because "profession with the tongue is but an external thing" (L, 42, 11, p. 338).

52. "Ad fidem pertinet non solum credulitas cordis, sed etiam protestatio interioris fidei per exteriora verba et facta; nam confessio est actus fidei. Et per hunc etiam modum quaedam exteriora verba vel opera ad infidelitatem pertinet in quantum sunt infidelitatis signa, per modum quo signum sanitatis *sanum* dicitur." ST, II-II, 12.1 and 2.

Chapter 4 Positive Law

in the Analytical Positivism

of John Austin

THE LAST OF THE SCHOOLMEN

John Austin occupies a unique position in the history of the discourse of positive law: no legal theorist makes more use of the expression *positive law* than does Austin. Although Austin was in some respects a disciple of Jeremy Bentham, nowhere does he stray further from his master than in his discourse of "positive law," which, as we shall see, brings him closer to the concerns of Thomas Aquinas and Thomas Hobbes than to those of Bentham.[1] Bentham, after all, insisted above

1. Many commentators describe Austin simply as a disciple of Bentham: "Austin followed very much in Bentham's footsteps, though he did not command his master's powers of innovation in logic." H. L. A Hart, "Jhering's Heaven of Concepts," in *Essays in Jurisprudence and Philosophy* (Oxford: Clarendon Press, 1983), pp. 265–77, at 273. Obviously Hart is aware that, after the publication of his first lectures on jurisprudence, Austin distanced himself radically from Bentham's politics. For an assessment of this distance, see Lotte and Joseph Hamburger, *Troubled Lives: John and Sarah Austin* (Toronto: University of Toronto Press, 1985), chap. 9, "Did Austin Remain an Austinian?" But even in his early lectures on jurisprudence, Austin's commitment to rule utilitarianism and his grounding of utility in divine law show him marching out of

all upon sharply distinguishing the enterprise of expository jurisprudence (the science of law as it is) from the quite different enterprise of censorial jurisprudence (the science of law as it ought to be). Given that Austin famously limits the "province of jurisprudence" to "positive law,"[2] many of his students and commentators have wondered why he devotes three of his six published lectures to the topics of divine law and moral truth; why, in short, so much censorial jurisprudence in a treatise purporting to define the domain of expository jurisprudence?[3]

These Benthamite puzzles disappear when we see Austin's legal thought in relation to the traditional discourse of positive law, for, as we have seen, the discourse of positive law has always been inseparable from questions of natural law, divine law, and moral truth. Because Austin framed his expository jurisprudence in the language of positive law, he could not avoid the closely connected topics of moral truth and divine law. Austin's decision to build the notion of positive law into the framework of his legal thought brought him willy-nilly into all the quandaries of positivity from Plato through Aquinas and up to Hobbes. In short, Austin's bold "philosophy of positive law," far from emancipating him from the ancient traditions of legal thought, sucked him deeply into them. For these reasons, Austin's jurisprudence is much more traditional than Bentham's. Unfortunately, the Benthamite reading continues to dominate the interpretation of Austin, obscuring his deeper understanding of the relation of positive law to divine law and to natural law. As we shall see, Austin's conception of a general jurisprudence—what he calls "the philosophy of positive law"—deeply qualifies Bentham's careful separation of expository from censorial jurisprudence.

If anyone could be expected to cut through the conceptual knots of the dis-

---

step with Bentham. See Wilfrid Rumble, *The Thought of John Austin* (London: Athlone Press, 1985), chap. 3, "Divine Law, Utilitarian Ethics, and Positivist Jurisprudence."

2. Strictly speaking, jurisprudence on Austin's account takes in some nonpositive laws, such as declaratory, repealing, and imperfect laws.

3. Henry Sumner Maine led a chorus of complaints that Austin's lectures on utilitarianism were "the most serious blemish in the *Province of Jurisprudence Determined*" because "it is a discussion belonging not to the philosophy of law but to the philosophy of legislation." Maine, *Lectures on the Early History of Institutions* (New York: Henry Holt, 1975), pp. 369–70. Even today, Michael Lobban complains: "Austin created confusion by spending much time in the *Province of Jurisprudence Determined* discussing utilitarian theory. Yet this was irrelevant to *jurisprudence* . . . utility was clearly part of the science of ethics, and had nothing to do with law *as* law." *The Common Law and English Jurisprudence, 1760–1850* (Oxford: Clarendon Press, 1991), pp. 246 and 254.

course of positive law it would be John Austin. He is famous, if not infamous, for the contempt he poured on what he saw as verbal and conceptual confusion in other writers: "He disdained the 'mischievous and detestable abuse of articulate language,' and in his work he frequently complained about 'verbal ambiguities,' 'muddy speculation,' 'confusion of ideas' (by Fichte and Godwin) and 'double logical error' (by Bentham and various German writers), 'impenetrable obscurity' (of Blackstone and Hale), and the use of a term (by Locke and Bentham) that was 'pregnant with confusion and perplexity.'"[4] Austin deeply admired and aspired to employ "the language of logicians"—language, he said, "unrivalled for brevity, distinctness, and precision."[5] J. S. Mill reported that "Mr. Austin once said of himself, that if he had any special intellectual vocation, it was that of 'untying knots' . . . the clearing up of the puzzles arising from complex combinations of ideas confusedly apprehended, and not analysed into their elements." According to Mill, moreover, Austin's aspiration to precision and clarity were genuine achievements: "In this judgment he [Austin] estimated his own qualifications very correctly."[6]

Even Austin's severest critics praise the logical rigor and precision of his thought and language. Henry Maine praises his "rigidly consistent terminology," and John Chipman Gray admires "his unwillingness to let others juggle with words, or to juggle with them himself."[7] H. L. A. Hart memorably said that when Austin was clearly wrong, at least he was wrong clearly: "Austin was determined to use in his analysis only clear, hard, empirical terms intelligible to common sense, but for this laudable enterprise he chose the wrong fundamental notions."[8] Hart is thinking here of Austin's analysis of the elements of the concept of law, such as command, duty, sanction, habit, and sovereign. The term *positive* is as central to Austin's analysis of law as any other framework term, yet the discourse of law's "positivity" is anything but clear, hard, empiri-

4. Hamburger, *Troubled Lives,* p. 50.

5. Austin, *The Province of Jurisprudence Determined* [1832] (hereafter PJD), ed. H. L. A. Hart (London: Weidenfeld and Nicolson, 1954), p. 18.

6. J. S. Mill, "Review of Austin's *Lectures on Jurisprudence,*" *Edinburgh Review* 118 (1863): 222–44, at 223.

7. Maine, *Lectures on the Early History of Institutions,* p. 369; J. C. Gray, *The Nature and Sources of Law,* 2nd edition (Gloucester, Mass.: Peter Smith, 1972), p. 3.

8. "Like our own Austin . . . Holmes was sometimes clearly wrong; but again like Austin, when this was so he was always wrong clearly." Hart, "Positivism and the Separation of Law and Morals" in *Essays in Jurisprudence and Philosophy* (Oxford: Clarendon Press, 1983), pp. 49–87, at 49. See also Hart's introduction to Austin's PJD, p. xi.

cal, or commonsensical. Did Austin master the ambiguities of the discourse of positive law or was he mastered by them? What implications does the language of "positivity" have for Austin's conceptual clarity, doctrinal coherence, and theoretical aims?

Austin's analysis of sovereignty, command, sanction, and habit have all been subjected to searching critical scrutiny by his commentators, but his understanding of "positive" law and morality has largely escaped notice. Andreas Schwarz observed that Austin's use of the expression *positive law* is curious, since, although the expression can be found in Hobbes and Hume, "its use was not widespread and it seems not to occur as a technical term with Blackstone and Bentham." Actually, the expression *positive law* does occur as a technical term in Blackstone and Bentham, but Schwarz is right that Austin's first masters at law almost never use it.[9] Because the discourse of positive law has been ubiquitous in European juristic commentary since the twelfth century, Schwarz is no doubt right in asserting that "the expression 'positive law' had already become familiar to Austin before his German studies."[10] How could any student of law and jurisprudence not be familiar with the expression *positive law?* That Austin chose to make the discourse of positive law so central to his whole conceptual framework is puzzling—especially in light of the fact that his alleged master Bentham very carefully avoided doing so.

We must take seriously this elegiac reflection of Austin's: "I was born out of time and place. I ought to have been a schoolman of the twelfth century—or a German professor."[11] As we shall see, Austin's discourse of positive law reveals that, in many respects, he was a twelfth-century Schoolman, by way of being a German professor. Austin tells us that he borrowed his subtitle "the philosophy of positive law" from the German jurist Hugo (LJ, p. 32), and Schwarz usefully

9. Andreas B. Schwarz, "John Austin and the German Jurisprudence of His Time," *Politica* 1 (August 1934): 178–99, at 194n. For Blackstone's contrast of "natural duties" to "positive [legal] duties" and for his contrast of positive and common law, see *Blackstone,* 5th Edition, vol. 1, introduction, sec. 2, pp. 57–58, and sec. 3.10, p. 92. (Dublin: John Exshaw et al., 1773); for Bentham's use of "positive law," see *Deontology Together with A Table of the Springs of Action and the Article on Utilitarianism,* ed. Amnon Goldworth (Oxford: Clarendon Press, 1983), p. 34, and *Legislator of the World: Writings on Codification, Law and Education,* ed. Philip Schofield and Jonathan Harris (Oxford: Clarendon Press, 1998), pp. 29 and 203.

10. Schwarz, "John Austin and the German Jurisprudence of His Times," p. 194n.

11. John Austin's confession here is reported by Sarah Austin in her preface to his *Lectures on Jurisprudence: Or the Philosophy of Positive Law* (LJ), 5th edition, ed. Robert Campbell (London: John Murray, 1885), p. 12.

shows that several of the other German jurists studied by Austin also make positive law central to their analytical frameworks.[12] These contemporary German treatises on law represented the culmination of the whole medieval and early modern Scholastic tradition of commentary on Roman law; they were Austin's guide to the discourse of positive law among the medieval Schoolmen, for Austin tells us that by "positive" law he is translating the Latin "*positum*."[13] Indeed, his discourse of positive law often reads like a flat-footed translation of Scholastic Latin. For example, when he says, "Every positive law, or rule of positive law, exists *as such* by the pleasure of the sovereign" (LJ, p. 36), he is echoing standard Scholastic formulae.[14] Austin is much better understood as the last of the Schoolmen rather than the first of the Benthamites.

POSITIVE LAW AS LAW IMPOSED
BY THE SOVEREIGN

Our concern, however, is not with the origin of Austin's discourse but with its meaning and implications for his legal thought. What does Austin mean by positive law? Here, origin might well shed light on his meaning, since Austin twice tells us that in saying "positive" he means the Latin "*positum*," and we saw that Thomas Aquinas often uses this word and other variants of *pono* to refer to the act of imposing or laying down a statute.[15] Austin uses a variety of English expressions to render *ius positum*, such as law "set" or "established" or existing "by position." Each of these renderings manages to capture the Latin badly by means of awkward English. The closest that Austin comes to a formal or official

12. Schwarz cites not only Hugo's *Lehrbuch des Naturrechts, als eine Philosophie des positiven Rechts* (1798) but also Daniel Nettelbladt's *Systema elementare universae Jurisprudentiae positivae* and N. Falck's *Juristische Encyklopädie*, 5th edition, ed. R. Ihering (Leipzig: Verlags-magazin, 1851), in which Falck discusses positive divine law, positive civil law, and positive law of nations. See Schwarz, "John Austin and the German Jurisprudence of His Time," pp. 192 and 194.

13. Austin, "The Uses of the Study of Jurisprudence," in PJD, pp. 365–93, at 365; LJ, p. 548.

14. For example, Iacobus de Ravinis asks about a rule of contract law: "Si tu queras quare est speciale. Dico sic placuit legislatori . . . unde ius impositum est." *Lectura Super Codice C.* 2.3.10; like Austin, Iacobus identifies *ius positivum* with *ius impositum* (cf. *Lectura Super Codice C.* 4.64.3). Texts in James Gordley, *The Philosophical Origins of Modern Contract Doctrine* (Oxford: Clarendon Press, 1991), p. 43 n. 54.

15. In the *Thesaurus Linguae Latinae*, s.v. *positus*, we read: *respicitur potius action ponendi, quae fit: imponendo vel efficiendo;* similarly, the *OED* begins its definition of "positive" with "formally laid down or imposed."

definition of positive law is a set of formulae that he repeatedly deploys, verbatim, throughout the *Province of Jurisprudence Determined:* "Every positive law or every law simply and strictly so called, is set by a sovereign person, or a sovereign body of persons, to a member or members of the independent political society wherein that person or body is sovereign or supreme. Or (changing the phrase) it is set by a monarch, or sovereign number, to a person or persons in a state of subjection to its author" (PJD, pp. 9, 132, 193, 253–54, 350). Austin does not directly say here that positive law is imposed by sovereigns on their subjects, but that seems to be his intent. The concept *positum* strongly suggests the action of imposing or laying down something from above; this top-down action is only weakly conveyed by Austin's description of law "set [down]" by a sovereign (above) to persons "in a state of subjection [below]." Austin seems to mean "imposed" when he says "set": "A father may set a *rule* to his child or children: a guardian, to this ward: a master, to his slave or servant" (PJD, p. 22).[16] When Austin distinguishes positive law from natural law, he says: "The aggregate of the rules, established by political superiors, is frequently styled *positive* law, or law existing *by position*" (PJD, p. 11). What is law existing "by position"? Austin explains: "Every positive law exists *as positive law* through the position or institution given to it by a sovereign government" (LJ, p. 534). Thus, "by position" means "by the institution of that present sovereign in the character of political superior" (PJD, p. 193). Austin captures the top-down force of positive law when he says: "Laws, and other commands are said to proceed from *superiors,* and to bind or oblige *inferiors*" (PJD, p. 24).

As we have seen, positive law, in the sense of law imposed by sovereign statute, has always been implicitly or explicitly contrasted with law that grows up by custom. Is Austin's understanding of positive law shaped by this underlying contrast with custom? Austin's contrast of positive law with positive morality seems to have emerged from a concern to distinguish true law from mere custom. Austin thus twice refers to the contrast of positive law to positive morality as the contrast of *ius* (law) to *mos* (custom).[17] Law is imposed from above, while customary morality grows up from below. Austin attacks those jurists who imagine that custom "exists as *positive law,* apart from the legislator or judge, by the institution of the private persons who observed it in its customary

16. After Austin says that the laws of God are "set by God to his human creatures" he refers to the "duties imposed by the Divine laws" (PJD, p. 34); he also speaks of *"laws set* or *imposed by general opinion"* (PJD, p. 140).

17. See Austin's Advertisement for his Lectures and his Letter to Sir William Erle, in LJ, pp. 16–17.

state" (LJ, p. 36). Custom is not positive law because it grows up from below: "At its origin, a custom is a rule of conduct which the governed observe spontaneously" (PJD, p. 31). Austin even contrasts positive law to constitutional law on the grounds that positive law is deliberately imposed, while constitutional law grows up from custom. Since all positive law is imposed by the sovereign, the institution of sovereignty is a precondition for, and not a product of, positive law. In short, positive law is *made,* but the constitution, if not imposed by a foreign sovereign, has *grown:* "In most societies political and independent, the constitution of the supreme government has *grown*" (PJD, p. 337). For this reason, the law of England (the *corpus iuris*) includes not just positive law but also constitutional "law."[18]

When he refers to "positive" law or law "strictly so-called," Austin seems to mean those commands imposed by the sovereign superior upon his subjects. Austin's best commentators have also understood his positive law to mean imposed law. Hart observes that if Austin had understood law in terms of a rule of recognition rather than in terms of a command, then "*set by a sovereign* would no longer appear as a defining characteristic of positive law" (PJD, p. xii). Herbert Morris similarly explains what Austin means by positive laws: "They are positive laws, laws imposed on human beings by a person or group of persons in a sovereign position."[19] Indeed, Austin's seemingly relentless focus on positive law as sovereign command has led to frequent and unfair quips that he learned his jurisprudence in the army or that his paradigm of law is a criminal statute. More importantly, however, some fundamental features of what is understood as Austinian positivism seem logically dependant upon this view that positive law can be identified by facts about its adoption quite apart from any normative debates about its content. According to Austin, jurisprudence "is concerned with positive laws, or with laws strictly so called, as considered without regard to their goodness or badness" (PJD, p. 126). Jurisprudence can become an objective science, says Austin, only on the presumption that its object of inquiry, positive law, can be reliably identified by empirical criteria independent of disputable normative evaluation. Austinian positivism is usually understood as an attempt to develop criteria to identify positive law based on what Dworkin calls its "pedigree" rather than on its content. According to Morison,

18. "A description, therefore, of the law which regards the constitution of the State . . . is an essential part of a complete *corpus iuris,* although, properly speaking, that so-called law is not positive law" (LJ, p. 746).

19. Morris, "Verbal Disputes and the Legal Philosophy of John Austin," *U.C.L.A. Law Review* 7 (1959–60): 27–56, at 53.

Austin followed Bentham in describing jurisprudence as an historical science, since it focuses on the datable events that mark the adoption and development of positive legal rules.[20]

POSITIVE LAW AS CONTINGENT IN CONTENT

According to the standard interpretation of Austin, law's positivity stems wholly from empirical facts about its source in an act of sovereign stipulation. Because law is positive owing to its pedigree, a positive law might have any kind of content, whether morally good or morally bad. Austin strongly distinguishes the existence of a positive law from its merit or demerit and tells us that the content of positive law sometimes coincides and sometimes conflicts with divine law (PJD, p. 159). Austin's entire project of sharply distinguishing law as it is from law as it ought to be rests upon his view that law's positivity stems from its source in sovereign command. Given the centrality of this conception of positive law to Austin's key theoretical aims, it is rather astonishing that, in addition to this familiar sense of positive law, Austin should also speak of law's positivity in quite a different sense. For example, Schwarz examined Austin's personal copy of Blackstone (edited by E. Christian in 1809) and found this marginal note by Austin: "Distinction between moral and natural laws (laws which are dictated by utility in all times and places) and laws which are merely positive laws (that is, of transient or local utility)."[21] Here, by "positive" Austin clearly does not mean "imposed" laws but laws with a particular kind of content—a moral content that is not universally valid but only locally valid.

As we shall see, throughout his writings, Austin distinguishes, within positive law, a universal natural law from a local positive law. So by "positive" law Austin will refer to two very different contrasts to "natural" law. In the first sense, positive law is the law actually imposed by the civil sovereign as opposed to the natural law, meaning law as it ought to be. This is the familiar contrast between the science of jurisprudence focused on actual positive law and the science of legislation focused on the natural law or what law ought to be. The science of positive law is taken to be an empirical science about law actually existing, while the science of legislation is taken to be a moral science about what

20. "Austin was surely right in a sense, at least about this part of Bentham's theory, when he said that Bentham belonged to the historical school." W. L. Morison, *John Austin* (Palo Alto: Stanford University Press, 1982), p. 92.

21. Schwarz, "John Austin and the German Jurisprudence of His Time," p. 194n.

law ideally would be if it conformed to objective moral truth. But this simple set of oppositions between positive law and natural law, between what is and what ought to be, between empirical legal science and moral legal science, fails to capture Austin's deeper legal analysis. For Austin will go on to distinguish, within positive law imposed by the sovereign, a natural or universal law from a local or positive law. In other words, within every positive legal system we find natural (or universal) law and positive (or purely local) law. Here the distinction between natural and positive law is not the distinction between legal ideal and legal fact but the distinction between universal legal norms and merely local legal norms. In this second sense, "positive" picks out not law imposed by the sovereign but law with a certain kind of content, namely, a local content.

Austin's unfamiliar distinction between natural and positive law within positive law does not merely add a level of complexity to his overall account of law and of the science of law, I think it forces us to revise that overall account. For if every legal system must contain both natural and positive law, then positive law cannot simply be defined in terms of facts about its pedigree or adoption. If legal science must distinguish natural from positive law within positive law, then it must do so on analysis of the content of those legal norms, not simply on the formal facts of their imposition. Furthermore, Austin will describe at least a part of the universal natural law as "necessary" because it is a fundamental requirement of human nature. Since no merely empirical science of law could possibly establish the necessity of certain legal norms, Austin has now blurred his own emphatic distinction between the science of law as it is and the science of law as it ought to be. Certain kinds of legal institutions are necessary because of the moral requirements of human life and other human goods. Distinguishing the necessary from the merely contingent norms of human law demands a science of jurisprudence both empirical and moral.

In a variety of contexts, Austin uses the term *positive* to refer to the content of norms that are not necessary but only contingent. Thus, for example, he contrasts the necessity of Aristotelian logic to the mere contingency of Roman law: he says that the study of Aristotle's logic is more important than the study of Roman law because "Roman Law is not *necessary.*" Roman law is filled with purely local and morally contingent rules and, in that sense, Roman law is positive law: "The great Roman Lawyers are, in truth, expositors of a positive or technical system. Not Lord Coke himself is more purely technical."[22] So when Austin says that Roman law is positive and not necessary, he clearly refers to the

---

22. Austin, "The Uses of the Study of Jurisprudence," PJD, pp. 378 and 376.

content of Roman legal rules and institutions, which he claims are not logically or morally necessary but only contingent. An empirical science of law might be able to distinguish, within positive law, what is universal (or nearly so) from what is merely local; but no empirical science can distinguish what is necessary from what is contingent: that is inescapably a normative judgment.

Austin's understanding of the relationship of natural to positive law within every system of positive law stems from his understanding of the ancient Roman distinction between the local civil law (*ius civile*) and the universal law of nations (*ius gentium*). Gaius says in the *Institutes*, "All peoples who are ruled by laws and customs use law that is partly their own and partly common to all mankind. The law which each people makes for itself is special to itself. It is called 'state law,' the law peculiar to that state. But the law which natural reason makes for all mankind is applied in the same way everywhere. It is called 'the law of all peoples' because it is common to every nation."[23] Austin cites this text in Latin but also offers his own revealing paraphrase: "Every independent nation has a positive law and morality ('*leges et mores*'), which are peculiar to itself. . . . Every nation, moreover, has a positive law and morality which it shares with every other nation."[24]

What does Austin make of this distinction? Austin tells us that Gaius's opening contrast of civil law to the law of nations is merely window dressing meant to show his familiarity with Greek moral philosophy; in Justianian's compilations, he says, this distinction "is speculative rather than practical" because the Roman jurists draw almost no important legal conclusions from it: "As a legal distinction, that of *ius civile* and *ius gentium* is nearly barren." But Austin does tell us of one important consequence of this distinction in Justianian: some classes of persons, such as women, soldiers, and minors, are permitted the excuse of ignorance of the law. "They are exempt from liability (at least for certain purposes), not by reason of their general imbecility, but because it is presumed that their capacity is not adequate to a knowledge of the law." But here the jurists insist that such persons cannot "allege with effect their ignorance of the law, in case they have violated those parts of it which are founded upon the *ius gentium*. For the persons in question are not generally imbecile, and the *ius gentium* is knowable *naturali ratione*. With regard to the *ius civile*, or to those parts of the Roman Law which are peculiar to the system, they may allege with effect their ignorance of the law."

23. *The Institutes of Gaius*, I, 1. I have adopted the translation of W. M. Gordon and O. F. Robinson (Ithaca: Cornell University Press, 1988), p. 19.
24. Austin, LJ, p. 563.

Of course, that the Roman lawyers sometimes found this distinction legally significant does not mean that Austin does. But Austin immediately goes on to offer his own assessment: "This coincides with our distinction between *malum prohibitum* and *malum in se;* and the distinction is reasonable. For some laws are so obviously suggested by utility, that any person not insane would naturally surmise or guess their existence; which they could not be expected to do, where the utility of the law is not so obvious."[25] Of course, in other contexts Austin attacks the distinction between *malum prohibitum* and *malum in se,* just as in other contexts he attacks the distinction between natural law or the law of nations and positive or civil law. In both cases, he defends the legal significance of the distinction in practical jurisprudence while he attacks the interpretation of the distinction by moral philosophers, ancient and modern. As a utilitarian, Austin cannot admit any special "moral sense or instinct" by which natural law is distinguished from positive law. He rejects the whole idea of a special faculty of practical reason whereby some deeds are immediately seen to be intrinsically evil, while others are seen to be evil only because prohibited. For Austin, there is only the general faculty of reasoning that tests moral principles by their empirical consequences. So Austin's strategy is to attack the interpretation of the distinction between natural and positive law by Roman and modern jurists under the sway of a misguided Stoic or Aristotelian philosophy, but to defend what is being distinguished when properly interpreted by the principles of utility.

Thus, although Austin attacks the Roman jurists for appealing to Greek philosophical notions of divine law or Aristotelian "natural right," Austin defends the importance of distinguishing universal from local law in the practical analysis of any legal system. He argues that the law of nations, far from arising out of Greek moral philosophy, actually arose from the practical necessity of Roman jurists to find a common legal framework within which to adjudicate mainly private law disputes between citizens of Rome proper and citizens of the many Italian and other cities coming under Roman political power. This quest for a common law intelligible to all the nations led to the development of legal principles that reflected general and widespread notions of what is fair and just, so that that law of nations became known as a law of equity. The civil law peculiar to the Romans, says Austin, was "barbarous" and the product of narrow experience; the law of nations, by contrast, was enlightened and the product of wide experience. "The *ius gentium,* therefore, was so conspicuously *better* than

25. Austin discusses the Roman doctrine of ignorance of law in LJ, p. 565 and pp. 484–85.

the proper Roman law that naturally it gradually passed into the latter."[26] In light of Austin's strong contrast between the science of what law is and the science of what law ought to be, it is revealing that Austin here, in explaining the history of actual Roman law, finds that he cannot make sense of that history without invoking the standard of what law ought to be. Austin goes on to tell us that the law of nations was administered by the praetors and hence passed into the *ius praetorium,* from which it continued to influence the other parts of the Roman law. So even though Austin is skeptical of the significance of Gaius's grandiose claims about the law of nations reflecting the moral law grasped by natural reason, Austin certainly recognizes the importance of the distinction between universal and local law within any legal system: "The distinction indeed between *ius civile* and *ius praetorium,* is as penetrating and as pregnant with consequences as our distinction between law and equity."[27]

After explaining the Roman distinction between the law of nations and the civil law as a distinction between universal and local parts of the Roman law as a whole, Austin translates this distinction into the vocabulary of modern philosophical jurisprudence. He says that "the positive laws, therefore, of any political community are divisible into two kinds. . . . Some are peculiar or proper to that single political community. . . . Others are common to all political communities. . . . The rationale of the distinction of positive laws into natural laws and positive laws, may therefore be stated thus. The former are common to all political societies, in the character of positive laws. . . . The latter are not common, as positive laws, to all political societies."[28] So in the sense of law as imposed, positive laws can also be natural; but in the sense of the contingent content of law, positive laws are opposed to natural.

Similarly, in the fourth lecture of his *Province of Jurisprudence Determined,* Austin says: "By modern writers on jurisprudence, positive law (or law, simply and strictly so called) is divided into *law natural* and *law positive*" (PJD, p. 101). In other words, of law positive in the sense of imposed by sovereign command, some is natural in content, while some is positive in content. According to these "modern" writers, says Austin, law natural in content defines crimes that are *mala in se,* whereas law positive in content defines crimes that are *mala quia prohibita*—all of this a commonplace of medieval jurisprudence, as we saw.

26. By "*better*" (his emphasis), Austin means morally better: he explains that the law of nations "was distinguished by a spirit of impartiality or fairness, or by its regard for the interests of the weak as well as for the interests of the strong." Austin, LJ, pp. 559–60.

27. Austin, LJ, p. 565.

28. Austin, LJ, pp. 568–69.

In Austin's discussion of the distinction, within positive law, between natural law and positive law, we see Austin both affirming and denying the validity of that distinction. Because, he says, the traditional discourse of natural and positive law usually presupposes a false theory of an innate moral sense or special faculty of practical reason, Austin is wary of any appeal to the distinction of natural and positive law, within law imposed by the sovereign. "I must remark that the distinction of positive rules into natural and positive seems to rest exclusively (or nearly exclusively) on the supposition of a moral instinct; or (as this real or imaginary endowment is named by the Roman Lawyers and by various modern writers), a natural reason, or a universal and practical reason."[29] Nonetheless, if we can avoid any suggestion that human beings possess some innate special faculty for distinguishing natural from positive moral and legal norms, then Austin is prepared to admit the validity of a distinction between natural and positive law, within positive law: "The distinction of law and morality into natural and positive, is a needless and futile subtilty: but still the distinction is founded on a real and manifest difference" (PJD, p. 179). No doubt, this is a grudging and back-handed compliment to the traditional discourse of natural and positive law, but by comparison to Bentham's unalloyed contempt for natural law, Austin's qualified acceptance is quite remarkable.

Indeed, Austin tells us that even assuming that the principle of utility is the only index to the natural law, the distinction, within positive law, between natural and positive laws "is not unmeaning."[30] If we begin with a proper understanding of morality in terms of utility, we can see that "as some of the dictates of utility are always and everywhere the same, and are also so plain and glaring that they hardly admit of mistake, there are legal and moral rules which are nearly or quite *universal,* and the expediency of which must be seen by merely *natural* reason, or by reason without the lights of extensive experience and observation" (PJD, p. 178). Thus, quite apart from any alleged moral sense, simple observation and natural reason are sufficient to grasp reliably the utility of universal and natural moral and legal rules.[31]

Austin makes it clear that what he objects to in the traditional theory of natural law is not the valid observation that some law is universal and, hence, natural but the interpretation of the basis of that universality: "The *jus naturale* or

29. Austin, LJ, p. 571.
30. Austin, LJ, lect. 32, p. 571.
31. "With regard to actions of a few classes, the dictates of utility are the same at all times and places, and are also so obvious that they hardly admit of mistake or doubt." PJD, p. 100.

gentium would be liable to little objection if it were not supposed to be the offspring of a moral instinct or sense, or of innate practical principles" (PJD, p. 179).[32] By using the categories of Roman legal thought, Austin signals his agreement with the Roman inference that what is common to all nations must in some way be natural: the law of nations (*ius gentium*) is our best guide to what is morally necessary in law (*ius naturale*). In one place, Austin says that the Romans were right to assume that everyone has a knowledge of the *ius gentium* from natural reason (*naturali ratione*) because "some laws are so obviously suggested by utility, that any person not insane would naturally surmise or guess their existence"; by contrast, the Romans did not assume that everyone knew the particular rules of the *ius civile,* "where the utility of the law is not so obvious" (LJ, p. 485).

While Austin rejects the traditional conception of these concepts, he accepts a distinction, properly understood, between universal natural law and particular positive law within the science of positive law. "The portion of positive law which is parcel of the *law of nature* (or, in the language of the classical jurists, which is parcel of the *ius gentium*) is often supposed to emanate, even as positive law, from a Divine or Natural Source. But (admitting the distinction of positive law into law natural and law positive) it is manifest that law natural, considered as a portion of positive, is the creature of human sovereigns, and not of the Divine monarch" (PJD, p. 164). Natural law belongs to the science of jurisprudence only insofar as it has been incorporated into the positive law by the civil sovereign.

We must note that by distinguishing, within positive law, between positive law and natural law, Austin is not here restating his distinction between positive law as it is and positive law as it ought to be. When he divides positive law into natural and positive law, Austin is not dividing positive law into good law and bad law, moral law and immoral law; nor is he distinguishing the science of legislation from the science of jurisprudence. Rather, he is distinguishing universal and (presumptively) morally necessary law from local and (presumptively) not morally necessary law—a distinction that he defends as a part of the science of jurisprudence. Austin says that there are strong reasons for supposing that universal legal rules are more likely to be morally justified by utility than are local

32. Yet Austin doubts whether the distinction between natural and positive law can ever be separated in practice from the false theory of a moral instinct: "But, since it is closely allied (as I shall show hereafter) to that misleading and pernicious jargon, it ought to be expelled, with the *natural law* of the moderns, from the sciences of jurisprudence and morality." PJD, p. 179.

and contingent moral rules. Still, these reasons are presumptive and not conclusive because, as he notes, slavery was part of the law of nations (LJ, p. 573), yet hardly justified, in his view, by true morality. Conversely, Austin also observes that utility demands the adaptation of most legal rules to unique, local, and transient circumstances. Being morally contingent does not imply being immoral: "Rules which are peculiar to particular countries may be just as *useful* as rules which are common to all countries" (LJ, p. 571). In short, within positive law, natural law might well be immoral, while positive law might well be moral.

Austin brings his formidable powers of analysis to explicate the ambiguity of "natural" in a way in which he never does with respect to "positive" law. In one sense, natural law refers to a part of positive law: "It signifies certain rules of human position; namely the human or positive rules which are common to *all* societies" (LJ, p. 573). Here, the distinction between law natural and law positive belongs to what Austin calls "General (or comparative) Jurisprudence, or the philosophy (or general principles) of positive law." What Austin means by general jurisprudence is "the science concerned with the exposition of the principles, notions, and distinctions which are common to systems of law."[33] One of the distinctions common to every system of positive law is the distinction between universal natural law and contingent positive law. This means that the science of jurisprudence—that is, the science of law as it is—necessarily involves not just the identification of positive legal rules according to their pedigree—that is, according to facts about their adoption and development—but also the identification of positive legal rules according to their content, in particular, whether that content is universal and necessary or merely local and contingent. While the identification of positive law by pedigree might aspire to objectivity and precision, the identification of positive law by its content must always remain uncertain: "For no one (I presume) can determine exactly, what positive rules are strictly universal, and which of them are merely particular" (LJ, p. 571). This last comment reveals that Austin, like Aquinas, often assumes that human legal norms might somehow be sorted into mutually exclusive classes of natural and positive precepts. Christopher St. German, by contrast, thought that the challenge was not to sort legal precepts but to see the natural law in every positive law.

In another sense, natural law refers to the objective moral standard or test by which we judge what positive law ought to be.[34] In this sense, natural law be-

---

33. Austin, "The Uses of the Study of Jurisprudence," PJD, pp. 365 and 367.
34. "But taken with another meaning, it signifies the laws which are set to mankind by Na-

longs to the science of legislation, which, based upon the moral science of utility, "affects to determine the test or standard . . . by which positive law ought to be made, or to which positive law ought to be adjusted."[35] Natural law is the standard by which we judge the morality of all positive law, including both law natural and law positive: "So that all positive rules, particular as well as universal, which may be deemed beneficent, may also be deemed *natural* laws, or laws of Nature or the Deity which men have adopted and sanctioned" (LJ, p. 571). Still, even though Austin is quite clear in his lecture 32 that the distinction between moral and immoral laws cuts across the distinction between universal (natural) and particular (positive) laws, he is also aware that these two sets of distinctions are easily confused. To begin with, Austin himself admits that universality is a good presumptive, though not conclusive, sign of genuine moral utility: "For as some of the dictates of general utility are exactly or nearly the same at all times and places, and also are so strikingly obvious that they can hardly be overlooked or misconstrued, there are positive or human rules which are absolutely or nearly universal, and the expediency of which must be seen by merely natural reason, or reason without the lights of extensive experience and observation" (LJ, p. 571).

Although Austin concedes the presumptive moral force of universal positive laws, he is worried that this presumption might undermine the authority of merely particular positive laws: "So confused and perverse are the moral principles of the vulgar, that many an honest man, who would boggle at a theft, shall cheat the public revenue with a perfectly tranquil conscience" (LJ, p. 572). Austin here seems unduly condescending to the "vulgar" in light of the fact that he himself concedes the greater presumptive moral force of universal positive laws. Nevertheless, Austin's fear that the distinction between law natural and law positive might undermine the authority of merely positive law leads him to doubt, if not the intelligibility, then at least the utility of that distinction: "But if the principle of general utility be the only index to the laws of the Deity, the distinction, though not unmeaning, seems to be utterly or nearly purposeless" (LJ, p. 571).

Inasmuch as Austin only grants presumptive moral force to the universal and natural law within positive law, it seems that he can retain his neat separation of

---

ture or the Deity, or more generally, it signifies the standard (whether that standard be the laws of the Deity, or a standard of man's imagining) to which, in the opinion of the writer, human or positive rules *ought* to conform." LJ, p. 573.

35. Austin, "The Uses of the Study of Jurisprudence," PJD, p. 366.

the science of jurisprudence from the science of legislation. After all, as we have seen, his distinction between what law is and what law ought to be cuts across his distinction between universal natural law and local positive law. Law that is universal (as slavery once was thought to be) might well be immoral, just as law that is merely local might well be morally justified. The distinction between universal and local law, although it refers to the content of laws, seems to be subject to empirical methods of inquiry, and so pose no threat to the science of positive law. Indeed, we have seen Austin call the science of the universal principles of positive law "General (or comparative) Jurisprudence, or the philosophy (or general principles) of positive law."[36] He says that this science of general or comparative jurisprudence will have no immediate concern with the goodness or badness of laws.

But even general jurisprudence seems to exceed its empirical bounds when Austin claims that the object of inquiry of general jurisprudence is not only what happens to be universal in all legal systems but also what is necessarily so: "Of the principles, notions, and distinctions which are the subjects of general jurisprudence, some may be esteemed necessary. For we cannot imagine coherently a system of law (or a system of law as evolved in a refined society), without conceiving them as constituent parts of it." What makes these principles of positive law both universal and necessary is that they are "bottomed in the common nature of man."[37] Hart, in his discussion of Austin's views here, says that this natural necessity includes a moral necessity: the natural legal rules, he says, "overlap with basic moral principles vetoing murder, violence, and theft; and so we can add to the factual statement that all legal systems in fact coincide with morality at such vital points, the statement that this is, in this sense, necessarily so. And why not call it a 'natural' necessity?"[38] But this transition from factual universality to moral necessity takes us beyond Austin's neat distinction between what law is and what law ought to be or his claim that the "*science of jurisprudence* . . . is concerned with positive laws, or with laws strictly so called, as considered without regard to their goodness or badness" (PJD, p. 126). For Austin, like Hart after him, comes to the conclusion that a legal system cannot coherently exist or at least persist without some considerable protection of human life and other essential human goods. Austin claims that "inasmuch as the

---

36. Austin, "The Uses of the Study of Jurisprudence," PJD, p. 365.
37. Austin, "The Uses of the Study of Jurisprudence," PJD, pp. 367 and 373.
38. Hart's approving comment on Austin is in "Positivism and the Separation of Law and Morals," pp. 79–82.

knowledge of what ought to be, supposes a knowledge of what is, legislation supposes jurisprudence, but jurisprudence does not suppose legislation."[39] Yet a science of what law is that includes the identification of the morally necessary principles of positive law seems precisely to presuppose some important part of the science of what law ought to be.

AUSTIN'S CLASSIFICATION OF LAWS

We have seen that Austin uses positive law sometimes in contrast to customary law and sometimes in contrast to natural law; both of these contrasts will be at work in Austin's threefold classification of legal and moral norms into divine law, positive law, and positive morality. Now Austin tells us that his triad "tallies in the main" with Locke's triad of divine law, civil law, and the law of opinion or reputation (PJD, pp. 164–66). Austin's attempt to articulate this fundamental classification in terms of law's positivity will only produce deep muddles and confusion in his analysis.

Austin classifies norms first into laws proper and laws improper. Laws proper, of course, are general commands, and Austin's analysis of "command" shows an implied relation of superior to inferior, with the superior having the power to impose a sanction and the inferior having a duty to obey.[40] Every command, in short, must emanate from a determinate author (PJD, p. 133). There are three kinds of laws properly so called: divine laws emanating from God, "positive" laws emanating from sovereign superiors, and human laws emanating from nonsovereign superiors, such as the rules imposed by a club on its members (PJD, p. 140). Of laws improperly so called, the most important are the scientific laws of nature and customary norms. The function of the notion of "laws properly so called," therefore, is to exclude all laws that are not positive in the sense of imposed. Although divine law, sovereign law, and the by-laws of a club are all "positive" in the sense of deliberately imposed, Austin labels only one of them "positive" law. Despite the fact that Austin officially and frequently defines "positive" law as law imposed (*positum*) by the sovereign, in his official classification, all law "properly so called" is imposed, meaning that law called "positive" must be so for some other reason.

39. Austin, "The Uses of the Study of Jurisprudence," PJD, 372.
40. "A law . . . may be said to be a rule laid down for the guidance of an intelligent being by an intelligent being having power over him." PJD, p. 10.

Austin's muddle becomes apparent when he directly contradicts his official classification of laws by saying: "Strictly speaking, every law properly so called is a *positive* law. For it is *put* or set by its individual or collective author, or it exists by the *position* or institution of its individual or collective author" (PJD, p. 124). We should note that, in this sense of positive law, all divine law is positive law. If all law properly so called is positive "strictly speaking," then why does Austin always restrict the expression *positive law* in his official classifications to law imposed by the civil sovereign? Austin cannot decide if "positive law" names the genus of law properly so called or just one species of that genus, namely, law imposed by a sovereign. Austin is right that all law properly so called is positive in the sense of imposed, by contrast to rules that emerge from below by custom; by defining law as command, Austin has already built this sense of "positive" into his notion of law. It is purely redundant, at best, to say that all law properly so called is "positive." Austin admits this when he says that law imposed by the sovereign "might be named simply *law*" (PJD, p. 124).

Still, Austin cannot dispense with the discourse of positivity, because his legal theory requires him to distinguish "law strictly so called" not only from custom but also from divine or natural law. Law imposed by the sovereign differs from divine law not because it is imposed but because its content is morally contingent and adventitious: "As opposed to the law of nature (meaning the law of God), human law of the first capital class [law imposed by the sovereign] is styled by writers on jurisprudence '*positive* law'" (PJD, p. 124). Unfortunately, Austin does not explain that we are now using the term *positive* in a quite different sense. He tells us that the application of the term *positive* here is meant to obviate the confusion of human law with divine law, which is the test of human law (PJD, p. 124).

In this second sense of "positive," Austin distinguishes "positive" law from divine law and "positive" morality from divine law: for divine law is morally necessary and thus the standard or test of the morally contingent "positive" law and morality. Here by "positive" Austin marks the distinction between the divine and the human: human law and human morality lack the moral necessity of divine law. To my knowledge, E. C. Clark is the only commentator on Austin to notice how peculiar are these deployments of "positive." Clark says of positive law that it originally meant law that is "imposed"; but, as we have seen, "positive" has always had at least two quite distinct meanings. Still, Clark is right to note that, since Austin officially defines "positive" as imposed, it is rather odd for Austin then to claim that social customs are "positive," while divine laws are not.[41] As Clark says, in distinguishing the content of positive law and positive morality from divine law, "The term *human* would seem a better one, to express the distinction intended, than *positive*."[42] As it turns out, Austin's equation of what is positive with what is human finds its origin in the very earliest uses of the expression *positiva* among the theological humanists at Chartres.[43] And even Aquinas, in his mature legal theory of the *Summa Theologiae*, generally restricts the expression *positive law* to human law. Still, the term *positive* is poorly suited to mark the distinction between divine and human law, since, according to both Aquinas and Austin, divine law is imposed by God and includes precepts that lack moral necessity.

We can now see that the discourse of positivity has created what Austin calls in another context "a competition of opposite analogies"—a competition that pulls Austin's logic of classification in contrary directions.[44] Austin begins by telling us that he will classify legal and moral norms according to the kind of analogy by which they are related to "laws which are simply and strictly so called" (PJD, p. 1). The closest kind of analogy he calls "resemblance," more distant relations range from close or strong to remote or slender analogies, and most remote are merely metaphorical analogies. According to this logic, he says, "laws strictly so called" (that is, "positive" laws) most resemble divine law and those rules of positive morality that are laws properly so called (the rules of a club). By a close or strong analogy, positive laws are related to the rules of positive morality that are merely customary; by a merely remote or slender analogy, positive laws are related to metaphorical laws (PJD, pp. 1–2).[45] With these analogies, Austin hopes to array all legal and moral norms along a single dimension according to the degree of resemblance to his exemplar of "laws sim-

---

41. Of positive law, Clark says: "Its original juridical meaning appears to be that of *existing by position*, i.e. the *setting or ordaining* of some one. . . . In this meaning it is distinctly applicable to the Law of God: and it seems to me as distinctly inapplicable to any human law which exists, if such can be conceived as existing, independent of any presumable direct ordinance." E. C. Clark, *Practical Jurisprudence: A Comment on Austin* (Cambridge: Cambridge University Press, 1883), p. 132.

42. Clark, *Practical Jurisprudence,* p. 132.

43. Recall that in William of Conches's commentary on Chalcidius we read: "Positive [justice] is that which is contrived by men [*ab hominibus inventa*], such as the hanging of a thief." Latin text in Gagnér, *Studien zur Indeengeschichte der Gesetzgebung* (Stockholm: Almqvist and Wiksell, 1960), p. 231.

44. Austin discusses Paley's view that judges must somehow resolve "the competition of opposite analogies" generated by common law rules, in LJ, pp. 632–33 and 996–1001.

45. Austin's "Excursus on Analogy" is found in LJ, pp. 1001–1020.

ply and strictly so called." In this spatial array, divine laws and the laws of clubs are closest to positive laws, customary norms are more distant, and metaphorical laws are furthest removed.

If the positivity of law is irreducibly ambiguous, then we should expect that positive law in one sense will form quite different analogies from positive law in another sense. Indeed, these competing analogies are, as we have seen, pulling Austin's classification in contrary directions and leading him to inconsistent nomenclature. Positive laws, in the sense of laws imposed by a superior, obviously resemble divine laws and the by-laws of a club; this is why Austin calls all of these "laws properly so called" and even once says that "every" such law, including divine laws, is positive law (PJD, p. 124). But positive laws, in the sense of laws whose content is not necessarily moral, obviously resemble the rules of positive morality, whose content is also not necessarily moral; this is why Austin calls both of these legal and moral rules "positive." Since Austin never explicitly hierarchizes these two senses of "positive," his discourse of positivity generates a competition of opposed analogies and, hence, renders impossible any single or consistent array of relations among these legal and moral norms. Austin took the dilemmas posed by the "competition of opposed analogies" to be the most fundamental obstacle to logical consistency and predictability in judicial law making. It is ironic that the competition of opposed analogies would also pose a fundamental obstacle to the logical consistency of his own philosophy of positive law.

FROM VERBAL TO CONCEPTUAL AMBIGUITIES
AND INCONSISTENCIES

For someone who heaped withering contempt upon the verbal muddles of other theorists and whose alleged verbal clarity and terminological precision were taken by himself, his contemporaries, and his subsequent commentators to be his lasting achievement, the verbal confusions and logical inconsistencies we have noted in Austin are significant. Are these muddles of law's "positivity" merely at the surface of his verbal, definitional, and classificatory theory? How closely connected are his terms and his concepts, his language and his thought? Do his verbal muddles reflect or generate conceptual confusion as well?

We saw that Austin's distinction between natural and positive law within positive law deeply challenges his attempts neatly to separate the science of jurisprudence from the science of legislation. Are other deep aspects of his theory of law shaped by his discourse of positive law? Let us consider his understanding of what he calls "positive morality." Positive morality includes both laws proper, such as the by-laws of a club, and laws improper, such as customs, fashion, and social etiquette. What unites these two quite different classes of rules? The by-laws of social organizations are deliberately imposed and enforced by determinate authorities; they share with positive laws the quality of being commands imposed by a superior. By contrast, the rules of custom, fashion, and etiquette are not deliberately imposed and enforced by determinate authorities; what they share with positive law is a content that is not morally necessary. Austin's description of the source of customary social rules is curious: he says they "may be styled laws or rules set or imposed by opinion" (PJD, p. 1; cf. pp. 2, 8, 140, etc.). Put differently, Austin describes the institution of customs in exactly the same language as he describes the institution of statutes: they exist by *positum,* that is, by imposition from above to below. In other contexts, Austin describes customs as arising from below,[46] but in the context of defining customs as rules of positive morality, he seems to treat them as positive in the sense of deliberately "set or imposed by opinion," rather than positive in the sense of morally contingently in content.

Those who think of all human law as positive, in the sense of imposed, have a difficult time accounting for the legal force of some customs. Aquinas, for example, to account for the legal force of custom in nondemocratic societies, resorted to the Roman law fiction that "whatever the sovereign permits, he commands." In other words, despite appearances to the contrary, custom is positive law, imposed by the sovereign—albeit in a tacit, circuitous, and indirect way. The fiction that customs were tacit statutes was too much for Hobbes to swallow, so he simply denied that any custom had intrinsic legal force. Hobbes did resort to a similar fiction in his account of why judicial decisions had the force of law: they are actually the king's law, whosoever pens them. Austin agrees with Hobbes that no custom has intrinsic legal force and that customs can acquire legal force only when the sovereign legislature transmutes the custom into positive law. The sovereign may create positive law from custom either directly, through statutes based on custom, or indirectly, through judicial decisions based on customs: "Now when customs are turned into legal rules by decisions of subject judges, the legal rules which emerge from the customs are *tacit* commands of the sovereign legislature" (PJD, p. 32). Thus, in the discourse of posi-

---

46. "At its origin, a custom is a rule of conduct which the governed observe spontaneously." PJD, p. 31.

tive law, from Aquinas to Austin, customary law must be understood as a tacit or indirect statute.

Austin has frequently been attacked for his account of the legal force of customs on the grounds that he turns the judiciary into mere ministers of the sovereign. In the case of common law adjudication, this subordination of the judiciary to the legislature is especially implausible, since common law does not derive its authority from statute law any more than statute law derives its authority from common law. To say that all human law is positive is to assume a unitary chain of command in the legal order where none is to be found.[47] W. L. Morison points out that, even within the terms of Austin's own theory, Austin could have accounted for the legal force of customs much more plausibly if he had recognized that courts set forth general criteria defining when particular customs will have legal force; in this way, many particular customs obtain legal force well before they individually come before the courts.[48] As Morison points out, if courts could set forth general criteria in which custom is a source of law, then they could do the same for international law and juristic commentary; but such a multiplication of the sources of law would undermine Austin's fundamental claim that all law finds its source in sovereign imposition.[49]

Moreover, by describing judiciary laws as "tacit commands of the sovereign legislature," Austin assimilates them to the model of statutory law. Yet Austin's deeper account is that, although judiciary law and statutory law flow from the same source, they differ in the mode by which they originate, in how they are logically expressed, and in how they ought to be interpreted. Austin even marks these fundamental differences by a verbal distinction. Austin's commentators frequently point out that, whereas Bentham scathingly assailed what he called "judge-made" law, Austin defends the necessity and the merits of "judge-made" law.[50] However, Austin breaks with Bentham not only in his normative assess-

47. As W. L. Morison says: "To attempt to find a comprehensive or omnipotent center of control is anti-empirical, for we just do not observe this kind of phenomenon by ordinary means." *John Austin,* p. 182.

48. "What if the courts have let it be known that they will recognize customs which are established to exist in particular ways, at least under certain conditions, and the sovereign has issued no counter-command despite this? It would seem that in such circumstances a custom which can be so established, and in fact meets the conditions, is positive law and positive morality by coincidence even before it individually comes before any court." Morison, *John Austin,* p. 75.

49. Morison, *John Austin,* p. 100.

50. Morison says: "For Austin, tacit sovereign approval could be operating on well-formed

ment of "judge-made" law but also in his conceptualization of it: Austin tells us that, although Bentham's expression *judge-made* law is pithy and homely, he rejects it precisely on the grounds that it suggests that the judge makes law just as a legislator makes statutes. A judge, says Austin, makes law only indirectly or obliquely in the course of deciding cases. Austin strongly distinguishes law established in a legislative manner (what he calls *gesetzgebend*) from law established in a judicial manner (*richtend*). The issue is not who makes the law but rather how the law is made, with what logical generality, and how it ought to be interpreted (LJ, pp. 532–33; 620–41). All of this reveals a sophistication in Austin's understanding of judiciary law not manifest in his appeal to the transparent fiction that such law is the tacit command of the sovereign legislator.

The discourse of "positivity," as we saw, first arose in Greek philosophical debates about language. In our discussion of the legacy of Plato's *Cratylus,* we saw how Aristotle's understanding of linguistic meaning as an implicit covenant (*kata synthēkēn*) between speaker and listener became transformed by Boethius into a positivist account in which linguistic meaning was imposed by the will of the speaker (*ad placitum*). Similarly, in legal philosophy, some theorists understand law in terms of an implicit covenant between the lawgiver and the citizen, while other theorists understand law simply in terms of the will of the lawgiver. Lon Fuller famously criticized Austin and other positivists for conceptualizing the legal system purely in a top-down fashion; and indeed, as we have seen, "positive" law often implies precisely this exclusively top-down action. Fuller quotes Georg Simmel on the implicit understanding between rulers and subjects about the rule of law: "By enacting laws government says to the citizen, 'These are the rules we ask you to follow. If you obey them, you have our promise that they are the rules we will apply to your conduct.'"[51] Where Fuller sees the rule of law as an implicit covenant between ruler and subject, the discourse of law's positivity focuses instead upon the will of the ruler.

Even those theorists, such as Aquinas, who follow Boethius in describing law as stemming from the will and reason of the lawgiver nonetheless acknowledge the implicit covenant between ruler and subject by emphasizing the importance of the promulgation of law. To insist that law be promulgated acknowledges the rightful demand of citizens to be able to know the law to which they

---

judge-made laws." *John Austin,* p. 131. Rumble says of Austin: "He imputed many of the evils of judge-made law to the covert mode in which it has been introduced." See *The Thought of John Austin,* p. 122. Rumble does discuss Austin's distinctions between judiciary and statutory law.

51. Fuller, *The Morality of Law* (New Haven: Yale University Press, 1964), pp. 216–17.

are subject. Law must be promulgated, says Aquinas, if it is to guide the conduct of rational creatures. Hobbes goes further and says that not only must the content of a law be promulgated but so must the identity of its author, since law gets its authority from the will of the sovereign alone. Austin also follows Aquinas and Hobbes in defining law as "the pleasure" (*ad placitum*) of the sovereign (LJ, p. 36), but Austin alone takes this top-down logic to its conclusion by insisting that law need not be made known to those who are bound to follow it.[52] Austin is not opposed to the promulgation of law and, as a good utilitarian, he would no doubt recommend a general policy of promulgation. Nonetheless, the authority and validity of law does not depend, in his view, upon its promulgation. The sovereign has no legal duty to his subjects to make his law known, even though his subjects will be subject to that law.

It is curious that Austin denies that laws must be promulgated, since he says that commands must be promulgated, and laws are but a species of command. A command is a signification of a desire, either an expression or an intimation of a wish, combined with an intention to enforce that wish with a sanction (PJD, p. 14). The content of a command is a wish, and that wish must be expressed visibly or audibly: a command involves "an expression or intimation of the wish by words or other signs" (PJD, p. 17). The evil that the commander intends to visit upon a disobedient subject need not be expressed by words or other signs. Austin observes that the pragmatics of power relations often make it clear that "my wish is your command," so that the sanction may be understood without any need for explicit promulgation (PJD, p. 14). Still, if the promulgation of a wish is necessary for that wish to become a command, then it would seem that the promulgation of the content of a legal command would be necessary for it to be a law.

Of course, Austin could agree that, being commands, all laws must be expressed in words or other signs without agreeing that those words or signs must be published or promulgated. Could the concept of a secret law be more coherent than that of a secret command? Moreover, every positive law is a species of law in its most general and literal sense, namely, a "rule laid down for the guidance of an intelligent being by an intelligent being having power over him" (PJD, p. 10). It is hard to understand how a rule might be laid down for the guidance of an intelligent being without being promulgated.

52. "Laws established immediately by sovereign authors are not necessarily *promulged:* that is, published or made known, orally or in writing, for the information and guidance of those who are bound to obey them." LJ, p. 526.

Austin's extreme top-down understanding of positive law is evident in his view that law need not be promulgated, for to assert the necessity of promulgation is to acknowledge some degree of reciprocity between rulers and subjects. Even if Austin were to concede that law must be promulgated, he would still insist that those subject to a promulgated law are bound by it even if they are not aware of its existence. Indeed, Austin defends the traditional maxim that "ignorance of the law is no excuse" by saying that everyone has a duty to know the law even though no one can possibly in fact know all the law to which one is bound (LJ, p. 482). Our duty to know the law does not imply that we can know the law. Instead, says Austin, the maxim that "ignorance of the law is no excuse" finds its only justification in the fact that "if ignorance of law were admitted as a ground of exemption, the Courts would be involved in questions which it were scarcely possible to solve, and which would render the administration of justice next to impracticable" (LJ, p. 482).

That ignorance of the law is no excuse reveals a specific difference between legal commands and generic commands. Austin makes it clear that ordinary commands impose duties only insofar as those subject to them grasp both the content of the command and the relation of that content to the evil of a sanction: "Being liable to evil from you if I comply not with a wish which you signify, I am *bound* or *obliged* by your command, or I lie under a *duty* to obey it. If, in spite of that evil in prospect, I comply not with the wish which you signify, I am said to disobey your command, or to violate the duty which it imposes" (PJD, p. 14). Austin often describes the duty imposed by a command in terms of a subject being "liable to" or "obnoxious to" its sanction (PJD, p. 160), but these expressions misleadingly create the impression that a duty arises merely because of the objective probability of a sanction when Austin's actual view is that the subjective prospect of a sanction is also necessary, as when he says above "in spite of that evil in prospect." In short, a duty arises, on his account, when someone is both objectively liable to a sanction and when he fears that sanction: "The party is *bound* or *obliged* to do or forbear, because he is obnoxious to the evil, and because he fears the evil" (LJ, p. 444).

Austin's recognition of the subjective and psychological dimension of having a duty is important because many of his commentators are misled by his imprecise language into supposing that, for Austin, one incurs a duty simply by virtue of the objective liability to suffer a sanction. Hart, in particular, famously denies that Austin grasped the "internal aspect" of following commands or rules. Hart says that Austin "treats statements of obligation not as psychological statements but as predictions or assessments of changes of incurring punishments or 'evil.'"[53] Since Austin does understand duty in psychological terms as the subjective "prospect" of incurring a sanction, Hart should not say that Austin completely disregards "a person's beliefs, fears, and motives" but that Austin focuses on the wrong beliefs, fears, and motives in his analysis of having an obligation. Nonetheless, it is not clear how much this analysis of a sanction in general applies to specifically legal sanctions, given that we have legal duties and are subject to legal sanctions whether or not we are subjectively aware of them, since ignorance of the law is no excuse. For a theory of law so resolutely focused on sanctions, it is rather astonishing that Austin never tells us what, if anything, is distinctive about legal sanctions. He often speaks generally about sanctions, and occasionally he lists specifically moral, religious, and legal sanctions. But we never learn whether the sanctions associated with positive law are in any way unique. Perhaps Austin might have distinguished positive law from positive morality and from divine law simply on the basis of the different kinds of sanction associated with each.

AUSTIN'S DIVINE-COMMAND THEORY OF LAW

As we saw, the discourse of law's positivity arose mainly in the context of the medieval attempt to distinguish God's natural from his positive law. Aquinas was particularly concerned with discerning which parts of Mosaic law were natural, and hence also binding on Christians, and which parts were merely positive and hence only binding on ancient Israel. Hobbes also devoted a large portion of his *Leviathan* and other works to a largely unsuccessful attempt consistently to distinguish natural from positive divine law. Nowhere does Austin break more radically with Bentham and recur more deeply to the concerns of Aquinas and Hobbes than in his discussion of divine law. True, Austin does follow Bentham in distinguishing God's revealed will from his unrevealed will and in seeing utility as an index to God's unrevealed or presumptive will, but Bentham grounds the normative force of morality in pleasure and pain as fundamental principles of human nature, while Austin grounds the normative force

---

53. "Some theorists, Austin among them, seeing perhaps the general irrelevance of the person's beliefs, fears, and motives to the question whether he had an obligation to do something, have defined this notion not in terms of these subjective facts, but in terms of the *chance* or *likelihood* that the person having the obligation will suffer a punishment or 'evil' at the hands of others in the event of disobedience." H. L. A. Hart, *The Concept of Law,* 2nd edition (Oxford: Clarendon Press, 1994), p. 83.

of all morality and all law in God's power to inflict infinite suffering on his subjects.

Nowhere does the Benthamite reading of Austin distort his thought more than in relation to divine will, divine command, and divine law. Bentham simply sets aside the revealed will of God, and he treats the unrevealed will of God as merely redundant of the conclusions of utility.[54] J. S. Mill pioneered the Benthamite misreading of Austin by warning us not to conclude that Austin "regarded the binding force of the morals of utility as depending altogether upon the express or implied commands of God." Mill seeks to reassure us that Austin does not harbor a dark view about God's unfathomable will as the source of moral and legal obligation. Mill says that for Austin the distinction between right and wrong is not constituted by the divine will; rather the divine will merely recognizes and sanctions the conclusions of utility.[55] Lest we fear that Austin believes that whatever God wills is right because he wills it, Mill assures us that Austin follows Bentham's complacent view that "whatever is right is conformable to the will of God." If God merely sanctions the conclusions of utility, then the content of divine law has no independent moral force. Once we are sure that God simply sanctions what we know from utility to be right, we may quietly set aside the whole question of what the divine will is and how we might discover it. Nonetheless, Austin does not set aside or dismiss the independent moral force of the divine will; indeed, Austin thinks that God's revealed will and, where that is silent, his unrevealed will are the ultimate measure and test of all rules of human conduct. True, he says that utility is the ultimate test of the unrevealed divine law, but divine law includes both revealed and unrevealed law; we cannot understand how utility relates to divine law until we understand how revealed relates to unrevealed divine law. We shall see how Austin can claim that divine law is the ultimate standard and test of human conduct even while utility is the ultimate standard and test of unrevealed divine law.

For Austin, divine law is the test or standard of what positive law ought to be.

54. "The *will* of God here meant cannot be his revealed will, as contained in the sacred writings." And, "We may be perfectly sure, indeed, that whatever is right is conformable to the will of God." Bentham, *An Introduction to the Principles of Morals and Legislation*, ed. J. H. Burns and H. L. A. Hart (London: Athlone Press, 1970), p. 31.

55. Mill says of Austin: "If he could have been suspected of encouraging a mere worship of power, by representing the distinction of right and wrong as constituted by the Divine will, instead of merely recognized and sanctioned by it." Mill, "Austin on Jurisprudence," p. 228.

Although he does see the point of distinguishing "natural" from "positive" law within human law, he never refers to a part of divine law as "positive." Since Austin uses the term *positive* to distinguish human law and morality from divine law, he no doubt resisted using the term in connection with divine law. Yet what makes much of human law and morality "positive" is that it lacks moral necessity; the same is traditionally said of much of divine law, especially of the divine law revealed in the Bible. Since the distinction between natural and positive divine law is at the core of the traditional discourse of positive law, it would be surprising if Austin did not in any way acknowledge this distinction. The whole problem of divine law in Austin's theory raises deep and unresolved issues about the foundation of morality in divine command, about the duty to obey positive law, and about God's sovereignty.

As "laws properly so called," God's laws, says Austin, are "set" or imposed on men, just as positive laws are set by men to men. So all of divine law is positive in Austin's sense of *positum,* and, indeed, we saw that in one place Austin simply says that all laws properly so called are "positive" laws. At the same time, Austin often suggests that all of divine law is natural, in the sense of morally necessary, as when he frequently says that "the divine law is the measure or test of positive law" (PJD, p. 6); or when he says that the expression *natural law* has literal sense only if it means "the divine law."[56] These passages seem to deny any conceptual space for a positive divine law. But in other passages, Austin clearly creates space for a positive divine law: "The whole or a portion of the laws set by God to men is frequently styled the laws of nature" (PJD, p. 10).[57] At a minimum, Austin's language is often inconsistent on the question of whether there is more than one kind of divine law.

Although Austin does not explicitly distinguish natural from positive divine law, he does distinguish revealed from unrevealed divine law. "Of the Divine laws, or the laws of God, some are *revealed* or promulged, and others are *unrevealed*" (PJD, p. 34). He also says that some divine law is express and other di-

---

56. Austin rejects the misleading connotations of the expression *natural law,* but he thinks it intelligible when we take it to mean Divine law: "Rejecting the appellation Law of Nature as ambiguous and misleading, I name those laws or rules, as considered collectively or in a mass, the *Divine law,* or the *law of God.* . . . as contradistinguished to *natural* law, or to the law of *nature* (meaning, by those expressions, the law of God)." PJD, pp. 10–11.

57. "And certain of God's *laws* were as binding on the first man, as they are binding at this hour on the millions who have sprung from his loins." PJD, p. 22. "I proceed to distinguish laws set by men to men from those Divine laws which are the ultimate test of human." PJD, p. 34.

vine law is tacit (PJD, pp. 34 and 104). Austin is clear that the unrevealed or tacit divine law is natural law (PJD, p. 34); is the revealed or express divine law positive? Austin's description of the relation of revealed to unrevealed divine law very closely parallels a traditional juristic description of the relation between positive and natural law: Natural law is enforced as law in the absence of positive law, *cum deficit lex;* natural law serves as law in the interstices of positive law. Austin thus says of the unrevealed divine law: "These laws are binding upon us (who have access to the truths of Revelation), in so far as the revealed law has left our duties undetermined. For, though his express declarations are the clearest evidence of his will, we must look for many of the duties, which God has imposed upon us, to the marks or signs of his pleasure which are styled the *light of nature*" (PJD, p. 35). Since God's will is the ultimate measure and test of human conduct, and since the revealed divine law is the clearest evidence of his will, we resort to utility only when we lack guidance from the revealed divine law.

Austin understands the relation of the revealed law of God to the unrevealed very much like the relation of positive to natural law. To begin with, unrevealed law, grasped by the principle of utility and available to all men by natural reason, is inherently a matter of general principles, not the detailed specifications of positive law: "If the tendencies of actions be the index to the will of God, it follows that most of his commands are general or universal" (PJD, p. 40). These general principles of utility need not be expressly revealed, because they are available through natural reasoning about the tendencies of classes of acts; as natural law, they did not get their force or authority from an authoritative expression of the will of the sovereign. What matters for the grasp of natural law is not the interpretation of express language but the discovery of whether the tendencies of classes of acts are conducive to the general happiness or not. On the other hand, the revealed law of God need not be general or universal in scope; indeed, we would expect the revealed law of God to be highly specific, detailed, and certain, for if the revealed divine law were general and universal, then it would be merely redundant or inconsistent with unrevealed divine law. Austin tells us that the revealed law is not inconsistent with unrevealed divine law, since both kinds of divine law aim at "the *general happiness* or *good* which is the object of the Divine Lawgiver in all his laws and commandments" (PJD, pp. 42–43). Nor is revealed divine law redundant of unrevealed divine law, since the revealed law is available only to those with access to Revelation (PJD, p. 35).

Moreover, we grasp the revealed divine law not by reasoning from principles of utility but by the literal construction of the exact language of the revealed statutes: "In so far as the laws of God are clearly and indisputably revealed, we are bound to guide our conduct by the plain meaning of their terms" (PJD, p. 42). Since the moral authority of the revealed law of God rests upon the precise language of its expression in Scripture, this revealed law must be at least partly positive in content, in the sense of specific and morally contingent (only binding at least in part because commanded by God). The commandment "keep holy the Sabbath" would seem to exemplify what Austin means by revealed divine law. Unrevealed or natural divine law might lead us to recognize a duty to honor God, but only through knowledge of God's express commandment could we know that honoring God requires a specific day of rest.[58] Our conduct must be guided in the first place by God's express or positive law; we resort to utility only where God's express law is silent. As Austin says, "The *whole* of our conduct should be guided by the principle of utility, in so far as the conduct to be pursued has not been determined by Revelation" (PJD, p. 43).

Thus, Austin seems to collapse the traditional distinction of natural and positive divine law into his distinction of unrevealed and revealed divine law. No one has argued that positive divine law could be unrevealed, since what is positive in content has its force from its deliberate enactment, so Austin seems justified in suggesting that all positive divine law must be revealed. However, Aquinas, Hobbes, and many other theorists of positive law have claimed that God's revealed law includes both natural and positive precepts. Austin seems to rule out the possibility that revealed divine law might include natural law because of his rule requiring the literal construction of revealed divine law, a canon of interpretation that makes no sense in dealing with natural law norms.[59] Revealed divine law gets its priority over unrevealed divine law for the same reason that we normally give priority to the clear and specific provisions of an express statute over the general and tacit principles of natural equity. A natural revealed divine law would not have the priority Austin accords it over the natural unrevealed divine law.

Because Austin says relatively little about revealed divine law and because he ventures not even one example of a precept of biblical law, it is tempting to infer that Austin has found a decorous way to follow Bentham by simply setting

---

58. Austin includes in natural law "the dictates of natural religion" in PJD, p. 34.
59. Austin says that Revelation tells us next to nothing about the unrevealed divine law: "These [rules known by "the light of nature or reason"] the revealed law supposes or assumes. It passes over them in silence, or with a brief and incidental notice." PJD, p. 35.

aside the revealed divine law. After all, Austin says that we are bound by biblical law "in so far as the laws of God are clearly and indisputably revealed" (PJD, p. 42), but almost every alleged biblical law has been notoriously disputed in endless sectarian controversy. Hobbes's manifest failure consistently to distinguish natural from positive divine law, despite his Herculean labors of biblical exegesis, was a cautionary tale for Austin. At best, it seems that the divine law, both revealed and unrevealed, is merely redundant of utility, which is the index of the unrevealed divine law (making that law itself superfluous) and the measure of the revealed divine law. Far from saying that the general happiness is good only because God commands it, Austin seems to say that God's commands are good only because they are consistent with utility: "If the laws set by the Deity were not generally useful, or if they did not promote the general happiness of his creatures, or if their great Author were not wise and benevolent, they would not be good, or worthy of praise, but were devilish and worthy of execration" (PJD, p. 129). So for Austin utility, not divine law, seems to be both the ultimate standard and the ultimate foundation for morality.

Nonetheless, once we explore Austin's understanding of the relation of moral and legal obligation to command and sanction, we shall find that, according to Austin, divine command is both the source and the ultimate test of all moral duty—including, crucially, the duty to obey the positive law. To say that we have a duty is to say that we are subject to a sanction for a failure to perform that duty. The evil that we are liable to suffer from the sanction is both the ground of our duty and our motive for performing it. This means that our duties may be ranked in objective moral force according to the expected disutility of their sanctions; where duties conflict, we are bound to perform the duty in which the expected disutility for nonperformance is greatest. "The evils which we are exposed to suffer from the hands of God as a consequence of disobeying His commands are the greatest evils to which we are obnoxious; the obligations which they impose are consequently paramount to those imposed by any other laws, and if human commands conflict with the Divine law, we ought to disobey the command which is enforced by the less powerful sanction" (PJD, p. 184).

Since God can inflict infinite suffering upon his creatures, no matter how infinitesimal our prospect of incurring his terrible sanctions, it still follows by mathematical necessity that "our motives to obey the laws which God has given us, are paramount to all others" (PJD, p. 42). Nor can we discount God's sanctions by assuming them limited to a dubious hereafter: Austin is clear that God's sanctions "consist of the evils, or pains, which we may suffer here or hereafter" (PJD, p. 34). Because Austin grounds all moral and legal obligation in the prospect of incurring a sanction, the ultimate ground of all duties is God's commands: "In each of these cases [revealed and unrevealed divine law] the *source* of our duties is the same; though the *proofs* by which we know them are different. The principle of general utility is the *index* to many of these duties; but the principle of general utility is not their *fountain* or *source*. For duties or obligations arise from commands and sanctions. And commands, it is manifest, proceed not from abstractions, but from living and rational beings" (PJD, p. 43).

Here Austin follows Hobbes in arguing that reason cannot command; all commands stem from the will of a commander. The deliverances of the utility calculus might be an index to the content of our moral duties, but they impose no moral duties. All moral and legal obligation stems from the commands of rational beings to other rational beings. Even if God's commands are the source of moral duty, if the content of that duty is provided by utility, then God's role becomes merely one of enforcing the requirements of utility. Utility remains the test or measure of moral goodness, while God's commands enforce obedience to that test or measure. Still, Austin says: "Strictly speaking, therefore, utility is not the *measure* to which our conduct should conform, nor is utility the *test* by which our conduct should be tried. . . . It is merely the *index* to the measure, the *index* to the test." The divine commands are the ultimate measure and the ultimate test (PJD, p. 104).

If Austin claims that utility is only the "proximate" measure and test of our conduct (PJD, p. 104), how can he then tell us that utility is also the ultimate measure and test of divine law? He explains, "We may style them [divine laws] good, or worthy of praise, inasmuch as they agree with utility considered as an ultimate test" (PJD, p. 129). How can divine commands be the ultimate measure and test of human conduct if divine law itself is measured and tested by utility? Indeed, we saw Austin assert that "if the laws set by the Deity were not generally useful . . . they would not be good, or worthy of praise." One reason why utility cannot be the ultimate measure of our conduct is that utility is an index only of the unrevealed divine law: our conduct ought to be guided by the unrevealed divine law only where we lack guidance from the revealed divine law. So divine command is the ultimate measure and test of our conduct even though utility is the ultimate measure and test of divine law.

By erecting utility as a measure of the goodness of divine laws, Austin seems to deny those laws any independent moral content. This does not follow, for two reasons. First, by distinguishing law as it is from law as it ought to be, Austin is free to say that revealed divine law, no matter how devilish and execrable, is binding law, for the simple reason that in dealing with positive laws, divine or human, "we are bound to guide our conduct by the plain meaning of their terms"—regardless of whether those terms are morally good or bad.[60] Indeed, utility itself might indicate that general happiness is best served by a policy of obedience to all of God's clearly revealed laws, even if some of those laws happen to be morally bad. Second, even if utility is the ultimate measure of all divine laws, the revealed divine laws might retain important independent moral content as specifications of the general principles of utility. If revealed divine law provided authoritative specifications of the principles of utility, then they could provide moral guidance that is both consistent with utility but independent of it. So "keep holy the Sabbath" provides independent moral content to the principle of utility that we ought to honor God. In this way, utility remains the ultimate measure and test of divine law, while divine law remains the ultimate measure and test of human conduct. Since unrevealed divine law provides no guidance for human conduct apart from utility, only revealed divine law is capable of providing independent guidance for human conduct.

Bentham dismissed appeals to the revealed divine law by reason of the uncertainty of that law as manifested by the endless interpretive disputes among divines.[61] Austin admits this uncertainty but draws very different conclusions from it: "The laws of God are not always certain. All divines, at least all reasonable divines, admit that no scheme of duties perfectly complete and unambiguous was ever imparted to us by revelation" (PJD, pp. 185–86). To say that revelation does not provide a perfectly complete and unambiguous scheme of duties is far from asserting that revelation is irrelevant to the determination of our fundamental moral duties. Even this modest degree of uncertainty might amount to a serious disability if we had a more certain index of divine law by means of the science of utility, but Austin admits the grave uncertainty of utility: "As an index to the Divine will, utility is obviously insufficient. What appears pernicious to one person may appear beneficial to another" (PJD, p. 186). Austin has hopes for gradual improvements in the science of utility: "But, though they [principles of utility] may constantly approach, they certainly will never attain to a faultless system of ethics" (PJD, p. 80; cf. p. 87). Given the very

---

60. "In so far as the laws of God are clearly and indisputably revealed, we are bound to guide our conduct by the plain meaning of their terms." PJD, p. 42.

61. Bentham on revealed divine law: "Before it can be applied to the details of private conduct, it is universally allowed, by the most eminent divines of all persuasions, to stand in need of pretty ample interpretations; else to what use are the works of those divines?" Thus, he recommends, "setting revelation out of the question." *An Introduction to the Principles of Morals and Legislation,* p. 31.

different kinds of uncertainty that affect our grasp of both revealed and unrevealed divine law, it would seem to make sense on Austinian grounds to appeal to each as a check on the other.

Austin even considers the theological objection that the uncertainty of the principle of utility is inconsistent with the nature of God: "For it consists not with the known wisdom and the known benevolence of the Deity, that he should signify his commands defectively and obscurely to those upon whom they are binding" (PJD, p. 84). Austin responds that because God is a hidden and an inscrutable God, and because all the visible works of God are imperfect, we cannot expect his laws to be perfectly certain: "That the Deity should signify his commands defectively and obscurely, is strictly in keeping or unison with the rest of his inscrutable ways" (PJD, p. 84). According to Austin, the objector here is asserting that the evil of defectively signified divine laws is inconsistent with the perfection of God's goodness and wisdom. But, says Austin, the notion of evil and imperfection is built into our notions of law, duty, and sanction: "Law, like medicine, is a preventive or remedy of *evil:* and, if the world were free from evil, the notion and the name would be unknown" (PJD, p. 85). Whatever their merits, Austin's theological arguments do show that by admitting the uncertainty of our grasp of divine law, Austin was not implying that we need not look to divine law for fundamental moral guidance. God's infinite capacity to inflict suffering ought to provide sufficient warrant and motive to discover his will, even by the only proximate and uncertain measure of general utility: "We are bound by the awful sanctions with which his commands are armed, to adjust our conduct to rules formed on that proximate measure" (PJD, p. 116).

In principle, our religious duties and our legal duties should not conflict because obedience to morally good positive law is required by divine law,[62] and obedience to morally bad positive law is not always required by divine law.[63] Because citizens are normally "bound by the law of God to obey their temporal sovereign, a sovereign government has *rights divine* against its own subjects"

---

62. "The religious duties of the subjects towards the sovereign government, are creatures of the Divine law as known through the principle of utility. If it thoroughly accomplish the purpose for which it ought to exist, or further the general weal to the greatest possible extent, the subjects are bound religiously to pay it habitual obedience." PJD, p. 307.

63. Austin says that Hobbes "inculcates too absolutely the religious obligation of obedience to present or established government. He makes not the requisite allowance for the anomalous and excepted cases wherein disobedience is counseled by that very principle of utility which indicates the duty of submission." PJD, p. 277n.; cf. 307.

(PJD, p. 286); Austin further makes it clear that a sovereign government only has a divine right to do what is right: "An act which the government has a right to do, is an act which were generally useful" (PJD, p. 289). In practice, of course, our religious duties and our legal duties might well conflict, as when the government enforces pernicious laws; in this case, between obedience to the sovereign and obedience to God, we must, of course, choose God because of the incomparable severity of his sanctions.

POSITIVE LAW: SOVEREIGNTY
OR JURISDICTION?

If in obeying just rulers we are ultimately obeying God, and if in disobeying unjust rulers we are also obeying God, does not this habit of obedience reveal that God alone is truly sovereign? As we have seen, Austin tells us that God's commands are laws properly so called, that God is a determinate and common superior of man, and that God's laws are clothed in terrible sanctions. Is God an Austinian sovereign? Now, sovereignty is a species of superiority, and the specific difference of sovereign superiority is found in the notion of an independent political society implied by sovereignty (PJD, p. 193). A society is independent and political if it passes a positive and a negative test: "The *generality* of the given society must be in the *habit* of obedience to a *determinate* and *common* superior: whilst that determinate person, or determinate body of persons must *not* be habitually obedient to a determinate person or body" (PJD, p. 195; cf. p. 202, etc.). The question is: Given this twofold test, could the whole human community form an independent political society wherein God is sovereign? Austin admits that his test is quite imprecise and fallible due to the inherent vagueness of such terms as "generality" or "habitual." Does the generality of the human community habitually obey God? At first it seems obvious that, no, the generality of the human community obey their respective civil governments, but we noted that, according to Austin, to obey your civil government is normally to obey God. There are occasions, perhaps rare, when one cannot obey both one's government and God; in these situations people sometimes obey God, sometimes the government, and sometimes neither. All of this is consistent with the view that the "generality" of humans "habitually" obey God's command to obey one's government.

It is not plausible to suppose that the generality of the human race habitually obey God's revealed law, though Austin does not specify what parts of the Bible count as revealed law. If God's revealed law were limited to the Decalogue, then it might be the case that the generality of the human community habitually obey it. As for God's unrevealed law, it does seem plausible to suppose that the generality of the human community habitually obey God's unrevealed law, which simply asks that we follow the moral rules conducive to the general happiness. As for the negative test, Austin would certainly admit that God does not habitually obey any determinate superior. By Austin's avowedly imprecise positive and negative criteria, the human community under the sovereignty of God seems to count as an independent political society.

Austin is clearly aware of the possibility that his definition of a sovereign might suggest the Deity, so he attempts to exclude this outcome by introducing the word *human,* from time to time, at key points: "If a *determinate* human superior, *not* in a habit of obedience to a like superior, receive *habitual* obedience from the *bulk* of a given society, that determinate superior is sovereign in that society, and the society (including the superior) is a society political and independent" (PJD, p. 194). In this statement of his criteria defining an independent and political society, we discover that the determinate and common superior must be "human." Since this qualification appears only fitfully and without justification, we must ask if this is merely an arbitrary restriction upon the logical generality of his conceptual apparatus. Is there something inherent in the notion of sovereignty that excludes divine sovereignty?

We might note that Austin's formula above requires not only that the determinate superior be human but also that he "not be in a habit of obedience to a like [that is, human] superior." Austin explicitly allows here that human sovereigns might be in a habit of obedience to a common and determinate divine superior. Is this habit of obedience to divine law compatible with being a human sovereign? Is a human sovereign supreme if he habitually obeys divine commands? Why does it matter whether human sovereigns are in a habit of obedience to a common human superior or to a common divine superior? Austinian sovereignty is a jealous God: if God is truly sovereign, then no human may be, and if some human is sovereign, how could God be? Austin wants to affirm the sovereignty both of God and of certain human beings. However, sovereignty is one attribute that cannot be shared.

These questions cannot be answered within the framework of concepts by which Austin defines both sovereignty and positive law. Austin attempts to distinguish positive law from other kinds of law properly so called on the basis of sovereignty; he also attempts to define sovereignty on the basis of the concept of an independent political society. Within this framework of concepts, sovereignty cannot be distinguished from other kinds of superiority, and positive law cannot be distinguished from other kinds of law properly so called. Curiously, Austin himself concedes the inadequacy of the Austinian framework near the end of the *Province of Jurisprudence Determined*. After repeating, once again, verbatim his official definition of positive law,[64] Austin makes this remarkable concession: "This definition of a positive law is assumed expressly or tacitly throughout the foregoing lectures. But it only approaches to a perfectly complete and perfectly exact definition. It is open to certain correctives which I now will briefly suggest" (PJD, p. 350). For someone who places such emphasis on verbal and conceptual precision and rigor, to deploy an official definition throughout a treatise and then, at the end, to concede that the official definition is not just imperfect but even admits of correctives is astonishing. What is most admired in Austin's analytical jurisprudence is the strong dependence of his wide-ranging theory of ethics, politics, and law upon a few elementary concepts. Austin's whole imposing theoretical architecture rests upon the basic components of his official definition of positive law; any modification of those elements or the description of those elements will have profound effects upon the shape and character of the whole theoretical enterprise.

What led Austin to this dramatic avowal of doubts about his own official definition of positive law? Recall that Austin's formula asserts that sovereigns impose positive law only on members of their own independent political society; Austin later realized that positive law reaches not just members of a society but all persons within a particular jurisdiction: "In many cases, the positive law of a given independent community imposes a duty on a *stranger*: on a party who is *not* a member of a given independent community, or is only a member to certain limited purposes" (PJD, p. 351). This stranger is a member of a foreign independent political society and therefore, by Austin's definition, subject only to that foreign sovereign. Nonetheless, as a visitor or resident alien, our stranger is subject to the positive law of two countries: his country of origin and his country of residence. From the point of view of the aims of Austin's theory, this situation creates troubling uncertainties: our stranger is subject to two sovereigns, two legal systems, two chains of command. Austin argues that, in principle, "the enforcement of the law against the stranger is not inconsistent with the sovereignty of a foreign supreme government" (PJD, p. 353). The reality of the conflict of laws suggests that, in practice, the resident alien raises deep questions about the reach of legal systems and the nature of sovereign authority.

64. "Every positive law (or every law simply and strictly so called) is set, directly or circuitously, by a sovereign individual or body, to a member or members of the independent political society wherein its author is supreme." PJD, p. 350.

This quandary leads Austin to recognize the fundamental salience of the concept of jurisdiction to the theory of positive law. Austin briefly considers how his account of the authority, reach, and power of positive law might be gently modified and amended to accommodate the important role of jurisdiction. What Austin now argues it that positive law is law imposed not just on members of an independent political society but on any persons within a particular jurisdiction. The sovereign, in this new version, has authority to impose positive law and legal sanction not so much on a particular people as on a particular territory: "A party not a member of a given independent community, but living within its territory and within the jurisdiction of its sovereign, is bound or obliged, to a certain limited extent, by its positive law. Living within the territory, he is obnoxious to the legal sanctions by which the law is enforced" (PJD, p. 352). Thus, the case of a stranger led Austin to realize that no definition of positive law could be adequate without careful attention to the notion of jurisdictions.

Writers typically reach a full understanding of their own theoretical aims only toward the end of a project. Austin clearly regrets the incompleteness of his definition of positive law: "The definition is too narrow, or is defective or inadequate"(PJD, p. 354). Still, he says that despite these inadequacies "the truth of the positions and inferences contained by the preceding lectures is not, I believe, impaired, or is not impaired materially, by this omission and defect" (PJD, p. 355). Given the staggering labor, care, and aspiration to perfection that Austin evidently brought to this ever so preciously repeated formula defining positive law, his admission of its serious defects is deeply admirable.

We should not be surprised that Austin resisted the suggestion that he ought to go back and rethink, reformulate, and restructure his definition and analysis of positive law throughout his treatise. Austin's strategy for damage control involves three claims: first, that his definition of positive law is inadequate only at the margins and with what he calls "anomalous" cases: "To render that definition complete or adequate, a comprehensive summary of these anomalous cases . . . must be tacked to the definition in the way of a supplement" (PJD, p. 354); second, that his general theoretical claims are not impaired by the defects in their application to such anomalies: "They [such anomalies] hardly were appropriate matter for the foregoing *general* attempt to determine the province of jurisprudence" (PJD, p. 355); third, that the full exposition of the science of positive law "is really the ambitious aim of the entire Course of Lectures of which the foregoing attempt is merely the opening portion" (PJD, p. 354).

Austin's efforts here to protect the integrity of his own theoretical framework are certainly understandable but ultimately not defensible. In reflecting upon what makes the stranger subject to positive—that is, civil—law, Austin saw that what matters is not membership in an independent political society but falling within the reach of a legal sanction, which is to say, falling within a particular jurisdiction. If Austin had begun, rather than ended, his theory of positive law with an analysis of the notion of jurisdiction, much of his theory of sovereignty and of independent political societies would be superfluous. Is the example of a stranger or resident alien just an anomaly to the normal case of legal authority? Austin argues that normally positive law is imposed by the sovereign only on his subjects, that is, on members of the independent political society of which he is sovereign: "Now (speaking generally) a party who is obnoxious to a legal sanction, or to the might of the author of the law which the legal sanction enforces, is a member of the independent community wherein the author is sovereign" (PJD, p. 350). Austin still cannot limit the damage this insight does to this theory of positive law by claiming that the case of the stranger is a mere anomaly that might be "tacked to the definition in the way of a supplement" or that his general theory merely needs some additional specifying or that his introductory definitions can be perfected by his subsequent lectures. All of these proposals assume that Austin merely needs to add some new epicycles to his existing theory of positive law.

Austin is no doubt right that, as a factual matter, positive law is usually imposed only on members of a particular political society and only rarely on other persons, such as resident aliens. But the question is whether positive law is applied by courts upon persons qua members of an independent political society or upon persons qua subject to a particular jurisdiction. Some tribunals have jurisdiction only over citizens of a polity; other tribunals have jurisdiction only over members of particular religions. So membership of various kinds is only one possible basis for defining jurisdiction, which is why law should be defined in terms of jurisdiction rather than in terms of membership. One commentator proposed a revised Austinian jurisprudence in which the concepts of sovereignty and membership in independent political societies are replaced with concepts of jurisdiction and legal sanction: "A legal system is a set of rules laid down for the guidance of human beings, by a determinate person or group of persons having power over them by virtue of their effective monopolization of the physical sanctions within a particular jurisdiction (however defined)."[65]

---

65. Anonymous, "Hart, Austin, and the Concept of a Legal System: The Primacy of Sanctions," *Yale Law Journal* 84 (1975): 584–607, at 606.

We shall never know what direction an Austinian jurisprudence would take if it focused on the notion of jurisdiction rather than on the notion of sovereignty. But there are reasons to think that it might have taken Austin very far from his philosophy of positive law. As we have seen, Austin's theory of positive law is fundamentally a theory of legislative sovereignty: positive law is the creation of the sovereign legislator and is imposed by the political power of that sovereign over the members of the independent political society of which he is sovereign. In this legislative model of a legal system, law emerging from the judiciary is described as a tacit or indirect mode of sovereign legislation. So when Austin attempts to bring the notion of jurisdiction into his scheme, he does so in such a way as to preserve his basic top-down approach by speaking of the "jurisdiction of the sovereign." And even the commentator quoted above, while substituting the concept of jurisdiction for the concept of sovereignty, nonetheless preserved the top-down legislative-command structure of Austin's thought.

But jurisdiction is a judicial, not a legislative, concept. Roman jurists distinguished *ius dare,* the legislative function of giving the law, from *ius dicere,* the judicial function of declaring the law. As *Black's Law Dictionary* says: "Jurisdiction defines the powers of courts to inquire into facts, apply the law, make decisions, and declare judgment." Of course, the rules defining the jurisdiction of courts might originate in a legislature, though they need not. Jurisdiction defines the competence and scope of courts to resolve disputes and thereby to create and to enforce legitimate expectations in the coordination of individual and group conduct. The logical core of a legal system is the rules defining the jurisdiction of courts to settle disputes; those rules of jurisdiction might well be customary, and the basis of the judicial process could range from the unconstrained discretion of judges to fixed principles arising from precedents to reliance on a comprehensive national legal code. Legislation is not logically necessary to the rule of law; in both primitive legal systems and international law, legislation plays in practice a very small role. In all complex societies, no doubt, legislation is of great practical importance, especially legislation defining the jurisdiction of courts.

How could jurisdiction be a logically fundamental part of a legal system when jurisdiction already presupposes law? Even if Austin were to focus on jurisdiction, wouldn't he still first have to define law? If so, then how does a focus on jurisdiction imply a fundamentally different understanding of a legal system? Actually, law presupposes jurisdiction, but jurisdiction does not presuppose law. If tribunals have a customary right to settle certain kinds of disputes,

then they may settle them on the basis of the fixed and predetermined principles of law or on the basis of nonlegal judicial discretion, mediation, or arbitration.[66]

In sketching the possible implications of a focus on jurisdiction for Austinian positivism, I am not suggesting either that Austin developed his theory in
this direction or that he would have.[67] I only aim to suggest that such a focus
could have led Austin to a radically different model of the legal system, one focused not on sovereign legislative command but on the role of courts in bringing their own legal traditions to bear on resolving disputes. There is something
poignant in the final pages of Austin's *Province of Jurisprudence Determined:* just
as he is putting the final touches on his elaborate and delicate theoretical mechanism, the whole machine falls apart in his hands. If Austin really believed that
he could salvage the Austinian theory of law by means of supplemental clauses
to cover anomalies, or further detailed specifications and applications of his
general theory, then we should expect to see him do so in the subsequent *Lectures on Jurisprudence,* as he promises. It is notorious, however, that Austin
never did develop, supplement, specify, or apply his general theory in his subsequent work, much to the disappointment of himself, his wife, and his friends.
We shall never know precisely why Austin chose neither to complete the Austinian theory of law nor to develop a new theory of law focused on the notion
of jurisdiction. Still, we can only sympathize with the plight of a perfectionist
faced with a choice between attempting to salvage his own deeply flawed theory
or attempting to mount an entirely new theoretical enterprise.

Because of Austin's remarkable avowal at the end of *The Province of Jurisprudence Determined* that the definitions setting forth the conceptual framework
assumed throughout that work were incomplete and inadequate, and because
this avowal itself led him to a deeper recognition of the importance of the concepts of legal sanction and jurisdiction, it is deeply misleading to reduce
Austin's legal thought to his official definitions. It simply will not do to say, as

66. Fred Schauer observes that rules of jurisdiction are logically fundamental in a legal sys-
    tem: "We can acknowledge that any legal system would need jurisdictional rules to cre-
    ate and to organize the institutions of decision making. Yet a system constituted and
    structured by a system of jurisdictional rules could still impose little in the way of sub-
    stantive constraint on the decisions its decision-makers were expected to reach." *Playing
    by the Rules* (Oxford: Clarendon Press, 1991), p. 169.
67. It might be revealing, however, that when Austin lays out the seven stages of "the natural
    or customary order in which the law of any country arises, or is founded," courts emerge
    in stage 2, while legislation arises only in stage 5. See LJ, pp. 635–36.

Hart does, that, according to Austin, "the 'essential difference' of *positive law* is found to be that it is set by a sovereign to the members of an independent political society" (PJD, p. x). As we saw, Austin explicitly distanced himself from this formula in the course of his reflections upon the legal status of the stranger in our midst. We must not turn Austin into a mere Austinian.

Although we shall never know why Austin did not more fully explore the implications of the notion of jurisdiction, certainly the discourse of law's positivity was a big obstacle. We do not know exactly when Austin began to conceptualize civil law as "positive" law, but it may have been quite early indeed.[68] To suppose that all civil law is positive is to suppose that all civil law finds its source in authoritative imposition and/or to suppose that the content of civil law is not morally necessary. Insofar as Austin thought of law's positivity in terms of authoritative imposition, he found it difficult to distinguish civil from divine law, since both were laws properly so called; insofar as Austin thought of law's positivity in terms of its morally contingent content, he found it difficult to distinguish law from positive morality. Therefore, in his official account, Austin chose to define law's positivity in terms of a command of a human sovereign to members of his own independent political society. But, in the end, Austin registers his dissatisfaction with the Austinian account of law's positivity. This is not to deny that Austin's attempts to find the essence of law through the concepts of positivity have been an illuminating failure: we have discovered a great deal about the family resemblances among religious, civil, and moral norms. Nonetheless, whatever doubts Austin expressed or harbored about the adequacy of his own official definitions of law, he could hardly have been expected to theorize in any way other than what he called "the philosophy of positive law." If his theory ultimately failed, it was not fundamentally his failure or the failure of his age: it is the failure of the philosophy of positive law from the first Schoolmen to the last.

68. Schwarz thinks that Austin's marginal note in his personal copy of Blackstone was quite early: "Distinction between moral and natural laws (laws which are dictated by utility in all times and places) and laws which are merely positive laws (that is, of transient or local utility)." Schwarz, "John Austin and the German Jurisprudence of His Time," p. 194n.

Conclusion: The Rise and Fall
of Positive Law

We have observed that, although the norms enforced by courts form only one small part of the larger universe of factual regularities and norms we call "law," nonetheless the norms enforced by courts are themselves quite heterogeneous in source and in content. The precise list of sources and the relations among them vary over time and place. Practical lawyers and jurists simply accept a fundamental heterogeneity in the various sources of the law enforced by courts, ranging from commercial customs, to statutes, to precedents, to learned commentary. Lawyers must learn how to identify, interpret, and apply norms from each of the main sources of law and how to harmonize conflicts among norms. What unites these distinctive springs into the one reservoir of law enforced by courts is simply the distinctive custom of each particular court. Even in civilian jurisdictions, where a national code claims to be the sole source of law, courts rely upon both precedents and learned commentary in order to interpret, apply, and harmonize various provisions of the code.

The philosophers of positive law, however, argue that above (or, to follow the metaphor, below) all of these distinct sources is a master spring from which all positive laws derive their authority. Yet, as we have seen, the claim that all human law is deliberately imposed by the supreme authority of a political community applies much better to some sources of law than to others. It works tolerably well for legislation but requires some rather Procrustean methods in order to accommodate the other sources of law. Because the supreme political authority often seems not to take any notice or to signal any approval of legal customs and judicial precedents, it is difficult to see how they were imposed by a sovereign. We saw all our philosophers attempt, for example, to redescribe custom and judicial precedents as tacit or indirect commands of the supreme authority. Often the fiction that "whatever the sovereign permits, he commands" was deployed to shoehorn in these sources of law. But we saw that the supreme authority of a political community might well have many reasons to permit the existence of legal norms that he does not approve of, let alone command. Or, as with Austin, the diverse familiar sources of law were redescribed as mere "causes" of law so that all law might have but one true source in sovereign command.

We often say that judges "lay down" the law, so perhaps judiciary law can be understood as positive law just as much as legislation? What are the obstacles to understanding judges as subordinate legislators? In the first place, to preserve the unity of the legal chain of command required by the philosophy of positive law, we must define courts as instruments of sovereign legislatures and judges as ministers of sovereign legislators. Yet the relation of courts to legislatures seems to vary widely over time and place; is there any reason to think that courts must necessarily be instruments of sovereign legislatures? In many jurisdictions there are customs and institutions protecting the independence of the judiciary, practices that prevent those courts precisely from becoming instruments of the sovereign legislature. Moreover, Austin warns us against defining judiciary law as "judge-made" law, as if judges were subordinate legislators. We must distinguish the law the judge lays down upon the parties before him from the law that arises from those decisions. For the force, scope, and meaning of the law of precedents stems not from what a particular judge "lays down" as law but from what subsequent judges "take up" from those precedents. Subsequent judges may take up the principle of the prior holding but not its exact language, they might take up factual elements of the case, they might take up obiter dicta, or even dissenting opinions. What seems to count is what successive judges take up, not so much what was once laid down.

All philosophers of positive law attempt to unify law by tracing it back to a single supreme legal source, but the conception of that supreme source has evolved and varied. For Aquinas, all law is imposed by "he who has care of the community": divine law by God and human law by the temporal authority. As we saw, sometimes Aquinas speaks of a divine positive law as well as of a human positive law. For if law gets its validity from the supreme authority in a political community, that authority might well be either divine or human. Aquinas tends to limit the expression *positive law* to human law in his mature theory, but there is nothing intrinsic about "law laid down" or "imposed" that limits it to human law. Indeed, on Aquinas's account, if any law could rightfully be said to be deliberately imposed by the supreme authority, it would seem to be divine law. For Hobbes and Austin, the tension between divine and human positive law becomes much greater because of their theory of sovereignty. Aquinas can accommodate both divine and human positive law because he accepts a division of temporal and spiritual authority and jurisdiction. But Hobbes and Austin are committed to a theory of one supreme, undivided, and legally illimitable sovereignty. If the temporal sovereign were subject to divine positive law, then he would no longer be sovereign; but if human beings are subject to no divine positive law, then God is no longer sovereign. Hobbes and Austin insist that the civil sovereign be subject, at most, to natural divine law and to reserve all rights of translating that divine law into human positive law. In this way, there is only one true sovereign, the civil sovereign. So although our philosophers often seek to use the term *positive* to demarcate specifically human law, the term and concept are not well suited to do so. All of divine law is positive in source, and much of it is positive in content, which is why Aquinas and Hobbes explicitly refer to divine positive law and Austin does so implicitly.

In response to the challenges posed by the complexity and heterogeneity of legal norms and institutions, the account of the unique source of positive law has evolved in other important ways as well. Aquinas, of course, traced human positive law primarily to the rational will of the supreme temporal authority within a political community, leaving open the possibility of a divine positive law stemming from the supreme spiritual authority within the same community. Certainly divided authority and divided legal jurisdiction can and did lead to profound conflict within political communities, so Hobbes, Austin, and Kelsen insist that all positive law must stem from a single, undivided, and legally illimitable temporal sovereign. Still, as it became increasingly evident that no identifiable human authority guaranteed the validity of all norms enforced by courts, Kelsen sought the source of legal validity not in political authority but in a logically basic norm that authorized all other norms. Here, all positive law finds its source not in a sovereign will but in a master norm defining the validity of all other norms. Positive law thus has a logical unity rather than the unity of command.

Hart developed Kelsen's basic norm into a "rule of recognition," a second-order master norm specifying how to identify and to change all valid first-order legal rules within a legal system. Nonetheless, the irreducible heterogeneity of the sources of law in complex legal systems has presented intractable obstacles to Kelsen's and Hart's aspirations. In Anglo-American jurisdictions, for example, common law and legislation seem to be two historically and logically independent sources of valid law in the sense that common law does not derive its validity from legislation, nor does legislation derive its legitimacy from common law. Thus, a leading contemporary legal positivist, Joseph Raz, argues that our complex legal systems do not necessarily rest upon a single rule of recognition identifying all of the law enforced by courts.[1] But if we require a distinct rule of recognition for each source of law, or even a distinct criterion for each source of law within a single rule of recognition, then we lose much of the theoretical parsimony that made the whole concept of the rule of recognition attractive. Instead of a single logically basic norm identifying all valid legal norms, we may have to settle for something resembling the traditional lists of the sources of law.

In addition to claims about the source of law, the philosophy of positive law makes claims about the content of law. Although our philosophers vary widely in their views of the relation of law to morality, they all agree that positive law must be distinguished from the natural moral law. True, Aquinas alone insists that positive law loses the character or essence of lawfulness where it violates natural law; yet Aquinas also condemns unjust laws, recognizing that even immoral laws are still lawful in some diminished sense. More important is the fact that all our philosophers evaluate positive law in the light of an objective moral standard of the natural law and that they all permit officials and citizens to disobey positive law where it directly violates fundamental principles of natural law. For Aquinas, if the directives of positive law are not consistent with the requirements of the natural law, then officials and citizens may lose the moral obligation to obey the law or even acquire a moral obligation to disobey it. Hobbes, of course, has a more restrictive account of the possible conflicts between positive and natural law, but even he admits that where positive law di-

---

1. According to Joseph Raz, "There is no reason to suppose that every legal system has just one rule of recognition. It may have more." *The Authority of Law* (Oxford: Clarendon Press, 1979), p. 95.

rectly threatens my life, then positive law loses all moral authority for me because the sovereign and I have returned to a state of nature. Positive law, for Hobbes, has authority in conscience only where it serves the fundamental moral command of the natural law to seek civil peace. Austin also strongly distinguishes positive from natural law: he criticizes Hobbes for emphasizing too strongly the duty to obey immoral positive law. Austin argues that where the demands of positive law are not compatible with the natural moral law (whose index is utility), then we may well be morally obliged to disobey the positive law. But even where positive law is compatible with natural law, our philosophers insist that positive law must provide much more detailed and specific guidance for human conduct than does the more open-ended moral law. As a set of conventions for coordinating a vast array of human activity, positive law must create sharp lines and clear expectations. But in strongly distinguishing the natural moral law from the specific directives of the positive law, our theorists sometimes attempt neatly to divide norms into either natural or positive. For example, all our philosophers, when distinguishing natural from positive law, appeal to the distinction between what the natural law forbids because it is intrinsically evil and what is evil because forbidden by the positive law. But this distinction suggests that wrongful conduct can be neatly divided into what is intrinsically wrong by natural law and what is wrong merely by positive enactment.

Having sharply distinguished natural from positive law, the philosophy of positive law wrestles mightily with the challenge of putting them back together again. One difficulty with attempting to distinguish natural from positive law is that the content of legal norms varies widely in degree of positivity. Some principles of common law, such as the principle that "no one ought to be enriched by his own wrongdoing," are very close to basic principles of the moral law. They can serve as guides to human conduct and can be enforced in court only in conjunction with much more precise rules defining the scope and force of such broad principles. Other legal rules are much more positive, such as rules about how, where, and when a will must be signed. Because the positivity of a law's content is a matter of degree, the claim that all human law is positive in content is vague and subject to conflicting interpretations. Is the claim that every law enforced by courts has some degree of positivity or that it is wholly positive? Since the content of norms enforced by courts has such a range of specificity, generalizations are hazardous. As we saw in the discourse of positive law, sometimes our philosophers attempt to divide up human law neatly into natural and positive precepts: Aquinas sometimes divides up both divine and human law into natural and positive precepts; Hobbes attempts to divide up divine law into natural and positive precepts; and Austin distinguishes, within positive law, law natural from law positive. But Aquinas insists that every positive law bears some intelligible relation to the natural law, and Hobbes insists that the natural law and the civil law contain each other. Thus, human law is neither purely positive nor purely natural. At its best, the discourse of positive law acknowledges the mixture of intrinsic moral force and legal specificity in virtually all human law.

What accounts for the remarkable emphasis on positive law we have observed in major legal theorists from Thomas Aquinas to Hans Kelsen? The work of legal anthropologists, historians, sociologists, and philosophers over the past two centuries has taught us that many of the procedures and norms that constitute the rule of law rest upon tacit legal knowledge and usage. Like all forms of tacit knowledge, our tacit knowledge of law is murky and difficult to bring into focus. As Michael Polanyi vividly observed, when we use a hammer we are aware not of our grip but of the object we aim to hit. The deliberate enactment of a statute, the deliberate decision of a court, and the deliberate drafting of an agreement represent the focal aim of the rule of law, and it is quite easy to overlook all of the tacit knowledge and usages that make these deliberate activities possible. Nothing is more common than defining a complex reality in terms of its most rational and purposive element—for example, defining a human being as a rational animal! Of the whole complex of tacit and deliberate procedures, assumptions, and aims that we call the rule of law, the positing of positive law is our most intentional, rational, and purposive activity; hence the temptation to describe all of law as positive law. When we attempt to export the rule of law to nations lacking the tacit dimensions of the rule of law, we often discover how much more there is to law than positive law. So this natural human tendency to focus on and to value our deliberate, over our tacit, knowledge and aims helps to account for the strange hold that positive law has exercised for so long on legal philosophers.

Both the source and the content of positive law contribute in different ways to its profound and long-standing hold upon the legal imagination. Positive law in the sense of law imposed by the political authorities often serves to focus and to trigger the immense coercive apparatus of government. What other instrument of political power has wrought such good and evil as positive law? Usually executive edicts and fiats are narrowly circumscribed by time and place; they rarely outlive their authors. Positive law, by contrast, usually has both a wider range and a longer life. As Hayek said: "Legislation, the deliberate making of law, has justly been described as among all inventions of man the one fraught with the gravest consequences, more far-reaching in its effects even than fire and gun-powder."[2] As a focal point of the coercive apparatus of government, positive law serves as both a symbol and an instrument of the immense power and prestige of political authority.

Positive law in the sense of law lacking any intrinsic connection to morality also attracts deep-seated fascination. Who is not awed by the capacity of positive law to create wholly new kinds of legal and/or moral obligation where before none existed? Until just the other day, taking a large quantity of cash abroad raised no legal or moral issues whatsoever; now, because a law was posited, I have a legal and, on some accounts, also a moral obligation not to do so. Of course, I can assume new obligations for myself where before none existed by practices of promising and of contracting, but positive law creates new obligations even for those who in no way consent to them. That is a remarkable and profound expression of human authority and power.

After a vibrant career of eight centuries, the discourse of positive law is now falling into desuetude. Even leading contemporary legal positivists, such as Hart, Raz, and Kramer, no longer refer to positive law. In part this is because the discourse of positive law was meant to distinguish the law enforced by courts from other kinds of law, especially divine law, customary law, and natural law. But today the term *law* is used almost solely to refer to the law enforced by human courts, so there is no need for the distinguishing qualifier "positive." When lawyers or philosophers today wish to contrast positive law with customary law or with natural law, they simply contrast law with custom or law with morality. Positive law no longer needs to be distinguished from divine law because, although Austin defined divine law as "law, properly so called," the whole question of divine law has been jettisoned from legal philosophy and relegated to sectarian theology. In this respect, the discourse of positive law has failed precisely through its success: if all genuine law is positive law, then the term *positive* becomes purely redundant.

But I think there is something deeper at work here. We have seen that the discourse of positive law embodies a legislative model of a legal system. Hart observes that Austin's legal positivism never enjoyed the direct influence on American legal thought that it enjoyed in England. Hart attributes this to the

---

2. Here Hayek is paraphrasing Bernhard Rehfeldt, *Die Wurzeln des Rechts* (Berlin: Duncker und Humblot, 1951). See Hayek, *Law, Legislation, and Liberty,* vol. 1 (Chicago: University of Chicago Press, 1973), p. 72.

"distinctive American insistence on the central importance of the Courts and the subordinate place of the legislature."[3] On this view, Austin's philosophy of positive law finds its natural home in the context of English traditions of Parliamentary supremacy and is foreign to American traditions of judicial independence. Even leading American "positivists" have long avoided the language of positive law: O. W. Holmes Jr., for example, famously said: "The object of our study, then, is prediction, the prediction of the incidence of public force through the instrumentality of the courts." John Chipman Gray, in his classic *The Nature and Sources of Law,* goes so far as to deny that statutes are even part of our law; he says they are only sources of law. For Gray, all law is the work of courts: "In truth, all Law is judge-made law."[4]

But this focus on the courts, rather than on the legislature, as the center of a legal system is more than simply a peculiarity of American legal traditions. With the rise of legal history, comparative jurisprudence, and legal anthropology, it became clear that tribunals have always and everywhere been more central to the origins and development of law than have legislatures. Although Henry Sumner Maine famously observed that "the most celebrated system of jurisprudence known to the world begins, as it ends, with a Code," he was well aware that the origins and main development of Roman law were to be found in the activities of courts: "It is certain that, in the infancy of mankind, no sort of legislature, not even a distinct author of law, is contemplated or conceived of. . . . The only authoritative statement of right and wrong is a judicial sentence after the facts."[5] Maine explicitly links the rise of modern legal positivism to the rise of legislation: "The capital fact in the mechanism of modern States is the energy of legislatures. Until the fact existed, I do not, as I have said, believe that the system of Hobbes, Bentham and Austin could have been conceived."[6] Similarly, James Carter argues that Austin's definition of law is actually a definition of legislation: "It properly defines *legislation*—that is, law consciously enacted by men."[7] Carter also strongly contrasts law with legislation and asserts that all law is custom. He traces the origins of legal systems to the emergence of methods of resolving disputes: customs create settled expectations, and dis-

3. Hart, introduction to Austin, *The Province of Jurisprudence Determined* (London: Weidenfeld and Nicolson, 1954), p. xvi.
4. Gray, *The Nature and Sources of the Law,* 2nd edition (Gloucester, MA: Peter Smith, 1972), p. 125.
5. Maine, *Ancient Law* (New York: Dorset Press, 1986), p. 6.
6. Maine, *Early History of Institutions* (New York: Henry Holt, 1875), p. 398.
7. Carter, *Law: Its Origin, Growth, and Function* (New York: G. P. Putnam, 1907), p. 182.

putes arise when these expectations are overturned. "This arbitration of quarrels is a near approach to the establishment of a court." Once disputants can be compelled to bring their quarrels to a particular tribunal, then we have moved from arbitration to a genuinely judicial process. What is essential, then, are norms of jurisdiction.[8] No doubt Carter and others, in reaction to the emphasis on legislation in the discourse of positive law, underestimate the role of legislation in legal history.[9] Legal anthropologists have confirmed the insights of the legal historians, finding law in the dispute-resolution mechanisms of simple societies.[10]

In response to the findings of comparative legal historians and anthropologists, jurists and legal philosophers have begun making courts the center of their analyses of law. Gray, as a student both of American legal institutions and of comparative legal history, was one of the first major jurists to insist upon treating the courts as the centerpiece of a legal system: "We can conceive of a society with judicial but no legislative organs."[11] Max Radin found another way to prove the logical priority of courts: "There is an infallible test for recognizing whether an imagined course of conduct is lawful or unlawful. This infallible test, in our system, is to submit the question to the judgment of a court. In other systems, exactly the same test is used, but it is often more difficult to recognize the court."[12] Law does not take determinate shape, does not come fully into focus, and is not completely made until interpreted and applied by a court. Raz distinguishes norm-creating institutions (such as legislatures), norm-applying institutions (such as courts), and norm-enforcing institutions (executive powers of a state). Raz then argues that only norm-applying institutions are logically necessary to every legal system.[13]

8. "All that needed to be added [to arbitration] to constitute a court was to create permanent arbitrators and compel disputants to keep the peace and provide a mode by which they should be forced to submit their differences to the decision of a tribunal." Carter, *Law,* p. 48.

9. "There are no Law-givers such as are reverenced in history. Moses, Lycurgus, and Solon took the customs of their time, and gave them form and furnished better methods of securing their enforcement." Carter is no doubt right that whatever laws we might ascribe to these legislators in large measure reflected existing customs, but they also might well have partially transformed those customs. Carter, *Law,* p. 49.

10. See, for one example, *The Disputing Process: Law in Ten Societies,* ed. Laura Nader and Harry F. Todd Jr. (New York: Columbia University Press, 1978).

11. Gray, *The Nature and Sources of Law,* p. 152.

12. Max Radin, "A Restatement of Hohfeld," *Harvard Law Review* 51 (1938): 1145.

13. See Raz, *The Authority of Law,* pp. 105–11.

A legal system without a legislature is not only conceivable but frequently observed in primitive societies and in the arena of international dispute resolution. But no legal system is possible without courts, since there must be some forum for resolving disputes. Nor is legislation necessary for creating new law, since new law emerges inevitably as a by-product of the application of existing law by courts. Raz attributes the rise of new law to mistakes by courts in the application of law, mistakes that are nonetheless binding on other courts. No doubt mistakes are one mechanism by which new law emerges as a by-product of adjudication, but by no means the only one. Edward Levi, as we have mentioned, reveals another such mechanism when he describes common law adjudication as a moving system of classification in which rules get their force and scope from the facts in which they are embedded; Levi denies that common law consists of fixed rules applied (or misapplied) to changing facts. He argues that, as the facts of new cases change, so do the meanings of the rules applied to them.[14] Finally, Raz also denies that institutions of norm enforcement are necessary to a legal system, since courts can, at least theoretically, rely upon self-help.

We have seen, in short, a dramatic transformation of the focus of legal philosophy from legislation in Aquinas, Hobbes, and Austin to judiciary law in Gray, Radin, and Raz. Jeremy Waldron is puzzled by this development. He notes that "although legal positivism has traditionally given pride of place to legislation as a basis for law, modern positivists are much less interested in this than they are in the process whereby law is developed in courts. . . . What is going on here?"[15] Waldron attributes this shift of focus to a deep contemporary suspicion of legislation: "Why this embarrassment about legislation?"[16] But I believe that legal philosophers, including legal positivists, have simply registered the cumulative findings of legal historians and anthropologists pointing to the historically prior and universal role of norm-applying institutions. Wal-

---

14. Of course, long before Levi's masterful discussion of this process, W. Jethro Brown had observed the same mechanism: "The most conservative and timid of judges, however strenuously seeking to shelter himself behind the authority of earlier decisions, is driven by a power beyond his control to take his place in the ranks of the makers of law!" Brown, *The Austinian Theory of Law* (London: J. Murray, 1906), p. 297.

15. Waldron, *The Dignity of Legislation* (Cambridge: Cambridge University Press, 1999), pp. 15–16.

16. "One possible explanation is to see this embarrassment about legislation as an instance of a more general nervousness about the role of deliberate intellectualization in politics." Waldron, *The Dignity of Legislation*, p. 17.

dron is right to draw attention to this profound shift in the focal analysis of legal philosophy, but he fails to note that the major theorists focused on legislation, apart from Bentham, deploy the discourse of positive law, while the major theorists focused on the judiciary do not. So perhaps this deep transformation of legal philosophy helps to explain why contemporary legal positivists no longer use the discourse of positive law.

We have seen that the discourse of positive law belongs to a deep contrast between top-down and bottom-up views of the nature of law. A focus on courts might enable us to emancipate legal philosophy from this age-old but inadequate antithesis of top-down positive law to bottom-up customary law. Plato and Aristotle frequently contrast the deliberately imposed "written" (meaning statutory) law with the spontaneously emerging "unwritten" law of custom. Written law is a deliberate artifact, capable of being adopted or revoked at the pleasure of the political authorities; unwritten law is often described as natural or "second nature" because of its resistance to deliberate manipulation: custom, like nature, operates by its own tacit logic. Those who understand law from the top down tend to see it as an instrument of political power, wielded to accomplish the purposes of a particular regime; those who understand law from the bottom up tend to see it as deeply entrenched in social habit and relatively immune from deliberate manipulation.

We can see the force of these two contrasting pictures of a legal system in the very different ways in which courts are understood. In the top-down model oriented toward legislation, courts are seen as instruments of the legislature and judges as ministers of the supreme lawgiver. In the Aristotelian tradition, as we have seen with Aquinas, law is the instrument of each particular regime, made by legislatures and simply applied by courts. Aristotle says that laws must be framed to serve the particular ends of each different kind of regime.[17] He says that "the laws are, and ought to be, framed with a view to the regime, and not the regime to the laws."[18] Aquinas agrees that "the rational essence of human law is that it should be instituted by the governor of the political community . . . and thus human laws can be distinguished according to the variety of

17. Not only do democracies and oligarchies need different laws, each kind of oligarchy and each kind of democracy also needs its own laws: "For the same laws cannot be equally suited to all oligarchies or to all democracies, since there is certainly more than one form both of democracy and of oligarchy." Aristotle, *Politics,* 1289a 22. Jowett translation, in *The Complete Works of Aristotle,* ed. Jonathan Barnes (Princeton: Princeton University Press, 1984).

18. Aristotle, *Politics,* 1289a 12. (Jowett's translation modified).

regimes."[19] Aristotle argues that legislation should regulate all matters it possibly can, leaving the courts to apply the relevant statutes. Where such an enforcement of the letter of the law would create a blatant injustice, the judge may relax the rigor of the letter of the law by means of the principles of equity. In so doing, the judge is simply following the intention of the legislator, who is assumed to intend equity.[20] Aquinas agrees that the task of judges is to apply the statutory law and that when there is doubt about the meaning of that law, he must always refer to the intention of the legislator. Aquinas agrees further that since the legislator is assumed to intend equity, when the letter of the law would create a blatant injustice, a judge must relax the letter of the law.[21] Hobbes follows this top-down understanding of courts when he argues that judicial decisions are "the king's law, whosoever pens them" and that judges must enforce principles of equity to fill gaps in the statutory law—again because equity is assumed to be the will of the sovereign. Austin also argues that judicial decisions are the tacit or indirect commands of the sovereign; and, although Austin sees some virtues to judiciary law, he favors a systematic codification of common law, thus formally subordinating the courts to the legislature.

This top-down understanding of the role of courts is familiar in the discourse of positive law, but there is a competing vision of courts championed by common lawyers and the historical school of jurisprudence. Here the courts are defined not by their relation to the sovereign legislator above but by their relation to custom below. St. German said that those customs of the realm neither against the law of God nor against the law of reason are properly called the common law.[22] Blackstone also defined common law in relation to the "unwritten law" of custom, saying that common law included general customs, particular customs, and certain particular laws. But Blackstone goes on to say that only general customs are "the common law, properly so called."[23] For Blackstone, the normative justification of common law stemmed largely from its origins in popular custom: "It is one of the characteristic marks of English liberty, that our common law depends upon custom; which carries this internal evidence of freedom along with it, that it probably was introduced by the vol-

---

19. Aquinas, ST, I-II, 95.4c.

20. Aristotle, *Ethics,* 1137b 23.

21. Aquinas, ST, II-II, 60.5 ad 2 and 120.2.

22. St. German, *Doctor and Student,* ed. T. F. T. Pluncknett and J. L. Barton (London: Selden Society, 1974), chap. 7.

23. *Blackstone's Commentaries,* 5th ed. (Dublin: John Exshaw et al. 1773), vol. 1, intro., sec. 3.

untary consent of the people."[24] Friedrich Karl von Savigny famously defined law as the moral conscience or consciousness of a people: "In the general consciousness (*Bewusstsein*) of peoples lives positive law and hence we have to call it people's law (*Volksrecht*)."[25] But the law of popular conscience is not visible, so we must rely on custom as the most reliable sign of the people's law: "Custom, therefore, is the mark (*Kennziechen*) of law and not the ground of origin of positive law."[26] Custom must be properly interpreted, harmonized, and systematized by the jurists into a body of law to be applied by the courts. Nonetheless, the law developed by the jurists (*Juristenrecht*) must be subordinated to the people's law (*Volksrecht*).[27]

Both these views of courts seem plausible: courts do, especially in civilian jurisdictions, concern themselves with the interpretation and application of statutes and codes. And almost everywhere, the jurisdiction of courts and the appointment of judges are established by acts of legislation. So, in this and in many other respects, courts do serve as instruments of sovereign legislators. Moreover, if courts are seen as instruments of legislative power, and judges as ministers of the sovereign, then judiciary law assumes whatever legitimacy is possessed by the sovereign legislator. Yet courts also, especially in common law jurisdictions, seem in some decisive respects independent of legislative power: in England, as in many American states, the common law does not get its authority from any explicit act of legislation. Moreover, both common law and criminal law courts in Anglo-American systems are profoundly shaped not only by legislation but also by the pressure of popular opinion and changing mores. For example, the content of many common law standards is defined by ever-changing customs of professional best practice and notions of reasonableness. When prosecutors decide which cases to pursue and which to drop, which to plea bargain and which to bring to trial, their decisions reflect not only the relevant statutes but also public opinion and moral sentiment.[28] And the very institution of the jury trial puts immense pressure on courts to conform law to evolving customary mores. Nonetheless, popular custom and moral sentiment

24. *Blackstone's Commentaries,* vol. 1, intro. sec. 3.
25. Savigny, *System des heutigen Römischen Rechts,* vol. 1 (Berlin: Veit und Comp, 1840), sec. 7.
26. Savigny, *System des heutigen Römischen Rechts,* vol. 1, sec. 12.
27. Savigny, *System des heutigen Römischen Rechts,* vol. 1, sec. 14.
28. For an anthropological study of how social mores shape prosecutorial discretion and defense lawyers' strategies, see Lynn Mather, *Plea Bargaining or Trial: The Process of Criminal-Case Disposition* (Lexington, MA: Lexington Books, 1979).

do not themselves determine judiciary law; after all, many customs and moral sentiments are themselves the creation of that law.

What both the top-down and the bottom-up views of courts miss is the role of the legal profession itself as a basis for judiciary law. No doubt courts must interpret and apply statutes from above and must interpret and apply customs from below, but courts do so by means of distinctively lawyerly bodies of legal principles and rules, some customary and some stipulated. Lawyers and judges are not merely ministers of the sovereign legislator or merely agents of the popular will: they are also guardians of a relatively independent tradition of legal ideals, methods, doctrines, principles, customs, and rules. Courts, and the legal profession more generally, mediate legislative pressure from above and popular sentiments from below. These legal traditions go back to the modern Roman law, as it was developed in, among other places, the medieval and modern universities of Europe and the English royal courts; these traditions unite the bar, bench, and academic branches of the legal profession. So, in addition to sovereign legislation from above and popular mores from below, the law of the courts is also decisively shaped by the commitment of lawyers and judges to preserve the integrity of their own legal traditions. Indeed, the tradition of legal professionalism shapes much more than just the law of the judiciary. Legislation itself can be partly a product of legal tradition insofar as it reflects lawyerly standards of draftsmanship and not simply sovereign political will or popular moral passion. Over time, of course, these legal traditions are and ought to be shaped by the development of new legislation and new popular mores. Ever since Bentham, it has been easy to be skeptical of the legitimacy of these essentially aristocratic legal traditions in a modern democratic polity. Nonetheless, the strength of professional legal traditions can serve to protect the law of the courts, at least in the short run, from the strong pressures to conform to the demands of either urgent legislation or urgent popular sentiment—demands, as we know, that do not always promote justice.

Index